The Intergenerational Transfer of Cognitive Skills

Volume I: Programs, Policy, and Research Issues

COGNITION AND LITERACY
Series Editor: Judith Orasanu
U.S. Army Research Institute

In preparation

The Intergenerational Transfer of Cognitive Skills

Volume I: Programs, Policy, and Research Issues

edited by

Thomas G. Sticht
Micheal J. Beeler
Barbara A. McDonald

ABLEX PUBLISHING CORPORATION
NORWOOD, NEW JERSEY

Library of Congress Cataloging-in-Publication Data

The Intergenerational transfer of cognitive skills / edited by Thomas
  G. Sticht, Micheal J. Beeler, Barbara A. McDonald.
    p. cm. — (Cognition and literacy)
  Includes bibliographical references and index.
  Contents: v. 1. Programs, policy and research issues — v.
  2. Theory and research in cognitive science.
  ISBN 0-89391-736-2
    1. Early childhood education—United States. 2. Cognition in
  children—United States. 3. Literacy programs—United States.
  I. Sticht, Thomas G. II. Beeler, Micheal J. III. McDonald, Barbara
  A. IV. Series.
  LB1139.25.I58 1991
  370.15′2—dc20   91-17779
                                                     CIP

Ablex Publishing Corporation
355 Chestnut Street
Norwood, New Jersey 07648

Table of Contents

Preface

Today there is widespread concern that the major tool for transmitting knowledge to new generations—the public schools—is failing. Numerous reports have noted that the dropout rate is high, and among those who drop out, there is a low level of cognitive achievement. Even among those who graduate from high school, it is estimated that 1 in 6 may be "functionally illiterate." Low literacy levels are related to unemployment, welfare, and poverty. These problems are considered to contribute to low productivity in the workplace, as well, which is a large concern as the United States appears to be losing it's competitive edge in the world marketplace.

Education problems loom even larger as the future is considered. Demographic projections show that the population of youth is declining, except for minority groups, the very group that constitutes the largest percentage of dropouts, unemployed, and welfare and poverty groups. As this trend materializes, the future workforce will be comprised of people with lower cognitive skills. Predictions of work in the future show that while many jobs will be available in the lower-level, low-paying range, many jobs will be created in accordance with advances in new technologies. Fewer young adults will be available with cognitive ability needed to keep the U.S. competitive in the marketplace, and there will be an ever-widening gap between the haves and the have-nots.

In the face of these educational and demographic trends, there have been widespread calls for education reforms, lifelong learning, retraining of workers, and, in general, a concern for the reinvention of education in America to improve the cognitive abilities of children, youth and adults.

Given the widespread concern for improving the nation's cognitive ability, it was decided that perhaps the relatively new field of cognitive science might offer new perspectives that would aid in the development of new, more effective interventions. Consequently, a *Conference on the Intergenerational Transfer of Cognitive Skills* was convened in April 1988 in San Diego, CA. The participants in the conference reviewed the results of previous intervention programs for children, youth, and adults to determine if simply expanding on present efforts might make a significant improvement in the nation's cognitive ability. Additionally, they discussed a wide range of issues regarding the nature of cognition, how cognitive ability develops, and what educational implications can be derived from this scientific study of the mind.

The present book is one of two volumes of papers that were commissioned for the San Diego conference. It reviews intervention studies of the last quarter century, and focuses on the emerging *intergenerational literacy programs* to explore the policy, practice, and research implications of such programs for meeting the nation's educational needs.

The second volume resulting from the San Diego conference presents a review of contemporary cognitive science and its implications for the intergenerational transfer of literacy and other cognitive skills.

The conference on the Intergenerational Transfer of Cognitive Skills and preparation of the books resulting from the conference was supported by a grant from the John D. and Catherine T. MacArthur Foundation to the Applied Behavioral & Cognitive Sciences, Inc. Much appreciation is given to Dr. Peter Gerber of the MacArthur Foundation for his encouragement and support of this project.

Thanks are also due to Mike Beeler and Debra Vella for their help in the conduct of the conference on the Intergenerational Transfer of Cognitive Skills and the preparation of materials for this book. Thanks are also given to Bill Armstrong, Richard Flyer, and Jane Wycoff who took copious notes at the conference and provided those notes to the editors for their use in preparing this book.

While acknowledging the help and assistance of these many colleagues, it should be noted that the opinions and conclusions given in this volume are those of the editors and authors. They do not necessarily represent the opinions or positions of the John D. and Catherine T. MacArthur Foundation or the Applied Behavioral & Cognitive Sciences, Inc.

Chapter 1

The Intergenerational Transfer of Cognitive Skills

Thomas G. Sticht

It is well established that many children arrive at kindergarten or first grade with knowledge, language, and cognitive skills that are different from those needed to acquire higher levels of literacy, mathematics, and critical thinking abilities within the cultural context of mainstream public education. These children frequently fall behind in school and later drop out. They become the marginally literate and marginally employable youth and adults that comprise some one-fifth to one-third of the adult population in the United States. As many as 40 percent of minority populations may fall into this group (Sticht, 1987).

Many of these young adults become parents of children and are unable to transmit educationally relevant preschool oral and written language skills, which are the foundation for later reading and writing skills, or to model reasoning and thinking skills, frequently using mathematical concepts. Without these basics in language, numeracy, and critical thinking, the children from these homes show up for school prepared to recapitulate the failure of their parents, and the cycle repeats itself (Sticht, 1983; Hess & Holloway, 1979).

Attempts to break this cycle have focused on early childhood and elementary-school-based interventions. Chapter I of the Education Consolidation and Improvement Act (formerly Title I of the Elementary and Secondary Education Act initiated in 1965) for 1990 included appropriations for over $5.0 billion for childhood interventions. In comparison, efforts to further develop the literacy, learning, and thinking skills of adults have been and are trivial. The total effort in adult literacy in federal programs has recently been estimated at some $347.6 million. But these dollars are spread across 14 federal agencies, and most are for direct services such as adult basic education or general educational development to obtain a high school equivalency certificate, or perhaps for learning English as a second language (Kahn, 1986).

EARLY CHILDHOOD INTERVENTIONS
INVOLVING PARENTS

For decades it has been recognized that more literate, better educated, more highly intelligent parents somehow transfer cognitive skills to their children. In the early decades of this century, it was noted that more intelligent parents produced more intelligent children who achieved better in school and went on to become the better educated and achieving adults. It was thought that intelligence, defined operationally as the IQ, was largely an inherited and unchangeable trait that parents transmitted genetically to their children.

In the late 1950s, however, evidence was amassed to suggest that most of an adult's intelligence was developed by the time he or she was only 5 or 6 years old (e.g., Bloom, 1964), and that experience during this early period of childhood could be expected to change the child's IQ (e.g., Hunt, 1961). These ideas lead to the emphasis, during the War on Poverty of the mid-1960s, on early childhood interventions to break the cycles of low intelligence that lead to low school achievement that, in turn, were thought to lead to low employability and poverty-level employment.

In several of the early childhood intervention programs attention was focused on trying to educate parents (and particularly mothers) in ways to stimulate the intellectual growth of their children. In a review of 17 early compensatory education programs, Bryant and Ramey (1987) conclude, not only that such programs can provide intellectual benefits, but that "the most improvement in intellectual development is seen when children attend daycare and families receive parent training or other service" (p. 71).

Today, the movement in early childhood intervention is away from working only with children in educational facilities, toward working with families in home, school, and community settings (Klerman, 1985; McCubbin, Olson & Zimmerman, 1985; Zigler & Weiss, 1985).

ADULT LITERACY INTERVENTIONS
INVOLVING CHILDREN

While early childhood educators and researchers were shifting focus from the child to the family, a similar movement was taking place, though at a much slower pace, in adult literacy interventions. At the Association of American Publishers meeting in May, 1979, Sticht, who was then on the staff of the National Institute of Education of the U.S. Department of Education, presented data to suggest that "adult basic literacy development should be a high priority program for education policymakers not only because so many adults are living in marginal circumstances and have only marginal literacy skills to cope with our high information density culture, but also because the parent's educational achievement can be transferred to their children" (p. 7).

The presentation by Sticht was a part of the planning process of the National Institute of Education. Later on, after Sticht left the NIE, Dr. Mary Cross (n.d.) picked up the planning for research on "The Intergenerational Transmission of Literacy Skills." This planning bore fruit in 1983, when President Reagan announced the National Adult Literacy Initiative. As a part of that initiative, then Secretary of Education Bell called for the use of Work-Study students in colleges to work on problems of adult illiteracy. In response, Boston University initiated the Collaborations for Literacy project, under the direction of Dr. Ruth Nickse, and funded by the new Office of Education Research and Improvement that replaced the National Institute of Education, to teach "parents to read to children in an effort to break the cycle of intergenerational illiteracy" (see her chapter in this volume).

The concept of the intergenerational transfer of literacy from adult literacy students to their children was further elaborated (Sticht, 1983) and picked up by education reformist Jonathan Kozol (1985, p. 60), who, along with Sticht, presented testimony to the United States Congress in October 1985 regarding the links between the education of parents and their children. At the time, Congressman William Goodling had started drafting a federal bill called "Even Start," which combined adult basic education for parents and school readiness training for their children (Hartman, this volume). The Even Start legislation was subsequently included as Part B of Chapter I of the Education Consolidation and Improvement Act reauthorization of 1987. Even Start was passed by the House of Representatives and passed to the Senate in the late spring of 1987. When finally passed by the Senate in 1988, Even Start provided $15 million a year (or more) for fiscal year 1988–1989.

On Tuesday, March 18, 1986, the General Assembly of Kentucky reported a bill from the House to the Senate (House Bill No. 662) providing grants for developing and providing model programs of instruction for preschool children and their parents (Heberle, this volume). The bill was subsequently passed and funded. Called the Parent and Child Education Program (PACE) by the Kentucky Department of Education, the goal of the Kentucky program is

> to break the intergenerational cycle of under-education by uniting parents and children in a positive experience that can improve:
>
> 1. Parent's basic skills and attitudes toward education.
> 2. Children's learning skills.
> 3. Parents' child care skills. (Heberle, this volume, p. 136)

In February of 1987, the John D. and Catherine T. MacArthur Foundation announced the award of a grant for up to $700,000 over 3 years to The Home and School Institute, Inc. to support a pilot program called "New Partnerships for Student Achievement." Headed by Dorothy Rich, the New Partnerships project aims to work through various groups to "improve the performance and motivation of school children through work with their families."

Thus, as with the childhood interventions that started out focusing on the child, and which then expanded to include the family as the unit of intervention, there is currently a movement for programs that have been focused on adult literacy development to reorient toward family-oriented interventions.

A NEED FOR KNOWLEDGE SYNTHESIS, DISSEMINATION, AND GENERATION

Though the convergence of adult and childhood intervention programs on the family as the basis for action is a promising trend, there are some serious problems that must be overcome if such programs are to have a consequential and measurable effect on the cognitive skills of both adults and their children.

A major problem is that the knowledge base on which to develop programs that aim to improve both adult's cognitive skills and such skills in the adult's children is very meager, if not nonexistent altogether. Understanding of adult cognitive skill development, particularly among the least able, is very limited. Unlike childhood cognitive development and education during the school years, where well over a billion dollars have been spent in the last decade and a half on basic and applied research, next to nothing has been spent to further our basic knowledge of the cognitive development of adults, particularly undereducated, out-of-school youth and adults. Furthermore, when research has been conducted on the cognitive development of adults, it has been of limited scope and usually of very low quality. Research has usually been accomplished by those trained as professional educators, not by cognitive scientists or other discipline-based investigators.

To be sure, there have been billions of dollars put into job training and creation efforts, such as the Comprehensive Education and Training Act (CETA) and current Job Training Partnership Act (JTPA) programs. But these efforts have not supported basic research on the cognitive development of people in their programs. Repeatedly, program after program of youth remediation and job preparation has been developed, implemented, and soon discarded for lack of achievement of substantive improvements in learning. Literacy programs for adults are lucky to retain adults for 50 or so hours of education. The residential Job Corps program attracts students for only up to 90 to 180 days, and then most have left (Levitan & Gallo, 1987). Typically, only 1 or 2 "years" of growth in reading or mathematics is achieved, with nothing said of writing or critical thinking. And even the growth reported is suspect, due to the use of inadequate assessment tools. Outside the military services, little systematic research has addressed the learning abilities of undereducated youth and adults (Sticht, Armstrong, Hickey, & Caylor, 1987). And, though some projects have suggested that the education of parents in such "parenting" activities as reading to their preschool children may bring about improvements in their children's achievement in reading in school (Maughan & Rutter, 1985) research has not been found on the extent to which adults can be educated to improve their own cognitive ability and how the new competence of the parents can be transferred to their children (Sticht, 1983).

The need for carefully planned and executed research in this area is indicated by the fact that recent testimony before the U.S. Senate Committee on Labor and Human Resources called for policy and funding in the hundreds of millions of dollars on the basis of a belief that "each grade more skills of parents in one generation yields an equal increment in the skills of the next generation . . ." (Taggart, 1987, p. 28). The recommendation calls for the large-scale extension of a particular education program to bring about at least a 1-year gain in adult basic skills, with the expectation that this new competence of adults would transfer intergenerationally to the adult's children . . . with no mechanism for this transfer planned or elucidated.

A further problem with research on cognitive development, especially among undereducated youth and adults, is that it has typically been short-term research, accomplished by researchers who have come into a community, conducted the research and then left. Indigenous capacity for continuing the research in the community-based projects that are at work by the thousands throughout the nation is not developed and sustained. There are only limited efforts by "outsiders" to "put research into practice" without the long-term, sustained enquiry needed to usefully understand the functional contexts of adults in the local area and to improve the capacity of local organizations to design learning environments that promote cognitive growth in both adults and their children. This has the effect of failing to inculcate even the most rudimentary respect for measurement and evaluation in such programs. This shows itself in many ways, including a disdain for the collection of program outcome data, misuse of test instruments, and failure to learn from mistakes (Sticht, 1988).

Though, as indicated above, there is action in the policy, program, and research arenas to establish new models for the interruption of the intergenerational transmission of poverty and low cognitive skills, these activities are limited, and many are just forming. There has not been a concerted effort to bring the knowledge obtained in the last 20 years of childhood interventions to bear on the newly emerging adult–child interventions. There is still controversy over the success of the childhood interventions (Glazer, 1986; Jencks, 1986). Among other things, this includes concerns over the shift from reliance on the IQ as the central measure of cognitive growth in childhood programs to the use of school-oriented achievement tests (reading, mathematics) or noncognitive factors such as being promoted rather than held back, fewer delinquency problems, and so forth.

In adult cognitive skills remediation, little attention has been paid to the findings of the late 1950s and early 1960s regarding the rapid growth of IQ up to age 5 or 6 and then the relative stability of the IQ over the lifespan (e.g., Honzik, 1986). This finding is what suggested that most of the problem of adult illiteracy or functional illiteracy should be addressed through prevention in early childhood interventions rather than through remediation in adult literacy and basic education programs. What is the status of this IQ controversy today, and how does it relate to the move toward combined adult–child intervention programs? How do the new conceptions of intelligence as information processing, "practical intelligence," and so forth (Wagner, this volume) relate to the current movement of cognitive intervention programs toward the family as the unit of action?

Not only are conceptions of intelligence different today from 20 years ago; additionally, conceptions of the so-called academic "basic skills" are different. Reading, writing, arithmetic, and higher-order, critical thinking skills are differently understood today than a quarter century ago. A very significant difference in the understanding of these processes is the role of knowledge. Today, as contrasted with 20 years ago, there is much more of a recognition of the role of what one knows, in a very specific sense, in one's ability to apply the "basic skills" to problem solving and task performance in and out of school. What are the implications of the understandings from the recently emerged, interdisciplinary field called *cognitive science* for policy, practice, and research in adult–child interventions?

REVIEW OF RESEARCH

Because of the significance of the current move toward a new approach to the intergenerational transfer of cognitive skills that is taking place in the field of adult literacy development, including the proposed expenditures of hundreds of millions of dollars in federal and state education funds, it is both timely and important to conduct an in-depth review of the policy, practice, and scientific issues involved in such interventions.

OVERVIEW OF VOLUME I

As a part of a larger project, a series of scholarly papers by nationally prominent researchers and practitioners, some with experience in policymaking at the federal level, were commissioned.

The papers were presented and discussed in April 1988 at a 3-day *Conference on the Intergenerational Transfer of Cognitive Skills*. The conference included a review of past attempts to influence the course of cognitive development and a review of cognitive science research relevant to the intergenerational transfer of cognitive skills. The present volume (Volume I) presents the papers dealing with past- and ongoing intervention programs to improve the cognitive skills of children, youth and adults, and problems and research issues that should be considered in the design and implementation of new intervention programs. The papers on cognitive science are presented in Volume II.

Regarding past intervention programs, most of these programs were initiated in the mid-1960s as a part of the War on Poverty and were targeted at improving one generation at a time. The papers for this part of the conference are presented in Part 1 of this volume.

Papers that describe ongoing programs to improve the cognitive skills of two generations, parents and their children, are presented in Part 2.

Part 3 presents the summaries from the working groups regarding policy, practice, and research issues involved in the intergenerational transfer of cognitive skills. The book concludes with comments on the intergenerational transfer of cognitive skills by Dan Wagner.

It will be noted that the papers are heterogeneous with regard to style, length, and content. They represent the diversity of professionals at the conference: policymakers, practitioners, and research scientists. But these professionals also represent a variety of ethnic groups: whites, blacks, Hispanics, and Native Americans. This diversity of cultural and professional backgrounds is what makes the United States of America unique.

It is impossible to consider the intergenerational transfer of cognitive skills through systematic interventions without attending to the influences of such diversity. While this makes the job more difficult than in a country with a more homogeneous population, it is also the particular strength of the United States. A general conclusion from the conference was that the United States needs to find ways to build on the strength of its cultural diversity to appreciate and enhance the cognitive abilities of its citizenry, and its standing in the international community.

REFERENCES

Bloom, B. S. (1964). *Stability and change in human characteristics.* New York: Wiley.

Bryant, D. M., & Ramey, C. T. (1987). An analysis of the effectiveness of early intervention programs for environmentally at-risk children. In M. J. Guralnick & F. C. Bennett (Eds.), *The effectiveness of early intervention for at-risk and handicapped children.* New York: Academic Press.

Cross, M. (n.d.). *Intergenerational transmission of literacy skills. Unpublished planning paper.* Washington, DC: National Institute of Education, U.S. Department of Health, Education, and Welfare.

Glazer, N. (1986). Education and training programs and poverty. In S. H. Danziger & D. H. Weinberg (Eds.), *Fighting poverty: What works and what doesn't.* Cambridge, MA: Harvard University Press.

Hess, R., & Holloway, S. (1979). *The intergenerational transmission of literacy* (Report prepared for the National Institute of Education). Washington, DC: U.S. Department of Health, Education, and Welfare.

Honzik, M. P. (1986). The role of the family in the development of mental abilities: A 50-year study. In N. Datan, A. L. Greene, & H. W. Reese (Eds.), *Life-span developmental psychology: Intergenerational relations.* Hillsdale, NJ: Erlbaum.

Hunt, J. M. (1961). *Intelligence and experience.* New York: Ronald Press.

Jencks, C. (1986). Comment [on the chapter by Glazer]. In S. H. Danziger & D. H. Weinberg (Eds.), *Fighting poverty: What works and what doesn't.* Cambridge, MA: Harvard University Press.

Kahn, M. E. (1986, May). *Literacy management information project report: Volume I* (Report for the Adult Literacy Initiative). Washington, DC: U.S. Department of Education.

Klerman, G. L. (1985). Community mental health: Developments in the United States. In R. N. Rapoport (Ed.), *Children youth, and families*. Cambridge, UK: Cambridge University Press.

Kozol, J. (1985). *Illiterate America*. New York: Doubleday.

Levitan, S. A., & Gallo, F. (1987). *A second chance: Training for jobs*. Kalamazoo, MI: W. E. Upjohn Institute for Employment Research.

Maughan, B., & Rutter, M. (1985). Education: Improving practice through increasing understanding. In R. N. Rapoport (Ed.), *Children, youth and families*. Cambridge, UK: Cambridge University Press.

McCubbin, H. I., Olson, D. H., & Zimmerman, S. L. (1985). Family dynamics: Strengthening families through action-research. In R. N. Rapoport (Ed.), *Children, youth and families*. Cambridge, UK: Cambridge University Press.

Sticht, T. (1979, May). *The cycles of marginal literacy and marginal living*. Paper presented at the Annual Meeting of the Association of American Publishers, Palm Beach, FL.

Sticht, T. (1983). *Literacy and human resources development at work: Investing in the education of adults to improve the educability of children* (HumRRO Professional Paper 2–83). Alexandria, VA: Human Resources Research Organization.

Sticht, T. (1987). *Functional context education: Workshop resource notebook*. San Diego, CA: Applied Behavioral & Cognitive Sciences, Inc.

Sticht, T. (1988). Adult literacy education. In E. Rothkopf (Ed.), *Review of research in education* (Vol 15). Washington, DC: American Educational Research Association.

Sticht, T., Armstrong, W., Hickey, D., & Caylor, J. (1987). *Cast-off youth: Policy and training methods from the military experience*. New York: Praeger.

Taggart, R. (1987, January). *Solving the basic skills crisis* (Testimony before the U.S. Senate Committee on Labor and Human Resources). Washington, DC: Remediation and Training Institute.

Zigler, E., & Weiss, H. (1985). Family support systems: An ecological approach to child development. In R. N. Rapoport (Ed.), *Children, youth, and families*. Cambridge, UK: Cambridge University Press.

Part I

Intervention to Improve Cognitive Skills of One Generation

Chapter 2

Introduction to Part I

Micheal J. Beeler

During the 1960s, there was increasing recognition of inequalities in status, wealth, and income in the United States. This perception of inequality was in direct contrast with the ideology of our nation that "all men are created equal." The United States as a whole was experiencing unparalleled prosperity, and yet "pockets of poverty" defined nearly one-fifth of the population. In 1964 the Johnson Administration responded to this social crisis and began a War on Poverty. A single line of reasoning was often used to both rationalize the broad variability in wealth and explain how social programs might reduce this variability. Jencks (1972) summarized this chain of thought as follows:

1. Social and economic differences between blacks and whites and between rich and poor derive in good part from differences in their cognitive skills.
2. Cognitive skills can be measured with at least moderate precision by standardized tests of "intelligence, verbal ability, reading comprehension, mathematical skills," and so forth.
3. Differences in people's performance on cognitive tests can be partly explained by differences in the amount and quality of schooling they get.
4. Equalizing educational opportunity would therefore be an important step toward equalizing blacks and whites, rich and poor, and people in general. (p. 52)

Following this line of reasoning, the War on Poverty initiated programs of childhood compensatory education, youth and adult education and job training, and family and community development. The criteria for participation in most of these programs was low income.

The chapters that make up Part I provide critiques of some of the educational research and interventions that were spawned during this nation's War on Poverty. The interventions include federally sponsored programs (both civilian and military) which were designed and implemented to bring an emerging underclass of poor and minority citizens into the mainstream culture. The strategy, as expressed by government policy, was to improve economic and social conditions via education, or cognitive skills development. These programs can usefully be categorized as early childhood interventions, job training programs directed toward teenage youths and adults, and programs designed to benefit families and communities.

An all too frequent result of the early childhood interventions discussed in Part I was an initial increase in IQ for program participants that unfortunately was typically lost within 3 to 4 years following the intervention. This had the effect of calling into question the use of the IQ as the sole determinant of success or failure for these programs. It also called attention to the importance of other cognitive skills and measures of competence as indicators of program success.

Youth and adult job training programs, in general, found similar immediate postintervention gains in their central measure of employment. However, these gains typically faded, leaving no evidence of long-term gain in terms of employment, increased economic opportunity, or cognitive skills development.

Family and community interventions have been judged to have had an impact, albeit an unanticipated impact. For instance, Community Action Programs (CAPs), which were designed to function as a mechanism for the distribution of social services, also became vehicles for black political representation.

In Chapter 3, Spitz considers the theoretical foundations of many early childhood interventions. He notes that a conceptualization of human competence as malleable, is by no means new. In fact, this issue is grounded in one of the longest running debates of social science: nature vs. nurture in the development of intellectual ability. In his chapter, Spitz expresses concern with many of the conceptual, theoretical, statistical, and ethical practices of the early childhood interventionists. His central thesis is that, to date, empirical evidence of the capacity to modify IQ has not been published.

In Chapter 4, Paul provides an important perspective for understanding the past 20 years of early childhood interventions. Among the insights presented in this chapter are: (a) that positive outcomes occurred when evidence of institutional change was in conjunction with individual change; and (b) that need exists to bridge segmented components of this society's social structure (e.g., school and home). Paul believes that progress in cognitive skills development can be made with children from low-income minority families via early intervention programs. She insists, however, that anthropological research findings can assist in designing more effective programs.

Chapter 5 moves beyond early childhood interventions to those interventions designed for our nation's school-aged youth and adult population. Datta, an organizing participant of the Follow-Through planned variation experiment, provides us with some fresh light on past outcomes, and future hopes for programs such as Job Corps, YEDPA, CETA, and those programs administered under the Educational Improvement Act of 1982. Some education reforms that have come about as a result of the past research that Datta notes in this chapter are an increase in the number and breadth of courses required to complete high school, the establishment in many states of statewide achievement tests, and lastly, the development of teacher competency tests. The recommendations that Datta provides for future programs includes program networking, returning education to a functional context, and utilizing multiple measures and metaanalysis in the evaluation of programs.

In Chapter 6, Duffy suggests that past interventions could have benefitted from better designed instruction. In reviewing past and present military literacy programs, Duffy discusses the importance of content knowledge and discourages commitment to a "general literacy" model of reading. He also notes the need to consider divergent reading strategies, dependent upon the reader's purposes.

Concentrating on programs designed to affect the family and community, Scott-Jones, in Chapter 7, points out the theoretical foundation for many of these programs, and many of the inherent foibles that emerge as a policy design gets put into practice. She comments on several important aspects of intervention policies and programs, including the effects of government policy on scientific research, the failure of programs to generalize across subcultures, and the need to design programs that take a lifespan perspective.

In the final chapter of Part 1, Laosa notes the importance of explicit dialogue. He suggests that interventions can benefit from the explicit statement of assumptions, tacit models, and the rationale for interventions proposed. Laosa also comments on "tensions" in the field that remain unresolved (e.g., appropriate unit of analysis, segment of the life cycle in which to intervene). He concludes that, oftentimes, politics, as opposed to substantive considerations, have determined the approach of interventions. The final issue that Laosa deals with is the generalizability of research findings or, as he puts it, population validity. Laosa points out that population validity in applied work is more than a scientific issue. He contends that population validity is an ethical issue that, because of our growing cultural diversity, will be encountered with greater frequency in the future, and demands a framework for understanding the limits of generalization.

REFERENCE

Jencks, C. (1972). *Inequality: A reassessment of the effect of family and schooling in America*. New York: Harper.

Chapter 3

Early Childhood Intervention

Herman H. Spitz
E. R. Johnstone Training and Research Center*

It is always helpful to place current psychological issues into historical perspective, in order to see how they fit into the continuing flow of issues that have intrigued those who are interested in human thought and behavior. Such an approach increases our understanding immensely, and inevitably informs us that many of the concerns of our predecessors remain with us today, albeit refitted in modern clothing. This is certainly the case with the nature-nurture debate which—in many different guises—dates back to the golden age of Greece, to Protagoras, Plato, Socrates, and Aristotle.

But I have chosen (in Spitz, 1986) to take up the issue as it was in the year 1800, when French physicians, tutored in Philosophy, realized that the feral child seen running wild and naked in the woods in the province of Aveyron provided a natural test of the empiricist philosophy of Locke and Condillac. It was fitting that Jean-Marc-Gaspard Itard was given the task of training the child, for Itard was a firm empiricist who believed in the Lockian doctrine that the mind is—with minor exceptions—blank at birth (a *tabula rasa*), until sensory experience produced ideas. This view contrasted with Descarte's rationalism, which stressed innate properties of the mind acting upon and organizing incoming sensations.

Although initially successful in taming the "Wild Boy of Aveyron," Itard finally gave up in despair. Empiricism nevertheless survived and prospered, finding perhaps its fullest expression in Russian Lamarck-

---

* Now at 389 Terhune Rd., Princeton, NJ 08540

ism, British associationism, and American behaviorism. The reasoning is that if the mind at birth is a blank slate, then intelligence level is determined almost exclusively by environmental forces. Of course few workers today adhere to this extreme position, preferring instead some form of interactionism—the view that level of intelligence results from the interaction of innate intellectual potential with environmental shaping. Consequently, a major area of study and contention now centers on the characteristics of this interaction, and the relative extent to which heredity or environment are influential.

It was during the period (from the 1930s to the 1940s) when behaviorism was dominant that psychology somehow was renamed behavioral science and psychologists were transformed into behavioral scientists. And it was in this heady period that many psychologists actually believed that with proper response-reward contingencies the human mind would be like putty in our hands. In this atmosphere hundreds of childhood intervention projects were begun, with the aid of substantial federal funding. Here I will discuss briefly just two of these projects, the Perry Preschool Project and the Milwaukee Project. This will be followed by a brief discussion of environmental and genetic sources of variance in ability, with special emphasis on the implications of the findings reported by developmental behavioral geneticists.

THE PERRY PRESCHOOL PROJECT

The Perry Preschool Project (and the High/Scope Educational Research Foundation which it spawned) is—in terms of longevity, influence, and independence—one of the most successful early intervention projects ever developed. Here is how David Weikart, who directed the project and is president of the Foundation, described this success in a 1983 paper.

> Impossible to plan for in advance, but an accident of history finds that a carefully designed and executed project in a small midwestern city has the right data at the right time 20 years later to actually affect social policy at a national (and increasingly international) level. While I would like to claim the foresight and wisdom for achieving this success, it actually appears to be luck. (p. 194)

But Dr. Weikart is too modest. Luck had very little to do with the success of this project. It succeeded, in my view, because of Dr. Weikart's energy, persistence, and personality, and in particular his organizational and public relations abilities. The best evidence for this is in his proud description (in the Spring, 1985 issue of *High/Scope ReSource,* a newsletter published by the Foundation) of the hiring of a public relations firm in Washington, DC to stimulate interest in a news conference to publicize the publication of their monograph, *Changed Lives,* which it did quite successfully (see Spitz, 1986, pp. 104–105, for a description of these events). Since that time the High/ Scope Foundation and its Perry Preschool Project have continued in the spotlight. As just a small example of media coverage, it was featured in the April, 1987 issue of the *APA Monitor,* and is frequently mentioned very favorably in the Editorial pages and Education sections of the *New York Times.* (It should be noted that the Foundation has published a book edited by F. M. Hechinger, a *Times* education columnist.)

Still, all this would be of minor importance if it reflected good, objective evidence that the Perry Project has advanced the science and art of early childhood education. After all, most of its publications have been privately published monographs and a few invited chapters in books, and consequently they have not been subjected to the peer review process that most of us have to live through, and which serves as one of the safeguards in the scientific process. So we have to scrutinize with extra care the publications that are available.

In 1958 and 1959, David Weikart, as director of the Special Services Department, conducted a series of studies of the Ypsilanti Public Schools and reported to the curriculum council and the principals of the school system that, among other things, children in the lower-class schools were performing much more poorly than were children in the middle-class schools. There was general agreement that no further productive changes could be made within the school system, and an ad hoc committee decided to develop a compensatory preschool program for disadvantaged black children, designed to prevent the deficits from occurring.

Initiated in September 1962, with state and local funds, the project acquired additional support along the way, including a grant from the U.S. Office of Education (Weikart, Deloria, Lawser, & Wiegerink, 1970). The curriculum changed over the course of the study. From initially trying to teach Piagetian tasks, there evolved the most significant curriculum change of all: "The devolution of responsibility for initiating learning experience from the teacher alone, to the child and teacher together" (Weikart, 1983, p. 185), which became known as the "Cognitively Oriented Curriculum." In the early 1970s another major change was made when the classroom program was organized around a set of key experiences. Over the course of two decades the theoretical orientation had changed from one which implicitly viewed the child as a *tabula rasa* on which the teacher wrote the necessary experiences, to one in which teaching "was directed toward helping children use the preschool and home environment to accomplish their own activities and goals" (Weikart, 1983, p. 186), and no doubt the curriculum continues to evolve.

Commendable as this evolution is, it raises one very serious problem: The claims of success for this project, based as they are on the performance and life adjustment 19 years later of the children in the original groups, are irrelevant for predicting success for children presently in the preschool program, who receive an entirely different curriculum.

But then, perhaps *what* is taught is not important, as long as it is—in the words of the project directors—of "high quality." Indeed, at age 15 there were no IQ or school achievement differences between children receiving the Cognitively Oriented Curriculum and children receiving two other, different curriculums (Schweinhart, Weikart, & Larner, 1986). All three programs combined to produce a remarkable mean IQ gain of 27 points during the first year of the preschool program, which dropped 7 points during the second preschool year, and slipped further in the following years, typical of intervention programs. But there was, in fact, one significant finding from this study: Children who had attended the two preschool programs that used mostly child-initiated activities reported fewer delinquent behaviors. However, self-reports such as these are not always reliable; there were no differences in the rate of arrest.

Searching for a reason for why all three curriculums were, in general, equally effective, Weikart (1983) suggested certain common threads, such as (a) the consistency not only of the curriculum, but also of the supervision and inservice training, (b) the fostering of team teaching and planning by the staff, and (c) what Weikart termed a "catch bag" of components, including such things as the involvement of parents, adequate supplies and equipment, administrative support, and a system of program evaluation.

This, as far as I can see, is what it has come down to, and it's not very inspiring. After a careful reading of the history of this project, it is difficult, for me at least, to accept the special claims that have been made for it. Weikart and his colleagues very honestly and clearly demonstrated in their original study that although the mean IQ of the preschool children was initially raised considerably compared with that of the control groups, these differences dissipated by the time the children were 8 years old. Consequently, a host of other variables were emphasized. I have analyzed these in some detail elsewhere (Spitz,

1986). In general, they are not very persuasive. The one thing that stands out is that there is no correlation between attendance in the preschool and positive outcome measures; all the attempts to show relationships are indirect and strained (Berrueta-Clement, Schweinhart, Barnett, Epstein, & Weikart, 1984).

There is also an attempt to show that a cost-benefit analysis favors the preschool children, but this analysis depends on subjective judgments of the financial value of social outcomes, as well as on *projections* that the preschool children will earn more than the control children. In any case, results thus far are very clear in one respect: interventions, such as the Perry Preschool Project, have yet to show that they can interrupt the cycle of poverty. When the preschool children reached 19 years of age (in 1977 through 1981), their median income was $2,772 (Berrueta-Clement et al., 1984).

Finally, we should always be cognizant of the fact that the original Perry Preschool Project spawned the High/Scope Educational Research Foundation. This Foundation engages in a large number of ancillary activities and is very frankly in the business of selling preschool education. It is no longer an objective, scientific enterprise because it has so large an invested interest in the results of any study it might undertake, a vested interest that is reflected in the way it has reported its findings, and in its manipulation of the media.

THE MILWAUKEE PROJECT

At the same time that the Perry Preschool Project was underway in the early 1960s, a group of workers at the University of Wisconsin Rehabilitation Research and Training Center in Mental Retardation began to examine the characteristics of a population that was at high risk for mental retardation. The resulting survey suggested that so-called "cultural-familial" mental retardation might be prevented "by a program of family intervention begun during early infancy" (Heber & Garber, 1975, p. 400). Consequently in 1968, supported by federal funds, they began a project designed to intervene with "at risk" infants before they were 6 months old. The intervention was not only early, it was pervasive: all day, 5 days a week, 12 months of the year. Concurrently, there was a rehabilitation program with the infants' mothers, all of whom were below 75 IQ. Seven years later, when the project children were entering their first year of public school, "a final . . . comprehensive report" (p. 400) was promised. Thirteen years after this promise, a Final Report was finally published as a monograph by the American Association on Mental Retardation (Garber, 1988).

As with the Perry Project, the Milwaukee Project (as it came to be known) reported its findings at conferences, in book chapters, and in their own printed progress reports. At 10 months of age there was a small difference between experimental (intervention) and control infants on the Gesell Development Schedule, but by 22 months the differences were very large, with "the performance of the Experimental group . . . clearly accelerated while the Control group performs at or slightly below norms for the four scales" (Heber & Garber, 1975, p. 418). The control group continued to decline a bit, whereas the experimental group maintained its high performance. Based on the Cattell and Stanford-Binet, the discrepancy varied "from a minimum of 25 IQ points at 24 months to 30 IQ points at 60 months" (Heber, Garber, Harrington, Hoffman, & Falender, 1972, p. 50). At 5 years of age, the mean IQ of the 17 experimental subjects who remained in the project was 124, compared with the mean IQ of 94 obtained by the 18 remaining control subjects. Early intervention had resulted in a mean IQ difference of 30 points. Little wonder that the Milwaukee Project became so celebrated, was glowingly reported in the media, and was included approvingly in many textbooks on developmental, abnormal, educational, and general psychology.

However, despite these remarkable results, this project was to have a far different fate than did the Perry Preschool Project. Whereas the Perry Project developed into a flourishing Foundation, the Milwaukee Project fell into disrepute when its director and his assistant were jailed for depositing conference registration fees into their personal bank accounts when these fees should have been deposited into the grant account. Needless to say, this money was not reported in their income tax returns. As the investigation developed there were other surprises, including the fact that the director of the Project was, during the course of the Project, difficult to reach and spent a great deal of time in pursuing other interests.

Sommer and Sommer (1984) conducted an interesting survey of how the Milwaukee Project was represented in textbooks in abnormal and developmental psychology. Their findings, reported in the *American Psychologist,* illustrated "how research data can appear in textbooks . . . and seep into the research literature without ever having gone through the journal review process" (p. 982). They suggested also that the diversion of funds casts doubt on the validity of the data. Howard Garber, who had taken over as director of the Project, took issue with this conclusion, as did another writer (see comments on the Sommer and Sommer article in the November, 1984 issue of the *American Psychologist,* pp. 1314–1319). One has to decide for oneself whether the unlawful behavior of the Project's director and his assistant raises doubts about the data. But Sommer and Sommer pointed out that a number of other problems converged to raise their concerns about the study and the incautious reporting of textbook authors. One such problem was that the Project staff rarely responded to letters, a frustration that I had also experienced.

Finally, the results were so extraordinary that they have to be scrutinized carefully. In the past, stable IQ differences of such magnitude have never held up under close examination (see, for example, the Schmidt study in Spitz, 1986); and an intervention project begun in 1972 in North Carolina, very similar in the promptness and extent of the intervention, produced nothing like the IQ differences reported for the Milwaukee Project (e.g., Ramey & Campbell, 1984; Spitz, 1986, pp. 110–112). The published results of the Milwaukee Project have been carefully analyzed by Ellis Page, a most vocal and persistent critic (see Page's chapter in Spitz, 1986), who found a host of problems, including questionable statistical procedures, contradictory and shifting numbers, "teaching of the test," and so on. Until the results are replicated in an open atmosphere in which there is reasonable confidence in the project staff, the Milwaukee Project must be followed always by a very large shadow of doubt.

A PERSISTENT PROBLEM IN EARLY INTERVENTION STUDIES

A number of difficulties that plague early intervention studies have been pointed out in the past, and bear repeating. One of these problems is particularly crucial: Why are early results so impressive only to lead inevitably to later disillusionment? The first, most obvious reason is that assessment during infancy and early childhood is not acceptably reliable or valid. Infant scales are measures primarily of motor and sensory development. Infants with cerebral palsy would score very poorly on these scales, yet we know that most persons with cerebral palsy are not mentally retarded. Recent research does raise the possibility that measures of infant attention, novelty preference, and visual recognition (e.g., Fagan, 1984a, 1984b), as well as of foresight and expectation (e.g., Wachs & DeRemer, 1978), are tapping more directly into general intellectual ability and will prove to be better predictors of later ability.

Related to this problem is the possibility that the abilities tapped by scales designed for very young children are easier to train than are the abilities tapped by later tests. Almost inevitably the curriculum for early intervention programs are loaded with tasks that are very similar to the content of assessment tests.

This brings up a theoretical issue of some importance. Empiricists believe that ability (intelligence) develops out of what has been learned, like a slope leading up to higher development. But another way of looking at this is that the central nervous system is genetically programmed to advance to sometimes radically different and more complex ways of dealing with the environment as the brain matures, and consequently being trained at one stage of development will not necessarily carry over to the next stage when entirely different concepts are required, although there is still an underlying general capacity that persons bring with them through the stages. The best physical analogy of this process is the bodily change that takes place during adolescence, a metamorphosis dependent on genetic programming and essentially unrelated to prior development, although the general physical nature of the individual is retained—an athlete at 10 usually is an athlete at 15, for example. (Whether one believes that *specific* capacities are programmed to emerge, or only general organizational properties of the brain interacting with the environment, depends on whether one is a Chomskyite or a Piagetian, respectively.)

Wilson's (1986) study comparing the Wechsler subtest patterns of monozygotic (MZ) and dizygotic (DZ) twins from ages 5 to 15 is instructive. The subtest patterns changed somewhat over the years, but the degree to which the patterns changed *together* was greater in the MZ (identical) than in the DZ (fraternal) twins. There was continuity (particularly on the Verbal Scale) as well as change, and both continuity and change were genetically influenced.

This viewpoint does suggest an explanation for why early intervention studies are bedeviled by the ephemeral nature of initial, large differences between experimental and control groups. Once the children mature to new stages that require very different abilities, they must in a sense start over again, with concepts progressively more complex and more difficult to train.

Some support for this viewpoint comes from the empiricists themselves. In their famous study, Skodak and Skeels (1949) found that the IQ correlation between adopted children and their true mothers gradually increased from zero when the children were 2.2 years old, to .28 at 4.3 years, and up to .44 at 13.5 years. Ample evidence from many studies (see Plomin, 1986) indicates that correlations between children and their parents increase as the children mature, so that the highest correlation would no doubt be obtained if individuals were to be tested at the same adult age as their parents had been. The early infant and children tests are measuring different abilities than the later tests, and the genetic influence is manifested more fully at later ages. This brings us back full circle to the nature/nurture problems, but today there are powerful new tools and an entirely new field of study, behavioral genetics. This new field is contributing some very exciting findings that I believe will have a major impact on our thinking.

NATURE/NURTURE . . . AGAIN

As its name implies, behavioral genetics is a field of study in which various techniques of genetic analysis are used in order to increase our understanding of behavioral characteristics. Its inception as a distinct discipline is traced by McClearn and DeFries (1973) to the book *Behavior Genetics,* published by Fuller and Thompson in 1960. Of particular interest to interventionists is the subsequent emergence of "developmental" behavioral genetics (Plomin, 1986). Behavioral geneticists have refined existing techniques and developed new ones in order to tease from human behavior the variance accounted for by genetic and environmental components and their interaction. Two examples follow.

The Minnesota Center for Twin and Adoption Research, located in the Psychology Department of the University of Minnesota, consists of five principal research programs. One of these, the Minnesota Study of Twins Reared Apart, has aroused a great deal of interest. In this project, identical, monozygotic (MZ) twins who had been reared apart and fraternal, dizygotic (DZ) twins who also had been reared apart are invited to the University for a week of extensive medical, psychophysiological, and psychological tests and interviews. The project will continue at least until 100 MZ and 50 DZ twins are examined, but in 1986, 44 MZ and 27 DZ reared-apart twin pairs had been tested. The median age at separation was 0.2 years, and the median separation period was 33.8 years (Telligen, Lykken, Bouchard, Wilcox, Segal, & Rich, 1988). Clearly the twins had been separated too early and were apart for too long to have been influenced to any extent by the same environment.

The primary interest of this program is in the behavior and test correlations of the MZ compared with the DZ twins (e.g., Bouchard, 1984; Segal, 1985). What has most impressed the investigators is the remarkable similarities of the MZ twins reared apart (MZA) when compared with the DZ twins, although they are quick to point out that the twins are also individuals, and there are always some distinct differences in every pair of MZ twins.

The MZ twins share the same genes, whereas the DZ twins, on

average, share about half of their genes in common, by descent. Consequently, on highly heritable traits, the intraclass correlations should be about twice as high in MZ as in DZ twins. For example, for fingerprint ridgecounts, the correlation is .98 for MZ twins reared together, .96 for MZ twins reared apart, and .46 for DZ twins (Lykken, 1982). The heritability can be estimated by doubling the difference between the correlations of the MZ and DZ pairs, in this case producing a heritability estimate of about 1, indicating that variance in this trait is entirely genetically influenced.

On physical and psychophysical traits "the various twin designs yield consistent and substantial heritabilities, in the range of .65 and .98" (Bouchard, 1984, p. 174); that is, to say, 65 to 98 percent of the variance is genetically influenced. "In the domain of intelligence, we find somewhat less consistent estimates of genetic influence, but the effects are still quite strong, somewhere in the range of .50 to .80" (p. 174).

Another program in the Center, the Minnesota Adoption Project, is designed to determine the degree to which similarity in rearing environments of the twins who were reared apart is associated with the similarities the twins exhibit. To accomplish this, a *sibling* is paired with the co-twin whom he or she was *not* reared with, and their similarities determined. Then, that same sibling will be paired with the co-twin he or she *was* reared with. If a common family environment is a strong factor, the sibling will perform much more like the co-twin that he or she was reared with.

Another way of measuring the effects of a common family environment is to compare the correlations obtained by MZ twins reared together (MZT) with the correlations obtained by MZ twins reared apart (MZA). For example, on personality measures the average correlation is .54 for MZA twins and .52 for MZT twins, which, contrary to popular opinion, suggests minimal influence of family environment on the variance in personality.

These results are duplicated in the other behavioral genetics programs that I wish to mention, programs that are outgrowths from the Institute for Behavioral Genetics at the University of Colorado, including the Hawaii Family Study of Cognition (DeFries et al., 1979) and in particular, the Colorado Adoption Study (Plomin & DeFries, 1985). (Note that Plomin has since moved to Pennsylvania State University.) Plomin (1986) repeatedly points out that "the best way to study the effects of environment on behavior is through the study of genetic influences employing the theory and method of quantitative genetics" (p. 3). In this regard, he suggests that perhaps "the single most important contribution of human behavioral genetics to date" is the finding that: "Environmental variance relevant to psychological development is not shared by members of a family" (p. 5), or, put another way, "environmental influences make two children in the same family as different from one another as are pairs of children selected randomly from the population" (Plomin & Daniels, 1987, p. 1).

Some of the evidence for this startling statement is derived from the Colorado Adoption Project, where pairs of adopted children were reared in the same family from early life. If these children are very much alike, then the shared family environment is, presumably, responsible, and indeed when adoptive siblings are young they produce some modest correlations in their performance. However, when adoptive siblings are tested in adolescence, their correlation for IQ and other traits is not significantly different from zero. Although shared family experiences have some influence in making siblings similar during childhood, this influence fades as individuals reach adolescence.

The environmental sources of variance which have the strongest effects on siblings are embedded in experiences siblings do *not* share (nonshared environment). These include not only differences in experiences outside the home and away from the family, but also derive from the fact that parents treat each of their children differently for many reasons, including the fact that the siblings *are* different and consequently differ from each other in their interactions with their parents. In sum, the influence of shared environments (such as the number of books in the family book shelf) is less relevant than the nonshared environments within and outside the family, which serve to increase sibling differences.

IMPLICATIONS FOR EARLY INTERVENTION

Nature abhors sameness, or, to express it inversely, nature demands variability. It is essential that there be variation in the characteristics of the individuals who make up a species. Variation consequent on sexual reproduction can protect a species from extinction. When there is a drastic change in the environment, diversity increases the survival chances of at least some members of a species (to the despair of exterminators). It is even possible to find tasks on which mentally retarded individuals perform more accurately than do college graduates (Spitz, Borys, & Webster, 1982).

Nature has many ways of assuring human diversity. There are many strongly genetic traits that will not necessarily run in families because they are determined by distinctive configurations and interactions of a number of independent or partly independent genes at different loci (Lykken, 1982). For this reason, child prodigies and geniuses can blossom in the most unexpected places.

The major difference between the domains of behavioral genetics and early childhood intervention is that behavioral geneticists focus on *variance*, whereas interventionists focus on *averages* (Plomin, 1987). Interventionists assess the outcome of their efforts by comparing the differences between the mean pre- and posttest performance of the experimental (intervention) group and the control (nonintervention) group, and variability in the groups is unwanted noise that decreases the chances of finding a statistically significant difference. Behavioral geneticists study the variability; that is, they are interested in finding the source of individual differences. This does not make one method better than the other, but the differences should be recognized and the implications of individual differences clearly understood.

For one thing, even when there is improvement in an experimental intervention group when compared with a control group, the variances usually remain the same, and therefore we can assume that the source of the group's improvement is not the same as the source of the individual variations. A genetic influence on individual differences in some trait cannot be generalized to implicate genetic influence on the group differences for that trait.

Most important for our present concerns is the finding that in a single family, going through the parents to reach the children requires that each child be treated differently, for each sibling brings to the world different genetic potentials and consequently interacts differently with the parents. This applies also of course to children from different families. Furthermore, differences outside the shared family environment are very influential. Yet traditional experimental designs require a standard set of procedures that treat all children pretty much the same, and herein lies a dilemma for intervention research, one among many challenges that must be met.

A trait's heritability does not doom an individual to an immutable destiny. Intervention can effect even traits that have high heritability. For example, if individuals whose genes would give them a height of, say, 5 feet, are given growth hormones, they might actually reach a height of 5 feet, 4 inches. Or individuals destined to be mentally retarded because of some enzyme deficiency will not, in fact, become retarded if they are placed on a special diet shortly after birth. But note that these examples involve biomedical intervention, treating the effects of a single gene. Intelligence, on the other hand, is probably polygenic. Perhaps this is one reason why the dramatic effects of medical intervention have not been duplicated by psychological or pedagogical intervention, although in principle there is no reason why they should not produce some positive effects, up to a limit. Even if the heritability is as high as 70 percent, there is enough remaining environmental contribution to allow for important changes; and in instances where social injustice has restricted the opportunities of entire groups, massive improvements are possible.

Consider also that the measurement of genetic influence derives from a population's *existing* genetic and environmental variation; if a child's environment is changed, the way his or her genetic propensity is expressed will also change. On the other hand, the more we approach a state in which the environment is the same for everyone, the greater will be the influence of genetic variance on individual differences in behavior.

SUMMARY

The philosophy of empiricism and its progeny, behaviorism, convinced many psychologists that individual differences in mental abilities result almost exclusively from individual differences in experiences. Consequently, early intervention studies were begun with great optimism. Many of these studies intervened with infants and young children who were assumed to be at risk for mental retardation, and in some of these the intervention was begun shortly after birth and was intensively continued. Two studies that have had high visibility were briefly examined.

A pervasive finding of intervention studies is that initially large differences between experimental and control groups dissipate as the children mature. It is suggested that one reason for this finding is that genes influence both continuity and change. Although children maintain their basic identity and character as they mature, their central nervous systems develop new capacities that provide them with new mental tools to deal with increasingly more complex challenges. Training simple skills in early childhood—sometimes including tasks that are part of the assessment instrument—is of little help when entirely different and less easily trained abilities are required at a later age.

The field of human behavioral genetics, which uses data from various kinship studies—including comparisons of monozygotic and dizygotic twins reared together and reared apart, family studies of various degrees of relationship, and studies of children adopted at an early age— has demonstrated that heritability accounts for at least 50 percent of the variance in cognitive ability.

Biology is not necessarily destiny, but by the same token biology cannot be ignored. We must, it seems to me, look carefully at the findings of behavioral geneticists for clues about where our interventions are most likely to have their greatest effect.

The most obvious desirable environmental intervention would be massive improvement in the economic and social conditions of the underclass, but even if this most desirable outcome were to be achieved, individual differences would remain; there would always be some people who would function at a low level of ability.

To quote again from Plomin (1987): "Genetic influence is embedded in the complexity of interactions among genes, physiology, and environment. It is probabilistic, not deterministic; it puts no constraints on what could be" (p. 19).

To ignore any one of the contributors to human variability is to invite further disillusionment.

REFERENCES

Berrueta-Clement, J. R., Schweinhart, L. J., Barnett, W. S., Epstein, A. S., & Weikart, D. P. (1984). Changed lives: The effects of the Perry Preschool Program on youths through age 19. *Monographs of the High/Scope Educational Research Foundation,* No. 8.

Bouchard, T. J., Jr. (1984). Twins reared together and apart: What they tell us about human diversity. In S. W. Fox (Ed.), *Individuality and determinism: Chemical and biological bases* (pp. 147-184). New York: Plenum.

DeFries, J. C., Johnson, R. C., Kuse, A. R., McClearn, G. E., Polovina, J., Vandenberg, S. G., & Wilson, J. R. (1979). Familial resemblance for specific cognitive abilities. *Behavior Genetics, 9,* 23-43.

Fagan, J. F. (1984a). The intelligent infant: Theoretical implications. *Intelligence, 8,* 1-9.

Fagan, J. F., III. (1984b). The relationship of novelty preferences during infancy to later intelligence and later recognition memory. *Intelligence, 8,* 339-346.

Fuller, J. L., & Thompson, W. R. (1960). *Behavior genetics.* New York: Wiley.

Garber, H. (1988). *The Milwaukee Project: Preventing mental retardation in children at risk.* Washington, DC: American Association on Mental Retardation.

Heber, R., & Garber, H. (1975). The Milwaukee Project: A study of the use of family intervention to prevent cultural-familial mental retardation. In B. Z. Friedlander, G. M. Sterritt, & G. E. Kirk (Eds.), *Exceptional infant* (Vol. 3, pp. 399-433). New York: Brunner/Mazel.

Heber, R., Garber, H., Harrington, S., Hoffman, C., & Falender, C. (1972). Rehabilitation of families at risk for mental retardation: Progress report. *Rehabilitation Research and Training Center in Mental Retardation.* Madison: University of Wisconsin.

Lykken, D. T. (1982). Research with twins: The concept of emergenesis. *Psychophysiology, 19,* 361-373.

McClearn, G. E., & DeFries, J. C. (1973). *Introduction to behavioral genetics.* San Francisco: Freeman.

Plomin, R. (1986). *Development, genetics, and psychology.* Hillsdale, NJ: Erlbaum.

Plomin, R. (1987). Behavioral genetics and intervention. In J. J. Gallagher & C. T. Ramey (Eds.), *The malleability of children* (pp. 15-24). Baltimore, MD: Brookes.

Plomin, R., & Daniels, D. (1987). Why are children in the same family so different from one another? *Behavioral and Brain Sciences, 10,* 1-60.

Plomin, R., & DeFries, J. C. (1985). *Origins of individual differences in infancy: The Colorado Adoption Project.* New York: Academic Press.

Ramey, C. T., & Campbell, F. A. (1984). Preventive education for high-risk children: Cognitive consequences of the Carolina Abecedarian Project. *American Journal of Mental Deficiency, 88,* 515-523.

Schweinhart, L. J., Weikart, D. P., & Larner, M. B. (1986). Consequences of three preschool curriculum models through age 15. *Early Childhood Research Quarterly, 1,* 15-45.

Segal, N. L. (1985). Monozygotic and dizygotic twins: A comparative analysis of mental ability profiles. *Child Development, 56,* 1051-1058.

Skodak, M., & Skeels, H. (1949). A final follow-up study of one hundred adopted children. *Journal of Genetic Psychology, 75,* 85-125.

Sommer, R., & Sommer, B. A. (1983). Mystery in Milwaukee: Early intervention, IQ, and psychology textbooks. *American Psychologist, 38,* 982-985.

Spitz, H. H. (1986). *The raising of intelligence: A selected history of attempts to raise retarded intelligence.* Hillsdale, NJ: Erlbaum.

Spitz, H. H., Borys, S. V., & Webster, N. A. (1982). Mentally retarded individuals outperform college graduates in judging the nonconservation of space and perimeter. *Intelligence, 6,* 417-426.

Telligan, A., Lykken, D. T., Bouchard, T. J., Jr., Wilcox, K. J., Segal, N. L., & Rich, S. (1988). Personality similarity in twins reared apart and together. *Journal of Personality and Social Psychology, 54,* 1031-1039.

Wachs, T. D., & DeRemer, P. (1978). Adaptive behavior and the Uzgiris-Hunt Scale performance of young developmentally disabled children. *Journal of Experimental Child Psychology, 24,* 108-128.

Weikart, D. P. (1983). A longitudinal view of a preschool research effort. In M. Perlmutter (Ed.), *Minnesota symposia on child development: Vol. 16. Development and policy concerning children with special needs* (pp. 175-196). Hillsdale, NJ: Erlbaum.

Weikart, D. P., Deloria, D. J., Lawser, S. A., & Wiegerink, R. (1970). Longitudinal results of the Ypsilanti Perry Preschool Project. *Monographs of the High/Scope Educational Research Foundation,* No. 1.

Wilson, R. S. (1986). Continuity and change in cognitive ability profile. *Behavior Genetics, 16,* 45-60.

Chapter 4

Two Decades of Early Childhood Intervention

Alice S. Paul
University of Arizona

The 1960s was a time of great concern in the U.S. government over the Soviet Union's military and technological advances. The launching of Sputnik marked the beginning of the race into space. Educators as well as government leaders began to question whether or not children in the United States were being taught the essentials for optimal achievement in school to deal with new technology and space exploration.

Also in this period, the civil rights movement was raising the country's consciousness regarding the inequality of treatment in all areas for minorities and the poor. Because of these important issues, the 1960s kindled a new interest in early childhood education. In part this reemphasis was an effort by the U.S. government to fight the "war on poverty."

Ellis D. Evans (1971) describes this new interest in early childhood education of the 1960s as follows:

> More than any other decade in American history, the sixties might be called the Decade of Early Childhood Education. Interest in and activity concerning the young child were sparked by the exciting idea that early human development is plastic and can be altered in significant ways. In particular, the notion that mental growth is cumulative and that later development of intelligence depends in part upon early intellectual stim-

ulation led to the emergence of a cognitive emphasis in early education. (p. vii)

It was the tenor of these times that launched Head Start as the longest running intervention program ever funded by the U.S. government. It was only one of many action programs supported by the government to break the cycle of poverty. At the time, poor people were seen as having characteristics of apathy and a lack of aspiration. However, the most important factor was a waste of human potential. The government leadership was supportive in providing funds to assist assimilation of the poor into the mainstream.

The concentration and study of the times indicated that the child's earliest years were also the time of the most rapid physical and mental growth. It was generally accepted that, in this early period of life, a child was most susceptible and responsive to environmental influences (Akers, 1972). To intervene in the education of children very early was supported by psychologists, educators, pediatricians, psychiatrists, and anthropologists, as well as nutritionists. The timing of events was such that Head Start began with strong support from every area.

HEAD START

Head Start was initiated for 4- and 5-year-olds as a summer program in 1964. The following year the program was expanded on a national scale as a year-round program prior to formal school entrance.

The initiation of Head Start represented a significant and concrete deployment of resources to provide comprehensive services to children from low-income families. The services provided, not only an educational component, but also medical, dental, nutritional, social services, psychological services, and parent involvement components. The health screening of children in Head Start served to identify problems early on and became preventive in nature as opposed to costly medical remediation efforts.

Studies describing the characteristics of Head Start children in the 1960s were oriented toward the discovery of response "deficits" rather than strengths. The information gained from large groups of children from differing social classes and ethnic groups did not necessarily generalize to all the populations being served. Much of the research did indicate a common factor that a year in Head Start might not be long enough to make a long-lasting difference (Hodges et al., 1980).

Other research concentrated on some important characteristics of teachers which were seen as assisting children in Head Start. Teachers who exhibited resourcefulness, flexibility, and supportiveness were identified as good teachers. Today these teacher characteristics are still regarded as good qualities of teachers. Evans (1971) also reported that intervention strategies which included efforts to actively involve and educate parents enhanced the success of the children. These efforts were seen as a bridge for continuity between home and school. Parents were taught and encouraged to use educational material at home to help their children. The indirect effect of increasing parental respect and feelings of self-worth was accepted as aiding all children in the home. Involvement of parents and volunteers in career programs provided many opportunities for economic advancement for them. Changes in parental behavior, and positive attitudes toward their children, in turn increased their support toward their children's successes in school.

In the late 1960s Head Start, serving as a resource in compensatory research, raised some critical psychological issues among scholars such as Hunt (1969), Kagan (1969), and Jensen (1969). And the nature–nurture controversy was reincarnated. Jensen argued that development was controlled by genetic mechanisms, and that too much was being expected from Head Start. Volumes were produced on challenges and counterarguments, because measurement of improvement was limited to what could be measured by conventional, standardized instruments.

The debate regarding nature–nurture gave rise to many other educational issues. Head Start, from its onset, has forced educators to take a hard look at the learning patterns and instructional problems of many children who had been regarded as unsuccessful and viewed as being at risk.

Early on, Head Start programs were patterned after the socialization approach for early education which was used in traditional nursery school practice. It was argued that curricula should move to include a more cognitively oriented approach to accommodate what was seen as standard expectation for all children.

The 1970s gave rise to a new perspective on the basis for compensatory programs such as Head Start. Baratz and Baratz (1970) contended that, instead of viewing poor children as basically inferior and lacking in cognitive competence, they instead should be seen as "different," possessing well-developed and functional cognitive competence, but a competence based on different experiences which were not school related. This new perspective gave educators the impetus to pursue a new approach in educating poor and minority students: to adapt instructional procedures and curricula to children whose cultural identification and competencies differed from white, middle-class American children. This approach was novel; for once the schools were being changed to meet the children's needs.

Jencks et al. (1972), in their book of the 1970s, *Inequality,* supported this contention. They stated, "The variations in what children learn in school depends largely on the variations in what they bring to school, not on variations in what the schools offer them" (p. 53).

Since its inception in 1965, Head Start has pioneered a successful approach to helping low-income children develop, learn and grow. The program has continued to improve children's health through prevention. Head Start has documented over and over the need for comprehensive services for low-income families to better their lives and increase their life chances.

Not only the children, but also their parents, have benefitted. Head Start has helped parents to see themselves as primary teachers and advocates for their children (Children's Defense Fund, 1989). This is a crucial step, as the family is the strongest determinant of children's behavior. Study after study has substantiated that a comprehensive program benefits both parents and children. In doing so, the effort yields substantial long-term dividends to our society.

FOLLOW THROUGH

In 1967, after 2 years and a summer session of Head Start implementation, the U.S. Department of Education initiated the National Follow Through Program. A large-scale study conducted by the Westinghouse Corporation indicated that gains made in Head Start were being washed out as the children became part of the elementary school system. To avoid continuing this washout effect, the U.S. Office of Education proposed Follow Through to assist Head Start children as they moved into kindergarten through the third grade in the public school system.

In the 1960s most educators subscribed to the "big bang" theory of reform. Their efforts sought to discover a technique or program that would solve the "problem" of low-income student failure and that could be disseminated all over the country, thereby solving all of the nation's social problems (House & Hutchins, 1979).

A "planned variation" experimental program was designed to evaluate different approaches to identifying and demonstrating alternatives that would make schooling more effective for low-income children and improve their life chances. Researchers and program developers from universities, national research centers, and regional laboratories were invited by the U.S. Office of Education to apply as Sponsors of the

National Follow Through Program. Each of these Sponsors differed in their philosophy and theory of early childhood development and education.

Each Follow Through Sponsor was to work in partnership with a number of local school districts that had been identified by state departments of education to implement their "model program," testing it in several school sites. Model sponsorship was a unique concept developed as part of planned variation.

The thrust of the Office of Education for the planned variation and inclusion of Sponsors was to build a national storehouse to bring theory and research together while improving school practices. A variety of theories and approaches in child development and practice were represented by the Sponsors. Some programs were highly structured, others were open-ended, and some were in between. Other model sponsors emphasized social-emotional growth. All programs had parent involvement in some form, and for some programs the parent was the primary focus for change.

The overall focus of the Follow Through "planned variation" experiment was for the government to support several types of early childhood models in a limited number of sites, and eventually to evaluate them to see which approach worked best.

The federal planners also set up the evaluation which would tell which model worked best, and at what cost. In keeping with the popular view at the time, the evaluation was set up as a massive, controlled experiment. A multimillion-dollar contract was awarded to the Stanford Research Institute (SRI) to conduct the research. SRI promised to evaluate all aspects of the program, including community involvement and institutional change.

Unfortunately, they were unable to develop new instruments to evaluate all aspects of implementation as they had promised; their primary outcome measures were children's standardized test scores. A more detailed record on the issues raised by the Follow Through evaluation can be found in Haney (1977) and House and Glass (1978).

In 1967, state departments of education throughout the country nominated 40 school districts to participate in a pilot program of Follow Through. It was not until 1968 that Sponsors and sites (local projects) were matched together for implementation of models.

By 1971, Follow Through had expanded from 40 to 173 local projects and from 12 to 22 Model Sponsors. The model programs provided services to children from kindergarten through third grade. At its peak in 1970, Follow Through was identified with 50 state educational agencies, 84,000 children and parents, and more than 4,000 teachers and ancillary school personnel. Since that time, Follow Through has been one of the longest and most studied early childhood intervention efforts ever conducted by the federal government.

The original design of Follow Through required all programs, regardless of variation in theory and approach, to include four components: an instructional model, parent involvement, staff development, and comprehensive services for the children. Although the original intent of Follow Through was that it continue to be a comprehensive service delivery program for children of low-income families, Follow Through funding restricted comprehensive services to a lower level than Head Start.

After 10 years of model implementation, Follow Through Model Sponsors summarized what they, as a group, considered to be successes of the program in primary schools (Hodges et al., 1980).

First, each Model Sponsor had documented improvement in academic achievement for some of its children, as well as improvements in school and home environments.

Second, advances were recognized by each Sponsor in the development of comprehensive instructional models.

Third, through sponsorship and their delivery systems, several alternatives were created for training and support of school faculty and staffs to implement change.

Fourth, much information had been gained and generated on how to involve parents in the educational and political processes of schooling.

Fifth, knowledge about the potential of model sponsorship (third party intervention) as a way of improving schooling had also increased.

Finally, much new information concerning evaluation methodology for large-scale field studies had been gained.

After two decades as a field-based program, Follow Through has had several types of long-term effects. There is evidence of institutional change within schools and school systems. Teacher training, staff training and student evaluations have undergone change. There have been changes in parent support and parent involvement in education. Follow Through has changed the lives of many low-income parents employed initially as paraprofessionals by the programs. Many, through career ladders, have completed high school, enrolled in college courses, and gained degrees. This type of long-term effect has implications for the individual, the family, and the community (Olmsted & Szegda, 1988).

The impact of the various Follow Through model programs cannot be restricted to standardized student achievement tests. Program outcomes must also reflect the development of motivation and positive attitudes toward schooling, as well as fostering self-concept.

An important message from Follow Through to educational researchers and program developers is that there is a critical need to continue to forge a two-directional link between research and school practices.

The lessons learned from Follow Through are still relevant as we examine the demographic trends of the future that predict increasing numbers of students who are from low-income families and considered at risk.

PARENT/FAMILY AND CULTURAL IMPACT

Historically, the view of the school toward parent participation has been limited. Today there are still people in school systems who believe parents should be "on call" and available when needed by the school. Too often the "call" to parents has been limited to supporting the school in disciplining their children, to supporting school functions, or to volunteering in the classroom.

Some schools today view parent participation as parent training, and much effort is exerted to provide parents with information about child development, nutrition, school expectations, and so on, topics that will contribute to better parenting skills.

Over the years of intervention, both Head Start and Follow Through have demonstrated that parents are their children's first teachers. Follow Through has fostered the view of parents as partners in providing successful experiences for their children, a view that is growing among some schools and communities. The directive by the government to include parent participation in federally funded programs has blossomed into a range of interpretations.

Parent groups have formed and have become legislatively involved in gaining a voice in decisions that affect their children. New funding today reflects the accepted importance of involving the family if intervention is to be successful.

An added dimension of single families—particularly those who are poor and members of minority groups—must also be considered. The view has been documented that the attitude of the family, and its acceptance or rejection of school policies and practices that children bring to school, does affect learning.

Ogbu (1985), in his anthropological research efforts to examine why some minority groups persistently fail in school, indicates that it is not bad teaching of uncooperative "bad" students, but that it is related to the ways majority groups have treated specific minorities, and how those minorities have responded to such treatment. Obgu's research demonstrates how group behaviors and beliefs can have powerful and complex effects on individual learning in school. Anthropological research for the past two decades has come to the view that a child can experience classroom learning difficulties if there is a difference between the child's culture and language and that of the school. The styles of communicating, learning, and interacting with adults and peers can be different from what is expected in school.

In addition, if minorities see themselves as different and opposed to the majority population who control the school, they often will have difficulty performing according to school norms, even when they possess the cognitive and language skills of the school.

SUMMARY

The implications of what has been learned in the last two decades of research and implementation of early childhood intervention programs provide strong evidence that changes can be made to assist low income minority children and families.

Evidence also indicates that progress can best be made when the families of the children being served are included in the planning, implementation, and evaluation of programs for change.

Much has been learned to indicate that better evaluation should take place, and on a much broader base than just standardized tests.

Finally, it is critical that we take under advisement the lessons learned from the past and incorporate them into our plans for future early childhood education intervention programs.

REFERENCES

Akers, M. E. (1972). Prologue: The why of early childhood education. In I. J. Gordon (Ed.), *Early childhood education* (pp. 1-12). Chicago: The National Society for the Study of Education.

Anderson, R. C., Hiebert, E. H., Scott, J. A., & Wilkinson, I. A. G. (Eds.). (1985). *Becoming a nation of readers: The report of the Commission on Reading*. Washington, DC: National Institute of Education.

Baratz, S. S., & Baratz, J. C. (1970). Early childhood intervention: The social science base of institutional racism. *Harvard Educational Review, 40*(1), 29-50.

Burke, C. (1985). Parenting, teaching and learning as a collaborative venture. *Language Arts, 62*(8), 836-843.

Children's Defense Fund. (1984). *A children's defense budget—An analysis of the President's FY 1985 budget and children*. Washington, DC: Author.

Children's Defense Fund. (1988). *A children's defense budget—FY 1989—An analysis of our nation's investment in children*. Washington, DC: Author.

Cole, M., & Bruner, J. S. (1972). Preliminaries to a theory of cultural differences. In I. J. Gordon (Ed.), *Early childhood education* (pp. 161-179). Chicago: The National Society for the Study of Education.

Evans, E. D. (1971). *Contemporary influences in early childhood education.* New York: Holt, Rinehart and Winston.

Flavell, J. H. (1977). *Cognitive development.* Englewood Cliffs, NJ: Prentice-Hall.

Haney, W. (1977). The Follow Through experiment: Summary of an analysis of major evaluation reports. *Curriculum Inquiry, 7*(3), 227-257.

Hodges, W., Branden, A., Feldman, R., Follins, J., Love, J., Sheehan, R., Lumbley, J., Osborn, J., Rentfrow, R. K., Houston, J., & Lee, C. (1980). *Follow Through—Forces for change in the primary schools.* Ypsilanti, MI: The High/Scope Press.

House, E. R., Glass, G. V., McLean, L. D., & Walker, D. F. (1978). No simple answer: Critique of the "Follow Through" evaluation. *Harvard Educational Review, 48,* 128-160.

House, E. R., & Hutchins, E. J. (1979). Issues raised by the Follow Through evaluation. In L. G. Katz (Ed.), *Current topics in early childhood education* (Vol. 2, pp. 1-11). Norwood, NJ: Ablex Publishing Corporation.

Human Development Services. (1983). *A review of Head Start research since 1970 and an annotated bibliography of the Head Start research since 1965.* Washington, DC: CSR, Incorporated.

Hunt, J. McV. (1969). *The challenge of incompetence and poverty: Papers on the role of early education.* Urbana, IL: University of Illinois Press.

Jensen, A. (1969). How much can we boost IQ and scholastic achievement? *Harvard Educational Review, 39,* 1-123.

Jencks, C., Smith, M., Acland, H., Bane, M. J., Cohen, D., Gintis, H., Heyns, B., & Michelson, S. (1972). *Inequality—A reassessment of the effect of family and schooling in America.* New York: Harper & Row.

Kagan, J. (1969). Inadequate evidence and illogical conclusions. *Harvard Educational Review, 39,* 274-277.

Ogbu, J. U. (1985). Research currents: Cultural-ecological influences on minority school learning. *Language Arts, 62*(8), 860-869.

Olmsted, P. P., & Szegda, M. J. (1988, April). *Long-term effects of Follow Through participation.* Paper presented at the annual conference of the American Educational Research Association, New Orleans, LA.

Paul, A. S. (1987). The transitional model—Bilingualism examined. In J. Roopnarine & J. Johnson (Eds.), *Educational models for young children* (pp. 179-196). Columbus, OH: Charles E. Merrill Publishing Co.

Soar, R. S., & Soar, R. M. (1972). An empirical analysis of selected Follow-Through programs: An example of a process approach to evaluation. In I. J. Gordon (Ed.), *Early childhood education* (pp. 229-260). Chicago: The National Society for the Study of Education.

Wang, M. C. (1988). *An analysis of the impact of the National Follow Through Program.* Paper presented at the annual conference of the American Educational Research Association, New Orleans, LA.

Chapter 5

Youth Interventions: Literacy

Lois-ellin Datta
U.S. General Accounting Office[1]

Many youth and adults face difficulties in their lives. Some may be handicapped from birth defects, accidents, or wars. Others may be at the wrong place at the wrong time when industries become uncompetitive, when natural disasters strike, or when new towns leave old towns economically bare. Still others may find themselves with family responsibilities they had not anticipated or without support they had counted on, as spouses divorce, parents age, or children are born.

The welfare of these persons is, of course, of great concern. Providing useful support can be costly; the best approaches to meeting their needs are not always clear or feasible. With one important exception, however, literacy is not a central source of their difficulties nor, usually, a major intervention in their assistance. (The exception is basic skills acquisition or recovery in the face of specific physiological problems such as deafness. The special topic of literacy development in special education or rehabilitation is beyond the scope of this chapter.) Thus, while more could be done, these situations are not the focus of this analysis.

The focus is on those youth and young adults who seem, despite other qualities, to be "born losers" academically and in regard to employment. These may form a permanent underclass. They contrib-

[1] Opinions expressed are the author's in her personal capacity. They are not to be interpreted or construed in any way as the views of the U.S. General Accounting Office.

41

ute to the cycle of poverty, transmitting problems with the law, dependency, and the like to their children and grandchildren. They account far beyond their proportion in the population to what are often perceived as social problems and costs (Wilson, 1987). The War on Poverty, begun in 1965, was geared to these people as well as to their children. Over two decades later, what have we learned about youth interventions?

Lessons learned can be considered under three themes, each of which will be discussed as part of the broader examination of program development, depending on information availability. These themes are:

- The content of the intervention (for example, what was taught, method of instruction, combination of services associated with the intervention).
- Implementation of the intervention (for example, responsibilities assigned to schools, community-based organizations and the private sector in design, funding and administration, and how these responsibilities were carried out; time required for and phases of implementation).
- The outcomes of the intervention (for example, intermediate attainments such as program participation and completion; intermediate achievements such as performance on measures of literacy and numeracy; longer-term attainments such as entry into and completion of post-secondary education and training; longer-term achievements such as hourly and monthly earnings; and long-term attainments and achievements, such as success in employment, avoidance of welfare dependency and arrests, and intergenerational progress).

THE INTERVENTION PROGRAMS

Since 1965, there have been three cycles of programs for out-of-school youth and three involving in-school youth.[2] Roughly speaking, they were concurrent in time, and shaped by similar assumptions.

---

[2] One source of information that is not extensively discussed comes from adult basic education programs, both projects supported through the Department of Education and those literacy campaigns that have reached so many people which are supported through private, often voluntary organizations. There is considerable descriptive information about the adult basic education programs, and some evaluations have been supported through Federal, state, and local resources (see, for example, Lerche, 1985). However,

Out-of-School Youth and Young Adults

1965 through 1972. During this period, the Job Corps was launched for hard-to-reach youth and young adults in nonschool settings. The Corps, open to low-income youth and young adults, provided remedial education, job training, and counseling in special locations, similar to the Civilian Conservation Corps camps of the late 1930s. Here, the community and home influences that might have tempted the youth through unwholesome peer pressure were reduced. The counselors could focus on intensive training, and deal with negative attitudes about working. Often studied, and often precariously continued, evaluations of the Job Corps over the years have shown that for *some* participants, skills could be acquired, the work ethic supported, and the transition successfully made to independent living. However, these studies also have shown that the approach was costly, as residential programs typically are, and it was difficult to predict who could benefit and who would not, so that the success rates could be improved. The response to such criticism was, of course, that Job Corps was notably cheaper than jail (true) and that giving high-risk youth and adults a chance was precisely what the Corps was all about (see, for example, Wholey, 1987).

The response was strong enough to save the Corps. It was not convincing enough to expand the program to serve all eligible youth.

1972 through 1982. Alternative programs to the Job Corps brought the youth and adults back into communities. The goal was to link program participation and employment.The Comprehensive Em-

---

these studies usually were completed in the 1970s. While new studies are planned, and some are in progress, the lessons learned are stronger in the areas of program implementation and of adapting instruction to the learning styles of adults—an important and valuable topic—than on specific aspects of literacy or on long-term results. It should be noted that a variety of long-term benefits *have* been reported by participants in some programs. These include being better able to help children with their homework, better job performance, being able to handle many tasks in everyday life, and being able to continue in further education and training. Among the features considered essential for effective programs are materials substantively geared to adults' interests, individualized instruction, frequent assessment of student progress with rapid feedback, and opportunities to try out skills in relatively low-risk, nonpunitive situations (see, for example, National Advisory Council on Adult Education, undated).

Still another source of lessons to be learned is the remedial reading and arithmetic programs offered by some large employers as a way of getting entry-level personnel and for upgrading and assisting the job progress of those who are marginally skilled. Some of these may be intensively evaluated within different corporations. Detailed data and results from these experiences are not as readily available as more general discussions of employer needs and approaches provided through the publications and meetings of groups such as the American Society of Training Administrators.

ployment and Training Act of 1973 (CETA) and the subsequent Youth Employment and Demonstrations Program Act of 1977 (YEDPA) launched a wave of first service and then more experimental programs, all aimed at reducing the problem of the transition between education and work. These programs were particularly aimed at economically disadvantaged, minority youth, and young adults who were out of school or who were at high risk of failure. The programs were arranged so that the training and counseling would be the minimum needed to enable employment. The communities would provide the multiple supports thought essential to helping the youth and adults stay on the job, once employment had been achieved. Enthusiasm ran high for coordinating existing services, and for highly targeted and condensed programs that would help the participants quickly achieve the minimum levels of literacy and numeracy, of proper behavior, and of work orientation needed.These programs, too, were evaluated, even more ambitiously and extensively than the earlier Job Corps. So many reports were produced in a fairly short time that the task of consolidating them has only recently been completed. The findings lead to the following reactions among reviewers such as the National Academy of Science panels and in the Congressional Research Service. First, there has been a general disappointment in the technical quality of the evaluations. Second, reviewers expressed concern for the unevenness of implementation when complex programs were expected to be up and running in months and the managerial and infrastructural capacities were exceeded. Third and most important, the summary analyses indicate dismay that with a few important exceptions, the CETA and YEDPA programs were not notably effective in helping very hard-to-reach youth and adults enter the labor market (e.g., Betsy et al., 1985; Smith, 1987).

1982 through 1988. The assumptions underlying programs of this period were that since people earn their living through working, the best thing is to put them to work, in part, learning on-the-job as they go. The experiments have included payment of the first six months of a high-risk employee's salary, guaranteeing jobs as an incentive for students to remain in school, and combining intensive training and child care with subsidized employment. The experiments evolved into state-wide programs in which welfare was contingent upon signing up for employment. The findings from these demonstrations suggest the feasibility of the approach and its effectiveness, particularly in reducing the welfare rolls for women formerly on Aid to Families with Dependent Children (AFDC). Such early evaluation reports contributed to the rapid spread of these work force programs.

Less publicized, however, were the failures of the demonstrations for low-income men. That is, the demonstrations originally involving unemployed men *and* women swiftly became a woman's program, with welfare dependency reduced not through the formation of two-worker families, but through getting women off AFDC and into the work force (Gueron, 1984, 1988).

In School Youth

1965 through 1972. The passage in 1964 of the Elementary and Secondary Education Act (ESEA) launched a period of attention to children from low-income families, children who were not prospering academically, and children at risk for academic failure. The funds, allocated by proportion of children in poverty, could be used for a variety of supplementary educational services, from speech therapists through inservice training to development of new curricula. Two factors influenced the shape of these programs.

First, the funds could not supplant existing services and the money had to be allocated only to eligible children. Second, as Madden and Slavin (1987) have noted, pull-out programs did or do outnumber in-class models by ratios as high as nine to one. The difficulties of managing the funding conditions in a regular classroom setting led to this overwhelming predominance of pull-out programs. Third, the emphasis in human development theory in the 1960s and early 1970s on the influence of the early years led to a concentration of resources at the elementary, rather than the secondary level.

Early evaluations of the major authority under the Act, Title I, failed to detect improvements on standard tests of reading and arithmetic, a result disappointing to some, although not surprising to others.

1972 through 1982. This period saw a continued focus on the elementary school years and a commitment to making compensatory education work. There was, however, a growing awareness of the importance of the secondary school (see, for example, Sewall et al., 1976; Wilson, 1980). This spark of concern for youth did not, however, jump the gap from ideas to implementation.

More specifically, initiatives at the elementary level included the (a) Follow Through program, which at one time included 23 different "models" of school management, instruction and curriculum; (b) expansion of the demonstration authority in Title IV of ESEA, which encouraged experimentation with instruction and curriculum; (c) the creation of the National Diffusion Network, aimed at recognizing effective programs and providing resources for other schools to learn about them and adapt them; and (d) support of basic and applied research on reading, writing, arithmetic and mathematics, learning and cognition, effective schools, school leadership, and assessment.

At the same time, the loss of gains from Title I and Follow Through after the third grade, in addition to increases in school problems among 12–13-year-olds and high rates of youth unemployment, stimulated attention to the secondary period. As examples,

- The effective schools "invisible college" held meetings to discuss generalizability of their elementary-level findings to the junior and senior high school levels, and to begin to design the next generation of necessary research and development.
- The National Assessment of Educational Progress and other testing programs continued to show fairly promising achievements in the basic or rote skills and fairly unpromising performance on more complex, abstract tasks, particularly the application of basic skills to problem solving and comprehension (Koretz, 1986).
- The development of functional tests of skills (NAEP, 1976) and of performance-based credentials for both high school and college-stimulated research on the nature and development of literacy and numeracy including studies of functional literacy by Cole, Scribner, and Sticht.
- The Youth Employment and Demonstration Programs Act of 1977 and the Vocational Education Amendments of 1976 both called for closer coordination between education and training communities; for example, about 22 percent of the YEDPA funds had to be spent through schools. In the process of designing the demonstration programs, attention was focused on how acquisition of literacy and numeracy could be infused into academic, vocational, and on-the-job training.

By 1980, many policy analysts identified the next frontier as secondary school improvement, particularly for youth who were doing poorly (for example, Hawley & Rosenholts, 1984). A high-level task force in the newly formed Department of Education spent almost a year planning a major initiative which focused on youth and secondary schools, particularly low-income, minority youth at special risk of school failure.

This initiative featured considerable local and state determination of how the resources would be spent, applying the lessons learned from studies of the implementation of federal programs (see, e.g., Berman & McLaughlin, 1978; McLaughlin, 1987; Pressman & Wildavsky, 1979). The notion was to be specific about the outcomes desired and flexible about how to achieve them. Among the outcomes emphasized were school retention, school completion, and achievement of good work habits, task orientation, literacy, numeracy, and more complex as well as basic skills. The scope of the work was anticipated to be as large as the original Title I, but directed to the secondary schools.

1982 to the present. Expending lots of new federal money for at-risk, poor, or minority youth in the schools was not a priority for the new administration. Since 1982, however, administration leadership, building on a reform momentum already underway in many states, has expended lots of federal attention to educational excellence (National Commission on Excellence in Education, 1982; Tomlinson & Walberg, 1986). Under this rubric, changes have included increasing the number and breadth of basic academic courses required for high school graduation, state-wide, standardized achievement tests for school progress and for graduation, and more recently, teacher competency tests as a basis for certification. These and other approaches have been talked about in all states, approved by the legislatures in many states, and actually implemented in some states. The changes, generally spoken of as "the educational reform movement," feature determined attention to reading and mathematics achievement.

This attention is, however, more in the traditional sense (for example, in federal promotion of phonics), rather than in the context of literacy and numeracy. It also is in the context of variation in whether special assistance is given to students likely to dropout or do poorly, beyond the encouragement given to all students in the form of higher expectations, increased homework, and the message that a relatively free ride toward a high school degree is over.

These reforms were largely extrapolations from basic research, from correlational studies (e.g., Coleman et al., 1982), and from a few small-scale pilot projects, plus an enormous shift in ideology. Until about 1987, they were not accompanied at the federal level by support for technical assistance development, testing or research.

The major federal education legislation, the Educational Improvement Act of 1982, was, in essence, similar to a block grant. It consolidated many categorical programs, eliminated reporting requirements, maximized local and state flexibility, and redistributed funds to private schools and middle-income students (Final Report from the National Assessment of Chapter One, 1987). Not surprisingly, the implementation and effects of educational reform are now being examined by at least five national studies. Among the questions is whether low-income and minority youth have prospered, held steady, or lost ground academically, relative to prior improvements and compared to middle-income and nonminority youth (Koretz, 1987).

These analyses are likely to be complex and full of pitfalls. Sebring (1987), for example, has used the variations in state requirements for high school graduation in 1980 and 1982 to examine the relationship between the amount of academic coursework completed and performance on the College Entrance Examination Board tests. She found consistent relationships, when aptitude was controlled statistically, between coursework and achievement, across all aptitude levels. Sebring notes that three other studies, using nationally representative samples, also determined that the alterable variable most strongly correlated with achievement was the amount of coursework. She observes, "the potential for the new requirements to help bridge the gap between general and vocational track students and academic track students . . . depends on the kinds of courses that are allowed to pass for academic courses. Offering general and vocational track students watered-down versions of academic subjects would do nothing to bridge the current gap between the tracks in academic training."

TODAY'S PROBLEMS

The concerns mentioned above for the achievement of low-income youth are coupled with somewhat alarming demographic projections for the United States. In a scant 10 years, minority and at-risk youth will be a far higher proportion of both the secondary school and entry-level worker population than ever before. This combination has stimulated a new examination of problems associated with low achievement and a new search for approaches that can be the foundation for public action (Committee for Economic Development, 1984; Elmore, 1986; Venezsky et al., 1987).

Attainment, Achievement and Economic Independence

Analysts have brought together an array of indicators, many of which tell a similar story: First, school achievement and attainment, however measured, continue to be associated with a wide array of post-school situations. These include:

- Much better chances of employment for those who have completed high school and college, relative to those who have not (see, for instance, Boris, 1984).
- Additional thousands of dollars annually in salaries for students who have completed high school or college, relative to those who have not.
- Much lower scores on measures of achievement for those who are on welfare or in jail, than for their age cohort.
- And, perhaps most seriously, strong evidence of a relatively small, but seriously troubled, group of persons who are forming a permanent underclass, with two and three generations characterized by

low school achievement and attainment, long-term welfare dependency, unemployment, drugs, and prolonged, serious criminal records.

Berlin and Sum (1988) describe these trends in an economic context of real income stagnation, with young workers, especially those with limited education, as most hurt. For example, between 1973 and 1984, workers without a high school diploma lost 41.6 percent in real income, compared to 11.0 percent for college graduates. Among those with no diploma, blacks lost 61.3 percent in real income, Hispanics 38.6 percent, and whites 38.7 percent. Further, they report that the decline in the manufacturing sector has had a devastating effect on those young people with deficiencies in education and basic skills, noting that "the silent firing of young workers—those who were never hired to replace retiring workers—is the big untold story underlying the decline of the manufacturing sector." These were, Berlin and Sum continue, "frequently the jobs in which one could earn enough to support a family, even if one did not have a strong education" (p. 12).

These conditions, in turn, cascaded to "deal a staggering blow" to family formation patterns. Between 1973 and 1984, for example, Hispanic and black males between 20 and 24 years of age who had earnings above the poverty line for a three-person group dropped from 55 percent to 23 percent, and from 61 percent to 34 percent, respectively. The percentage of 20- to 24-year-old men who were married and living with their spouses dropped, during this same period, from 39 to 22 percent for all men, but from 29 to 9 percent for black males. These patterns, Berlin and Sum conclude, in turn helped to increase the number of children living in poverty.

Further, an "intertwining" is found among teenage parenting, youth unemployment, dropping out of school, and poor basic skills. Berlin and Sum note that achievement determines attainment, which then determines employability and earnings, which influence the likelihood of marrying and bearing children within a two parent family. For example, on the AFQT, the percentile rankings in the basic skills distribution among youth were 32 for those arrested, 26 for the jobless, 24 for the dependent, 21 for unwed parents, 20 for dropouts, 18 for the poor and idle, 16 for the poor and dependent, and 15 for youth with three or more social problems (p. 29; see also Johnson & Sum, 1984, 1987).

There is, it should be noted, some dispute about the interpretation of these findings. Does achievement stand for "persistence" in employers' minds or does it represent true capacity needed for jobs? And if demand were higher and better wages offered, would "unemployable" youth become "employable" with no change in their skills? Likely, both assertions have more than a little truth. However, such nuances might be unconvincing to employers who are paying to teach basic skills and buying cash registers with pictures instead of numbers, and the military, who find that entry-level personnel with low scores cannot do the job. These examples argue for a notable component, at lower achievement levels, of lack of competence in explaining the correlations among school attainment and unemployment in legal and primary labor markets.

Attainment, Achievement, and Trends in Economic Independence

Achievement and attainment declined during the 1960s and early 1970s, then improved, somewhat. They now appear to be declining again for low-income and minority youth, both in absolute and relative terms.

- Performance on the most recent National Assessment of Educational Progress declined notably for all, and particularly for minority and low-income youth, a drop which has not been convincingly explained (see also Kirsch & Jungeblut, 1986; Applebee et al., 1988).
- Performance on the Armed Forces Qualifying examinations dropped and the gaps increased for low-income and minority youth.
- There are some reports that school retention and completion rates, as well as college matriculation and completion rates, are decreasing for at-risk youth.
- Unemployment rates, rates of teenage pregnancy, rates for child abuse and for homelessness—all factors associated with intergenerational transmission of academic problems—have either increased or held steady, without much progress being made.

While interpretation of any single indicator is open to alternatives, and the magnitude of the problem varies from indicator to indicator, overall a downward trend seems to be emerging.

TOMORROW'S SOLUTIONS?

The search is on for what lessons can be learned from past interventions and from promising programs. The places NOT to look may be programs sponsored by the traditional educational community, and the places to look may be approaches sponsored by the training community, the military, and private foundations.

Where not to look. The Department of Education has been in the forefront of a laudable effort to identify promising practices and to disseminate information. These efforts include national searches for exemplary schools, recognition programs for exceptional teachers, publication of readable articles in the "What Works" series, and an overhaul of the National Diffusion Network. Further, the Department recently has funded over 20 centers and mini-centers on educational issues including reading, writing, mathematics, history, citizenship, values and ethics, arts and the humanities, testing, urban schools, rural schools, teachers, postsecondary improvement, instructional improvement, state and local policies, effective schools, and effective principals. However, fewer lessons may be available than the lists of activities suggest.

First, closer examination of "what works" shows stale data. Much of the information was developed in the 1970s, much was obtained on a very small scale without tested replication in other sites, and much was done under conditions that may be significantly different from today. For example, many of the "programs that work" in the area of reading, writing, mathematics, arithmetic, literacy, or numeracy were approved *before* 1980, few have been revalidated and data do not seem to be available on their effectiveness in new sites (National Dissemination Study Group, 1987).

Second, with some exceptions, such as the centers on learning processes and on reading, the center and mini-center awards are too recent and too small to expect much applicable information for program design until the early 1990s. That is, the current lode of information from Department-sponsored research may be more useful for problem analysis—which is valuable—than for program design.

Where to look. Programs seen as having some applicability to improving literacy and to secondary school reform often have been supported through Department of Labor funds or private foundations. In one instance, the recent Ford Foundation report on basic skills (Berlin & Sum, 1988) identified as promising:

- The Perry Preschool (a high-quality program funded for many years by Carnegie and Ford Foundations)
- Title I of the old Elementary and Secondary Assistance Act
- Computer-based instruction
- A basic skills-oriented summer job program being tested in five demonstration sites
- The military's Project 100,000

- The Job Corps
- The remedial system used in about 250 community-based learning centers called the Comprehensive Competencies Program
- A school-to-work transition program, Jobs for America's graduates.

There are, of course, other examples. Concern for teen pregnancy has led to numerous analyses and demonstration programs (National Research Council, 1986). To cite only one, the Mott Foundation has supported for almost 10 years a multisite, well-evaluated demonstration program aimed first, at reducing teenage pregnancy, and second, at helping teenage parents stay in school and achieve at least employment-level skills. The reports of these programs have led to a comprehensive book on young families, including lessons learned about assessment of family functioning. While basic skills was one component among many of these programs, the database represents an exceptional opportunity for longitudinal and intergenerational studies of achievements and life chances for teen mothers.

Bottom of the barrel. As this suggests, efforts to learn from past experience reveal the consequences of limited attention to research, evaluation, and systematic program development in the education area for almost a decade. The examples of effective programs are often 20 years old, have not been replicated, have been studied by their own developers only or through studies with serious flaws. For example, the Perry Preschool Project, while yielding exceptional results in terms of school progress, school completion, employment, and independence has been successful *only* when implemented *and evaluated* by its developers (Berreuta-Clements et al., 1984). Replications have consistently failed to yield evidence of even short-term effectiveness when implemented by regular school systems and when evaluated by third parties. The military's Project 100,000 was news 10 years ago. Title I no longer exists, and was promising only in the short term and by inference from NAEP data of performance of youth in high- and low-concentration Title I eligible schools.

Lessons learned from demonstration projects may be clearer for program administration and management than for program design (see, for example, National Advisory Council on Adult Education, undated). As examples, among the administrative lessons, several analysts have identified the value of:

- The learning-from-each-other that comes from a network of demonstration programs, in contrast to unconnected, let-a-thousand-flowers-bloom approaches.

- Clear standards, monitoring, supervision, and technical assistance to assure that even the weakest programs are of acceptable quality.
- The importance of good accountability and documentation.

INFORMATION COMING ONLINE

There is, fortunately, information beginning to come online again, with reports that should be available by the early 1990s. In the area of education, the Perkins Act (P.L. 98-524, October 19, 1984) strengthened assurance that disadvantaged students can participate in quality vocational educational as an alternative to academic or general tracks, in part by targeting set-aside funds to districts with high concentrations of low-income families. A second emphasis is on "quality vocational education." This approach is consistent with the view that the problems of low-achieving youth are not too little vocational education, or too much, but rather that the low income youth are disproportionately in programs of low quality that do not prepare them for jobs that pay decent wages and have career possibilities (see, e.g., National Assessment of Vocational Education (NAVE), 1988).

There seems to be a long overdue, serious, effort stimulated by the Act and by the reform requirements, to improve academic and basic skills through vocational education. NAVE reports that New York and Ohio are redesigning their programs to strengthen academic content, that California is experimenting with a curriculum integrating academic and vocational education by "emphasizing practical applications of abstract concepts" (1988, pp. 5–12), and that the Southern Regional Educational Commission is sponsoring pilot projects aimed at improving basic skills in 13 states and 26 school districts.

What these redesigns involve may be illustrated by the specific practices seen as "successful ways of integrating academic and vocational education." Examples (Owens, 1988) include

- In a math class, students are required to measure the same lengths with several measuring tools that are used in home economics such as tapes, protractors, and T squares.
- A math teacher uses Ohm's law as an example in algebra.
- An industrial mechanics class has students learn sequencing to perform a job skill.
- In electronics class, juniors study direct circuits, while in science, they analyze electric motors.
- Vocational students are tested in math and those with low scores

are tutored twice weekly by volunteer students from their particular occupational areas.

* Vocational education teachers conduct informal classes several evenings for other teachers who want to learn more about vocational areas.
* As one way of gaining first-hand experience in writing, students in a cooperative Office Education Program interview secretaries or general office workers and request sample letters and memos for review.

The 1989 reauthorization of vocational education is to be accompanied by an extensive series of descriptive, implementation, and results studies of the programs supported by the Act and of special innovations in the reauthorization (National Assessment of Vocational Education, 1988). These will include studies examining functional literacy, and in some depth, the claims made by vocational educators that one of their unique functions is to encourage school retention and development of basic skills for youth who may not prosper in more formal academic settings. Preliminary results are being analyzed using fine-grained information about the extent to which functional literacy actually is being promoted. One study indicates that classes and programs providing this opportunity do have the benefits often claimed but not convincingly documented before (D. Schuler, personal communication, 1988).

As already mentioned, results from the small industry of studies examining the effects of educational reform should also be available in 1989 or the early 1990s. Because so many of the reforms affected school completion, these studies can be expected to have notably more information on secondary-level learning than prior work on compensatory education.

Still a third body of information comes from the welfare reform or work force experiments. These have been both developed and evaluated by a quasi-governmental organization, but in some instances, state-wide implementation of the reforms is being examined by state departments of evaluation and accountability. While the work force program emphasizes employment, counseling, childcare, and mandated, rather than optional or voluntary training, it nonetheless represents a quite remarkable source of natural variation data on different approaches to literacy-related training.

LEARNING ABOUT THE LESSONS LEARNED

What research shows is itself influenced by developments in evaluation methodology. Thus, lessons learned can be expected to be revised based on new ways of looking at older data. During the past 20 years, these developments have included:

- Attention to program implementation, fidelity and process as variables important in their own right for what they indicate about program replicability, and as essential in understanding variability in outcomes.
- The discovery that categorical measures of outcomes, such as school progress, school completion, welfare dependency, and repeat pregnancies could be, and often were, more sensitive to program effects than test scores, despite the theoretical links between the competencies the test scores represent and the categorical outcomes.
- Growing support for multiple measures in studies that describe the current situation, examine trends, or assess program effects.
- Development of quantitative and qualitative ways of "summing up" findings across many studies, techniques sometimes referred to as meta-evaluation. Pooling findings from scores of studies can help bracket the range of probable true effects, and permit examination of interactions among outcomes and learners, situations and curricula. Further, by comparing outcomes for studies in which weaknesses and strengths may be complementary, meta-evaluations can help increase the likelihood that the weak signals of a potentially useful approach are detected.
- Through studies permitting direct comparison of the outcomes of quasi-experimental or true experimental designs relative to regression-based and economic models, there has been an increase in willingness to take on the administratively more difficult experimental designs. The Department of Labor, for example, cut back a regression-based approach to some key JTPA demonstrations in order to start over with an experimental design.

SMALL WINS

Reexamination of lessons learned from programs and policies has led to another position: that of expecting small wins. The phrase is Weick's (1984), whose crystallization of "loose coupling" organized a decade of study on how change comes about. In elegant arguments derived from experience, from psychological theories of arousal, stress, and cognitive and affective limitations, and from politics, Weick noted,

A small win is a concrete, completed, implemented outcome of moderate importance. By itself, one small win may seem unimportant. A series of small wins at small but significant tasks, however, reveal a pattern that may attract allies, deter opponents, and lower resistance to subsequent proposals. (p. 43)

Weick's analysis of strategies for problem analysis and program design is echoed, more programatically, by Gueron (1988), summarizing the experience of many studies of welfare interventions. She observed,

Studies of welfare employment programs consistently indicated that effects are likely to be small when measured against expectations. Yet an important conclusion from the research is that small can be enough. (p. 25)

This theme—which appears in other "lessons learned" reviews (Bloom, Cordray, & Light, 1988) of employment and training programs, juvenile justice interventions, and direct cash housing assistance—is that effects of interventions or policies are likely to be small, but nonetheless may be important.

This insight may be useful both for learning lessons and designing programs. The analysis in this chapter, by relying in part on reviews across a fairly large body of data, is perhaps more skeptical about available evidence than if the thousands of individual evaluations since 1965 had been examined individually through the lens of small wins. The National Academy of Sciences review of the YEDPA studies, for example, used the strategy of relying on the methodologically strongest evaluations, of which there were relatively few when the high standards derived from the quasi-experimental and experimental canon were used. A small-wins view might have used and seen more.

Further, as a new wave of demonstration program develops, it may make sense to *design,* as Weick suggests, for achieving the intermediate victories and the moderate but important outcomes and to *evaluate* with expectations of small, but reliable, changes. This may provide a sounder basis than in the past, when promises were more fervent (and were known to be overpromises made for the sake of garnering support), the scale of interventions more sweeping, and the all-too-frequent results of the evaluation, macro-negative.

In Summary

In summary, the nation is faced with a growing proportion of the population at greatest risk of school failure, of long-term dependency and violent crime. The skein of causality includes lack of jobs in the areas where these groups live, low school attachment, availability of criminal subcultures for fast money, lack of school-related skills, lack of family environments which promote school achievement and learning, and schools where keeping minimum order is a task in itself. At the other extreme, the middle income and better-educated groups continue to seize opportunities traditionally available to them to upgrade their own skills and those of their children.

More than two decades of educational and training-related programs provides some guidance. Due in part to a shameful lack of "second generation" opportunities for building on the first round of program experience, the substantive lessons to be learned are suggestive, more than convincing. They *do* indicate the value, for some youth, of embedding academic and applied learning, and of attention to functional literacy and numeracy in both outcome and instructional senses. They show small, but consistent successes, particularly for women, and particularly for programs such as Job Corps, when implementation was mature and evaluation longitudinal.

It may be more possible now than in the past to develop secondary schools that offer different bases for learning. The efforts to retain racial balances, for example, have led to the acceptability and, in many instances, the apparent success of magnet schools. These schools may be oriented to science and mathematics, to the arts and music, to foreign languages, to academic subjects. The approaches of functional literacy could, of course, be infused in such schools, but also in more vocationally oriented high schools in areas large enough to support such school diversity.

Also, much may be learned from the work force, from demonstration programs for teenage mothers, and from the ongoing military and youth training and employment programs, as well as from a resource not examined in this chapter—basic research on learning and cognition.

Of special concern, however, is that in many of these studies, particularly in school settings, young men have received relatively little attention. Often the source of greatest disciplinary problems, they are most likely to drop out for academic reasons and to get in trouble with the law. Yet, the research on the causes of major social problems of the youth indicates that the lack of marriageable men cascades into problems of teenage pregnancy and subsequent poverty cycles when many babies are born, but stable, two-worker families are not formed. The supply of marriageable men arguably will not be remedied until we have learned how to reach—and teach—the young men, and assist them to find the employment needed, with the functional skills needed, for supporting themselves, their spouses, and their—and *our*—next generation.

REFERENCES

Applebee, A. N., Langer, J. A., & Mullis, I. V. S. (1988). *Who reads best?* Princeton, NJ: Educational Testing Service.

Berlin, G., & Sum, A. (1988). *Toward a more perfect union: Basic skills, poor families and our economic future.* New York: Ford Foundation.

Berman, P., & McLaughlin, M. W. (1978). *Federal programs supporting educational change.* Santa Monica, CA: The Rand Corporation.

Berrueta-Clement, J. R. et al. (1984). *Changed lives: The effects of the Perry pre-school program on youths through age 19.* Ypsilanti, MI: High/Scope Educational Research Foundation.

Betsy, A. C., Hollister, R. G., Jr., & Papgeorgiou, M. R. (Eds.). (1985). *Youth employment and training programs: The YEDPA years.* Washington, DC: National Academy Press.

Bloom, H. S., Cordray, D. S., & Light, R. J. (Eds.). (1988). *Lessons from selected program and policy areas.* San Francisco: Jossey Bass.

Boris, M. E. (Ed.). (1984). *Youth and the labor market: Analyses of the national longitudinal surveys.* Kalamazoo, MI: W. E. Upjohn Institute for Employment Research.

Coleman, J., Hoffer, T., & Kilgore, S. (1982). *High school achievement.* New York: Basic Books.

Coleman, J. S., & Hoffer, T. (1987). *Public and private high schools: The impact of communities.* New York: Basic Books.

Committee for Economic Development. (1984). *Strategy for U.S. industrial competitiveness.* New York: Committee for Economic Development.

Elmore, R. F. (1986). National policy and local delivery in three U.S. settings. In R. C. Rist (Ed.), *Finding work: Cross national perspectives on employment and training.* Philadelphia.

Final report from the National Assessment of Chapter One. (1987). Washington, DC: Office of Research, Office of Educational Research and Improvement.

Gueron, J. M. (1988, Spring). Work—Welfare programs. In H. S. Bloom, D. S. Cordray, & R. J. Light (Eds.), *Lessons from selected program and policy areas* (New Directions for Program Evaluation No. 37, pp. 7-28). San Francisco: Jossey Bass.

Gueron, J. (1984). *Lessons from a job guarantee: The youth incentive entitlement program.* New York: Pilot Projects, New York Manpower Research Demonstration Corporation.

Hawley, W. D., & Rosenholts, S. J. (1984). Good schools: What research says about improving student achievement. *Peabody Journal of Education, 61.*

Johnson, C., & Sum, A. (1987). Declining earnings of young men: Their relation to poverty, teen pregnancy and family formation. Washington, DC: Children's Defense Fund.

Kirsch, I. S., & Jungeblut, A. (1986). *Literacy: Profiles of America's young adults* (Final Report). Princeton, NJ: Educational Testing Service.

Koretz, D. (1986). *Trends in educational achievement.* Washington, DC: Congressional Budget Office.

Koretz, D. (1987). *Educational achievement: Explanations and implications of recent trends.* Washington, DC: Congressional Budget Office.

Lerche, R. (1985). *Effective adult literacy programs: A practitioner's guide.* New York: Cambridge Book Company.

McLaughlin, M. W. (1987). Learning from experience: lessons from policy implementation. *Educational Evaluation and Policy Analysis, 9*(2), 171-178.

National Advisory Council on Adult Education. (undated). *Illiteracy in America: Extent, causes, and suggested solutions.* Washington, DC: U.S. Government Printing Office.

National Assessment of Educational Process (NAEP). (1976). *Functional literacy and basic reading performance.* Washington, DC: U.S. Office of Education.

National Commission on Excellence in Education. (1983). *A nation at risk: The imperative for educational reform.* Washington, DC: U.S. Government Printing Office.

National Research Council. (1986). *Risking the future: Adolescent sexuality, pregnancy, and childbearing.* Washington, DC: National Academy Press.

National Assessment of Vocational Education. (1988). *First Interim Report.* Washington, DC: U.S. Department of Education.

National Dissemination Study Group. (1987). *Educational programs that work* (Thirteenth Ed.). Longmont, CO: Sopris West, Inc.

Owens, T. R. (1988). *Improving the collaboration of secondary vocational and academic educators.* Paper presented at the American Educational Research Association meeting, New Orleans, LA.

Pressman, J., & Wildavsky, A. (1979). *Implementation* (2nd ed.). Berkeley: University of California Press.

Rist, R. C. (1981). *Earning and learning: Youth employment policies and programs.* Beverly Hills, CA: Sage Publications.

Sebring, P. A. (1987). Consequences of differential amounts of high school course work: Will the new graduation requirements help? *Educational Evaluation and Policy Analysis, 9*(3), 258-273.

Sewell, W., Hauser, R., & Featherman, D. (Eds.). (1976). *Schooling and achievement in American society.* New York: Academic Press.

Smith, R. E. (1987). *Work-related programs for welfare recipients.* Washington, DC: Congressional Budget Office.

Tomlinson, T. M., & Walberg, H. J. (Eds.). (1986). *Academic work and educational excellence: Raising student productivity.* New York: McCutchan.

Venezky, R., Kaestle, C., & Sum, A. (1987). *The subtle danger: Reflections on the literacy abilities of America's young adults.* Princeton, NJ: Educational Testing Service.

Weick, K. E. (1984). Small wins: Redefining the scale of social problems. *American Psychologist, 39,* 40-49.

Wholey, J. S. (1987). The Job Corps: Congressional uses of evaluation findings.

In W. R. Shadish & C. S. Reichardt (Eds.), *Evaluation studies review annual* (Vol. 12, pp. 234-244). Beverly Hills, CA: Sage.

Wilson, W. (1980). *The declining significance of race.* Chicago: University of Chicago Press.

Wilson, W. J. (1987). *The truly disadvantaged: The inner city, the underclass and public policy.* Chicago: University of Chicago Press.

Chapter 6

What Makes a Difference in Instruction?

Thomas M. Duffy
Indiana University

Datta has presented us with some very sobering statistics on the intergenerational growth of a permanent underclass. She has also provided a comprehensive review of the programs offered by the Departments of Labor and Education to help young adults who are likely to become a part of that underclass.

I will begin my comments by first expanding on Datta's discussion of the implications of adult education and training for intergenerational transfer—the ways in which we might expect the programs to affect, not only the young adult being trained, but also his or her children. I will then examine and extend Datta's findings on the meager effects of the various job and education programs. The main thrust of this discussion will be the importance of identifying and focusing on the functional goal of an education or training program. As part of this discussion, I will review some military programs that have provided us bigger wins.

INTERGENERATIONAL TRANSFER

The growth of a permanent "underclass" is simply documented by Datta. For example, she reports that workers without a high school diploma lost over 41% in real income between 1973 and 1984 while college graduates lost only 11%. Further, the proportion of young black males with incomes below the poverty line for a family of three is now 77 percent—an increase of 22 percentage points over that same 10-year span. The poor do indeed get poorer! Datta also clearly identifies the consequences on youth—the intergenerational transfer—of this increasing poverty: larger number of single parent homes, more children raised in poverty, increased teen pregnancy, homelessness, a decline in school completions, and so on.

Adult education and training programs are meant to provide a direct route out of poverty. A high school diploma or job training means a far higher probability of a job, and "the job" is seen as the escape from poverty and the consequences of poverty described above. The "job" is the most obvious benefit of training. When an individual obtains a job for a living wage, he or she is raised above the poverty line and there is new potential for growth. The effect on the adults, and the transfer to the children, is straightforward. Indeed, education and training programs represent the *most obvious and potentially the most powerful strategy* for ending the intergenerational consequences of poverty.

Unfortunately, the findings reported by Datta, and the findings I will report, indicate that education and training programs have not been very effective in increasing skills or in providing the opportunity for jobs. Even when the programs lead to jobs, one may ask, "What kind of a job?" If the individual is receiving poverty-level wages, have we really broken the intergenerational transfer of poverty and the consequences of poverty? In sum the evidence suggests that the potentially very powerful direct effects of job training and education programs have been negligible. However, the potential is still there, and the bulk of my discussion will address what I feel is an essential ingredient required to begin realizing that potential.

The direct effect of training is expected to be an increase in a skill which in turn will increase employability. Before turning to these direct effects, let us briefly consider some of the potential indirect effects related to intergenerational transfer. These are effects that may be found even if training does not lead to a job. This intergenerational transfer is found in the new attitudes and the new skills that the adult introduces into the house and into the pattern of family interaction.

The first source of intergenerational transfer is in the attitude toward education introduced into the home. To the extent that the adults see the education or training program as valuable (relevant to their life needs), regardless of whether or not it leads to a job, they will present a positive attitude toward education. On the other hand, if the program is seen as the "same old stuff" that was rejected in school—

instruction they see as irrelevant to the real world and their needs—then they will certainly have difficulty encouraging their children to partake in the education process. Thus we may hypothesize that a functional context in education, where the instruction is based on real world tasks and is presented in the context of those tasks, will lead to a perception of education as valuable. This, in turn, will cause the parent to communicate a positive attitude toward education to the child. On the other hand, if instruction is abstract and divorced from the real world—as most literacy instruction and even vocational instruction tends to be—then the relevance and importance of education may be questioned.

The second potential intergenerational transfer effect is the development of schooling skills or learning skills. Resnick (1987) and Brown, Collins, and Duguid (1989) have emphasized the difference between learning in school and out of school. They emphasize that because of the differences in learning demands, there is little transfer from school to the real world. We think the lack of transfer in the opposite direction is equally important. That is, while children in the permanent underclass may be very capable in out of school learning environments because of the lack of similarity in the learning demands, there is little transfer into the classroom. In middle-class homes, in contrast, we may anticipate schooling kinds of learning demands as a regular part of daily interactions and hence greater transfer of that learning to the classroom.

For example, one might expect that the less literate and less schooled adult teaches the child how to do things by example. He or she will show the child how to do the dishes and will correct errors by demonstrating what should be done. As a consequence of schooling, however, the adults may more frequently use oral instructions to teach or correct behavior. Thus, the child will receive more experience with interpreting and responding to oral instructions. Since oral and written instructions are the primary means of teaching in the schools, this experience will provide the youngster with an essential skill for success in school.

Third, we may expect intergenerational transfer of the skills the parent learns in school. If the adult improves reading skills, he or she is more likely to use text or reading material to accomplish tasks in the home environment and thus serve as a literacy model for the child. The adult is also more likely to have books in the home and thus provide a more literate environment for the child. Finally, the adult may use his or her literacy skills in directly aiding the child in reading tasks and in completing homework.

It is very important for us to identify and capitalize on these more indirect effects when we design and evaluate education and training programs. As Datta's findings indicate, there is little evidence for a direct effect of the training. However, the indirect impact could be very significant—especially if we attended to those effects in designing the education and training programs. I hasten to emphasize my belief that these intergenerational transfer effects are dependent upon the adult seeing the relevance of the content and the learning tasks to the real world (Brown et al., 1989; Resnick, 1987).

INSTRUCTIONAL PROGRAMS

Datta very nicely summarizes the long history of government programs to provide job and basic skills training for youth and adults. She notes that virtually every intervention strategy possible has been tried. The occupational training has been for direct job skills and knowledge as well as for more general orientation or transition to work. The programs have been provided as: part time, neighborhood programs for out of school youth; residential programs that remove the young adult from the neighborhood environment and provide a wide range of counseling and job skill training; and employer-based, on-the-job training. There have also been programs for elementary school children and secondary school children.

While Datta suggests that findings soon to be released will offer us new hope, the summary from all of these past attempts is that there are minimal gains. While there is a reduction in criminal activity while the young people are in the residential Job Corps program, but other effects are weak at best.

Datta's description of the outcome of these youth programs reminds me of the review I did over 10 years ago of basic skills training programs in the military (Duffy, 1977). That review examined four existing literacy programs for low-literate military personnel. These programs were all administered during or shortly after recruit training and were aimed at providing the personnel with the reading and math skills necessary for success in follow-on job-training programs. Table 6.1 summarizes the findings from that review.

The four programs varied widely in character. The Navy1 program was professionally developed and instructed. The curriculum was organized around 129 well-specified instructional objectives; five pretests were administered to diagnose the student's instructional requirements. The Navy2 and Navy3 programs were designed by Navy personnel who had no experience in reading. They were simply college graduates who were interested in the assignment. The Marine Corps program was designed and taught by the local community college. It

Table 6.1 Summary of the Effectiveness of Four Department of Defense Literacy Programs. (Adapted from Duffy, 1975)

Training Program	Hours of Instruction	General Reading Scores		
		pre test	post test	gain
Marine Corps	120	3.5	5.7	2.2
Navy 1	60	4.5	6.3	1.8
Navy 2	92	4.2	6.0	1.8
Navy 3	69	4.2	6.1	1.9

was a general literacy program and part of the college's substantial adult literacy program.

In spite of these very significant differences in approach, the gain in reading score for all of the programs was between 1.8 and 2.2 grade levels on a general reading test. Thus, the approach to instruction and instructional design appears to make little difference, at least as indexed by the general reading test.

Rather than seeing the instruction as unsuccessful because of the lack of a differential effect of instructional methods, one might presume that all four programs were "successful"—they all produced a 1.8 to 2.2-grade-level gain. Unfortunately, there are at least two spurious effects that may account for a large part of those gains. In two of the programs (Navy1 and Navy2) students were admitted based on their low score on a test administered to a large segment of the recruit population. In retesting, even without intervention, we would expect an increase simply due to regression effects. Additionally, the Navy2 program conducted follow-up testing between 2 and 8 weeks after the trainees left the reading program and found that there was an average loss of 1.0 grade levels from the exit score (Duffy, 1977). This in spite of the fact that the recruits were spending half of their time in academic training where purportedly there were significant reading assignments. Thus more than half of the reading "gain" was lost, even though there was a call for the reading skill.

Back when I did this review, I concluded that *"within the confines of a short duration, instructor based, low literacy program, the amount of gain in general literacy is fixed and determined primarily by the simple exposure to the educational setting"* (Duffy, 1977). Furthermore, the gain seems to be about 1 year, or even less when regression and warmup effects are taken into account. Most importantly, the amount of instructional time (given it is a short duration program) does not seem to make a difference.

A General Accounting Office (1977) evaluation of the Army basic skills program also supports these conclusions. They found that 6 weeks of instruction, primarily in general literacy skills, yielded a

Table 6.2   Summary of Reading and Math Gains in Department of Labor Job and Literacy Training Programs. (From Department of Labor, 1986)

Training Program	Reading Inst.		Math Instruction	
	Hours	Gain	Hours	Gain
Comprehensive Competencies	30	1.10	28	1.30
Job Corps (1969)	75	.69	75	.70
Job Corps (1971–1975)				
Neighborhood	85/58	.80	85/58	1.00
Residential	100	1.30	100	1.30
Detention Facility	75	.70		
Air Force	173	1.40		
Job Corps	100	1.20	100	1.60

gain of 1.9 grade levels, much the same as the programs in Table 6.1. This minimal effect of the short-term literacy programs is not limited to the military. Kent (1973) administered tests at two times, 4 months apart, to a sample of 2,300 students in Adult Basic Education classes. The classes were in 90 different programs in 15 states. He found the average reading and math gains to be 0.5 and 0.3 grade levels, respectively.

Finally, the evaluation of the Department of Labor programs described by Datta also yield similar findings on literacy gains. The data are presented in Table 6.2. All of the programs listed in Table 6.2 were part of a more comprehensive job skills training program. Typically, reading and math would be taught in the morning and other job skills in the afternoon. As described earlier these courses were offered in a variety of settings and under a variety of restrictions (residential, neighborhood, etc.). As with the military programs, the literacy courses also reflected a variety of instructional approaches, including both computer and teacher based instruction. Indeed, the largest program, the Comprehensive Curriculum Program, offered a wide variety of reading materials and programs from which a program site could construct its own reading program.

As with the military programs, we find that the gain in reading does not seem to be related to the number of hours of instruction. *For these programs the average gain is slightly more than 1 grade level regardless of the number of hours of instruction, the type of instructional setting, or the type of instructional materials.* If we recall the Navy follow-up testing described above, we can also predict that these students will lose a significant portion of that gain within weeks of leaving the program.

MODELS OF READING INSTRUCTION

Datta argued that perhaps we need to be satisfied with small wins. I certainly agree with Datta that, many times, our goals are set too high. Students enter programs expecting to become quite literate in a few months. They often view attending classes as their primary responsibility in this learning effort. Many teachers, especially volunteer tutors, expect to have a meaningful impact on the learner's life in 6 months with only 2 to 4 hours of instruction per week. However, any consideration of the complexity of the reading process and of the time it takes youngsters to learn to read would suggest that significant gains in reading skills is by no means a short-term instructional process. In addition, as anyone who has taught these basic skills programs can attest, the complex of other problems in the lives of these students has a very significant, negative impact on the instructional process.

While many students, teachers, and administrators may have expected too big a win, I am nonetheless concerned with the acceptance of "small" wins. Should we be satisfied with the small wins of the literacy programs? Or should we be examining the programs closely to identify strategies for achieving bigger wins? The small win complacency might well lead one to excuse the small gains in the programs as being due to the short duration. "If the programs were only longer, the gains would be larger," one might argue.

Certainly time is an important factor. Literacy development is a life-long learning process. However, as we saw in the review of literacy programs, time alone is not the critical variable. The Pearson Product Moment correlation between hours of instruction and gain for the programs in Tables 6.1 and 6.2 is only .26. One might argue that these are all short duration, and, thus, that the correlation is restricted. However, the residential Job Corps programs can hardly be considered short duration. The average student enrollment in Job Corps is 7 months. This is 7 months in a full-time residential program with full days of basic skills and job skills training. While reading and math were only taught in the mornings, the students were in a learning and literacy environment for the entire time. Certainly we would expect a more significant impact from these programs.

Other literacy providers lament that "We could have a greater impact if we could only keep the students in the classes." Drop-out rates in adult literacy programs are typically in excess of 50 percent. This high drop-out rate is generally blamed on all of the competing obligations the adult student has. However, I would argue that we should be examining the literacy curriculum to understand the reasons for the drop-out rate. If instruction is seen as relevant and useful to everyday needs, I would certainly expect a higher proportion of the students to "stay with it." Unfortunately, most literacy curricula do not give any sense of relevance. Rather, the instruction follows an elementary school model of teaching the individual skills involved in academic reading.

The argument that I would like to advance is that our small wins are due, in large measure, to the failure to attend to the postinstructional tasks the students have to perform. This failure is reflected in the content specification, the instructional strategies, and the evaluation criteria of the programs.

The "General Literacy" Model of Reading

Datta suggested that all possible approaches to literacy instruction have been tried. This is clearly an accurate description of the management characteristics of the programs. However, the programs are homogeneous in terms of the basic instructional approach to reading. This approach reflects a general literacy model of reading.

The model basically follows the traditional elementary school approach in which reading is seen as decoding the text—getting the meaning from the text. The skills required for this are specifiable and thus instruction simply involves the development of these decoding skills. Once the skills are learned, it is thought that the student will be able to read any text as long as he or she has the necessary vocabulary. Readability formulas that address only word and sentence complexity are considered a good indicator of the difficulty a person will have in comprehending a text. If the words and the sentences are simple enough, then the person will be able to "comprehend" (Duffy, 1985).

The model also supports a decomposition approach to instruction. That is, reading is decomposed into its component skills, and those skills are taught individually. Since reading is simply the use of these skills, the emphasis is on the development of the fluent application of the skills. Once fluent, the skills will transfer to any reading task.

A Cognitive Science View of Reading

Research on the reading process clearly shows that the general reading skills model is inaccurate. Rather than a general process composed of a fixed set of skills, the ability to comprehend text is a function of the reader's knowledge of the content domain, the structure or genre of the text, and the particular reading task (Just & Carpenter, 1987). What concerns me is that, while we have extensive research data on the importance of these factors in reading and the theoretical framework is well established, there has been little impact on adult reading instruction, that is, the general skills model of reading has dominated. I will therefore review some of this research evidence to provide a foundation for the instructional approach I am advocating.

It is now generally recognized that reading involves building a representation that combines both the information in the text and the readers knowledge of the subject matter. That is, the reader not only decodes the text bottom up, but also uses knowledge of the subject matter in a top-down process of identifying key information, structuring the information for storage in long-term memory, filling in missing information, and making inferences. Recent research suggests that the text information and the information called up from long-term memory are combined in the memory trace from the reading activity such that the reader cannot distinguish the two sources of information (Masson, 1987).

Knowledge of the subject matter affects comprehension. Bransford and Johnson (1972) provided the classic demonstration of the importance of world knowledge with their "washer woman" passage. Learners' recall of a passage containing simple sentences and familiar vocabulary was dramatically improved simply by telling them the title of the passage. It is assumed that the title, "Washing Clothes," allowed the reader to tap a wide range of information and experiences in memory that could be used to structure the text information and fill in the gaps.

A more "real world" demonstration of the same phenomenon is provided in a study by Sticht et al. (1986). They developed readability formulas for predicting the ease of comprehension of text on electricity. Different readability formulas were developed for high, medium, and low background knowledge readers. When these formulas were used to predict the comprehensibility of texts, the formula based on the high background knowledge readers predicted a reading skill 5 years below that for the low background knowledge readers. If we use a simple model of reading, we can conclude that subject matter knowledge compensates for 5 years of reading skill, such as, persons with a fifth-grade reading skill can comprehend a tenth-grade text if they know the subject matter of the text.

The importance of subject matter knowledge in comprehension suggests that reading instruction should not be divorced from the content domain in which the reader will be working. At the most basic level, it means that the reading material used in instruction should be in the content domain relevant to the student's postinstructional reading needs. However, there is a more important implication. Reading is typically taught as a preparatory skill: The student "gets" reading skills so he or she can learn about some subject matter. However, the role of subject knowledge in comprehension suggests that reading instruction should follow or at least be coincident with content domain instruction. That is, the learners should develop content knowledge before working at reading in a content domain. The content knowledge will aid them in comprehending the text.

Knowledge of the text grammar affects comprehension. The structure of a text also has a significant influence on the ability of readers to abstract information. Story grammars have received considerable research attention, and we know that, if readers understand the structure of stories, they are better able to comprehend any particular story. At a common sense level, readers versed in fiction know that they can probably skip the first 20 pages or more without losing the thread of the story. They also know that they must watch for a central conflict that will be the focus of the book, a protagonist, an antagonist, and so on.

Expository texts also have structure: There are different structures for comparison and contrast, description, cause and effect, and so forth. Knowledge of those structures will facilitate comprehension by guiding the reader to key information and aiding the reader in structuring the information for storage in long-term memory (Mayer, 1987).

There are even more specific structural issues. For example, engineering text tends to have a very shallow structure where paragraphs are on a topic and every sentence in the paragraph is important. Main ideas are difficult to identify. In contrast, social sciences and humanities texts tend to emphasize cohesion and interlinking the information. A main idea with elaboration is easily identified. An engineer, used to very specific information in text, may well find it difficult to "comprehend" the social science text.

Technical manuals have specific organizational structures and cueing devices for readers to use, and there are even texts available to teach vocational students how to use a technical manual (Eisenberg, 1978). Indeed, familiarity with the structure may even compensate for poorly designed technical manuals. That is, technicians may be able to use a poorly designed manual more effectively than a well-designed one simply because of familiarity in using other manuals with the same poor structure (Duffy, Curran, & Sass, 1983).

The instructional implications of these findings are that the particular text structures relevant to the students' postinstructional goals must be taken into account in both the selection of reading material and the instruction on that reading material. It does no good to have the learners reading stories or even general expository text if, in fact, the goal of instruction is to prepare the learner to use technical manuals. The technical manuals, or at least abstracts from the manual, should form the basic instructional material. The instruction should focus on using the particular text structures in comprehending (Eisenberg, 1978).

Reading goals affect reading strategies and what is comprehended. Different reading strategies are required to achieve different goals. Sticht (1975) and Mikulecky (1982) have compared school and work reading tasks and found that most school reading tasks are reading-to-learn, in which the requirement is to identify key information (information that may be tested), build a representation of the information in the text, and store everything in long-term memory. In contrast, most reading on the job is reading-to-do, in which the task is typically to search for a fact or procedure and hold that information in short-term memory while it is being applied.

Clearly these two classes of reading tasks require different skills. Reading-to-learn places a high premium on the ability to synthesize information, to get the gist, and organize it and store it in long-term memory for later retrieval. In contrast, reading-to-do emphasizes the ability to identify information relevant to some specific goal and to understand the information in such a way that it can be applied. There is much less emphasis on long-term memory, on synthesizing information, and on identifying what the author or some other person might deem important.

The reading-to-do (job-oriented) and reading-to-learn (studying) tasks may be further distinguished in terms of the constraints placed on the reading activity. Studying is typically done at a time selected by the reader. The duration of the study activity is similarly determined by the reader. In contrast, job reading tasks are initiated by a specific need for job-related information. Hence, the job tends to determine the time and place of reading. Furthermore, Mikulecky and Ehlinger (1986) found that job reading tends to be accomplished in small spurts. Time for a leisurely perusal of the text is simply not available. This means that the reading strategies must be very efficient.

Reading-to-do and reading-to-learn represent two general classes of reading tasks. Under these general titles we can find a wide range of reading tasks, all calling for somewhat different reading strategies and skills, for example, understanding a concept rather than a whole chapter or book, understanding a procedure, locating and following a procedure, developing a strategy for accomplishing some goal, understanding an issue to guide later behavior, and so on. Kirsch and Guthrie (1982) outlined the variety of reading-to-do tasks engaged in by managers in the business community. The recent NAEP assessment of basic skills of young adults similarly identifies a range of functional reading tasks (Kirsch & Jungleblut, 1986).

TOWARD BIGGER WINS

The cognitive science view of reading and the research evidence supporting it suggests a rather dramatic revision in our approach to reading instruction. Reading is a complex cognitive activity requiring the selection of skills and strategies to match the particular reading task and the use of that knowledge to help guide the use of the text. If instruction is to address the needs of the learner, it must provide knowledge of the text structures and subject matter, and the student must learn how to use that knowledge when reading. If we know that those task characteristics are relevant to reading, and we can identify those aspects of the adult's reading tasks, it only makes sense to focus on those tasks in reading instruction. Indeed, common sense and any introductory psychology text will tell us that, if there is a particular type of (reading) task a person has to do, we will be more effective if we teach him or her how to do that task rather than some other task.

In the remainder of this chapter I will review several programs that have tried to take into account the cognitive features of the reading task. These programs can be divided into two groups. In the first group literacy instructional design is based on some analysis of the intended uses of literacy. That is, there is a content or task analysis guiding the design of instruction. The second group of design strategies are also based on a content or task analysis but also bring the context of the use of literacy—the functional context—into the literacy instruction. Hence, they represent integrated job and literacy training. This integration is an important consideration in instructional design. Reading is not just an isolated use of skills. Rather, successful reading involves the recognition of what reading tasks are required on the job and the successful integration of that reading into the job.

This integrated approach to defining and teaching has been described by a variety of labels. Brown et al. (1989) have described it as situated cognition while Bransford and his colleagues (Bransford, Sherwood, Hasselbring, et al., 1991) refer to anchored instruction.

Sticht (1987) has called it "functional context" instruction. Functional context education recognizes the integrated cognitive demands of the task and notes that transfer to the real world task will be maximal to the extent that the instruction reflects the cognitive features of the full task. As we progress to these whole task approaches, the emphasis is as much on the job task as it is on literacy. That is, reading and other literacy demands are just a component of the overall task.

Content/Task Relevant Approaches

Defining the content domain. Duffy and Hartz (1984) describe the most basic movement from general literacy to specific literacy instruction. The instruction was for less able readers entering fire control technician training in the Navy. Since the goal was to aid these individuals in reading in their technical area, sailors in each week of the technical training program were interviewed and asked to identify the vocabulary and the text they had trouble understanding that week. These difficult vocabulary and paragraphs of text became the focus of the reading instruction.

A computer-based drill and practice approach was used. An instructional unit consisted of learning vocabulary and then completing rather traditional reading exercises on five-sentence paragraphs. Thus, while the instruction utilized the relevant content domain, it did not actively teach the student how to use the domain knowledge to interpret the text. Furthermore, the instruction did not require the kinds of reading tasks the sailors had to do in training. It was simply traditional reading instruction using materials from the relevant content domain.

In spite of the simplicity of the approach, the instruction was very effective. A comparison was made between students attending 40 hours of this domain-relevant reading instruction and students in the traditional general literacy program. The latter group showed somewhat larger gains on a general literacy test for vocabulary and comprehension, but, as one might expect, they did not improve their knowledge of the vocabulary relevant to their technical area (neither technical vocabulary nor frequently occurring general vocabulary). The students in the domain-specific reading program, however, showed dramatic gains in knowledge of the vocabulary in their technical manuals and significant gains in the ability to answer questions based on text taken from those manuals (Duffy & Hartz, 1984).

The vocabulary tested was a subset from the 100 words the students had learned in the 2-week period. The texts they read were samples from their manual but had not been used during instruction. Thus, there was a transfer of comprehension skills to reading the manual in the way that will be required in the regular training program. The results simply state that the students get better at what they are taught. I only wonder why the general literacy programs do not attempt to teach relevant tasks.

Prerequisite skill instruction. The Army and Navy have long offered basic skills programs for low-ability recruits. These were general literacy programs and were described earlier in this chapter. These services have each introduced a replacement for the general literacy courses that is based on a detailed analysis of the specific basic skill requirements in the jobs the students will enter: the Job Oriented Basic Skills (JOBS) course in the Navy (Harding, Mogford, Melching, & Showel, 1981) and the Job Skills Education Program (JSEP) in the Army (Derry, Jacobs, & Murphy, 1986–1987). The courses are multi-stranded, so that a student enters a course specifically designed for his or her job area, that is, to prepare him or her for the specific literacy skills and knowledge considered prerequisite to successful performance in the job area.

Both programs identified prerequisite skills through a hierarchical task analysis. This amounts to identifying job tasks and then asking repeatedly, "What skills and knowledge are required to complete this task." I say "repeatedly" because this is done at deeper and deeper levels, such as, the skills and knowledge identified as part of the primary task are then analyzed in terms of their prerequisite skills and knowledge. This continues until we identify skills and knowledge that match the entry levels of the students.

Both the Army and Navy programs followed this path of creating a basic skills subject matter. There are 35 instructional modules in JSEP, and 25 modules in JOBS with between 3 and 11 lessons associated with each module. In both programs a student will only take a subset of the modules and lessons as determined by his or her job area. A sampling of the modules with a lesson topic is presented in Table 6.3 for both JOBS and JSEP.

Solid evaluation data are not available for either program. While the JOBS program was evaluated, a proper control group, where the JOBS-eligible students entered technical training directly, was not included in the design of the evaluation (Baker & Hamovitch, 1983). The JSEP program is currently undergoing a formal evaluation. In spite of the lack of evaluation data, the logic of the design of these programs suggests that they must be more effective than the general literacy programs they replaced. Not only is instruction in the right

Table 6.3   A Sample of Draft Module Titles and (Lessons) from the Army Job Skills Education Program (JSEP) and the Navy's Job Oriented Basic Skills (JOBS) Program.

JSEP Modules	JOBS Modules
Gage measurements	Fractions
(Read and Interpret scales with + and − demarcations)	(Divide fractions)
Geometry	Formulas and variational analysis
(Measure rectangular shaped solids)	(Current flow in a schematic)
Trigonometry	Trigonometry
(Use tables of trigonometric functions)	(Solve for unknown angles of right triangle)
Procedural directions	Comprehension of job specific material
(Select part of a text and visual material to complete an activity)	(Comprehension of electricity material)
Vocabulary	Taking notes
(Recognize the meaning of words from your job area)	(List the supporting ideas of a paragraph)
Illustrations	Locate key information in a schematic
(Use a map to communicate details of terrain and layout)	(Find the path of flow)
Outlining	Graphs
(Use letters and numbers to label topics in an outline)	(Determine a trend represented by a plotted line)
Editing	Follow independent study procedures
(Rewrite a paragraph by stating the main idea, etc.)	(Select an appropriate study strategy)
Recognition	Find information
(Identify objects by size shape color and markings).	(Alphabetize key words)

content domain, but they are working with the reading tasks and the text structures they will encounter in training and on the job. The instruction is obviously more relevant than the general literacy programs and more relevant than the simple domain specification in the Duffy and Hartz (1984) work.

Literacy task instruction. Sticht (1975) offered an alternative strategy to the labor-intensive hierarchical task analysis in developing yet another alternative to the Army general literacy programs. In designing the FLIT curriculum, he interviewed job incumbents, asking them to describe a reading task they had done on the job and one they had done in training during the last 24 hours. He collected the specific text materials used and the statement of the reading goal from each individual.

Rather than analyzing these tasks into prerequisite skills and knowledge, Sticht conducted a theoretical analysis to determine the specific cognitive and information processing requirements in the tasks. The instruction was then organized based on this theoretical account. In particular, Sticht distinguished between reading-to-do tasks and reading-to-learn tasks. Instruction in reading-to-do focused on strategies for searching for information in a variety of text structures: an index, table of contents, text, graphics, and text and graphics. Reading-to-learn focused on strategies for summarizing and rerepresenting information.

Instruction was on text structures and on strategies for achieving the particular reading goals using materials having those structures. Materials were matched to the job area so that instruction was in the context of the knowledge domain and the text structures relevant to the individuals job area.

The FLIT program was compared to one of the general literacy programs that it was designed to replace (Sticht, 1975). FLIT, like the Duffy and Hartz (1984) program, did not improve general literacy skills beyond what was obtained through general literacy instruction. However, the FLIT curriculum was very effective relative to the general literacy program in improving the ability of the students to use the technical material. This of course is only logical—the students were taught to work in the knowledge domain, with the particular text structures, to achieve the reading-to-learn and reading-to-do goals. We would expect the students to show the greatest gains in the tasks they were taught.

Integrated Job and Literacy Task Instruction

One of the shortcomings of the programs described thus far are that reading is taught as a prerequisite to job training rather than as just another part of the job. As a consequence, they fail to identify or teach these skills that make reading a part of the job—a job task. This integration is important for much the same reason that reading instruction should be based on the particular reading task the individual will face. Reading and other literacy tasks are driven by specific factors in the job context—the inability to perform the job task signals the need for the literacy task and the time available, the availability of co-workers, the diagnosis of the problem, and other context specific factors. Transfer to the job will be maximal to the extent that the job context is provided in training. In this section we will examine approaches to identifying the literacy demands in the context of the job. The three programs reflect three very distinctive approaches to defining the tasks.

Literacy task analysis. Mikulecky (1985) argues for the use of a modified version of traditional task analysis to identify the literacy instruction. Traditional task analysis procedures tend to ignore the literacy tasks of the job and focus on the specific job skills and knowledge that must be stored in the head. The approach also differs from the JOBS and JSEP approach in that the latter provided "prerequisite" skills instruction. The literacy prerequisites became an organizational factor, and, hence, instruction was decomposed.

In more recent applications of the approach, Mikulecky and his colleagues (Mikulecky & Ehlinger, 1986; Mikulecky & Winchester, 1983) are using contrasts between expert and novice incumbents to define the metacognitive components of the literacy tasks, that is, noticing when to use the literacy skills. These metacognitive aspects of performance, generally recognized as critical to successful performance, place even greater emphasis on the integration of job and literacy skills. As described by Mikulecky and co-workers, these skills amount to responding to implicit signals in the job context that call for specific literacy tasks. Sticht and Mikulecky (1984) report a job retraining program for water treatment workers in which literacy tasks were taught as part of the job tasks.

Cognitive task analysis. The Air Force shifted the emphasis from basic skills to basic cognitive skills. They developed an analysis strategy to identify the basic cognitive skills required on the job (Means, Roth, & Riegelhaupt, 1986). The cognitive tasks analysis procedure involves two stages: identifying key tasks, and analyzing the knowledge and strategies required in the performance of those tasks. The approach differs from traditional task analysis in two ways. First, not all job tasks are identified. Rather, the first stage identifies "key" tasks: tasks that are difficult to perform, tasks that are performed by many personnel, and tasks in which errors are costly. The learning of key tasks will involve literacy skills and domain specific skills and the integration of those skills in a model of the work environment. It is expected that those skills and the model will transfer to other job tasks.

The second difference from traditional task analysis is the emphasis on maintaining the task context during the analysis. The approach is one of knowledge engineering in which the analyst interviews experts to develop/describe an effective problem space for performing the job task. The experts are asked to work through the job task, thinking aloud as they do it. They are stopped periodically for questioning about alternative strategies for accomplishing each subgoal and for the knowledge and skills required for each decision. This is done with at least two expert job performers. The strategies, including alternate paths, are then confirmed by having the experts observe less experienced workers performing the same job tasks.

The result of these interviews and think-aloud protocols is a detailed network of decision options and alternate paths to the successful completion of the job. This includes identifying sources of information, the cues for signaling the information need, and the literacy tasks involved in obtaining the information. All of this can then be utilized in providing instruction in the basic cognitive skills required for the job task.

This approach was used recently to define the "effective problem space" for performing a troubleshooting analysis of an electronics test station (Means et al. 1986). Lesgold, LaJoie, Banzo, and Eggan (in press) then used the results of the analysis to provide basic skills instruction for recent graduates of the training program. The instruction involved a computer representation of the test station modules and a copy of all relevant schematics. An evaluation of the program suggested that 20 hours of this instruction resulted in job competency equivalent to 42 months of job experience (Nichols, Porkorny, Jones, Gott, & Alley, in press).

While the instruction for this particular task area did not place much emphasis on the literacy components of the job, the cognitive task analysis approach, in principle, a ideally suited to integrating literacy skill instruction with other job skills. The emphasis is not on the physical skills required for the job but rather the cognitive skills, including literacy skills, that are required. The approach can assist in identifying the specific reading tasks, the cues that elicit the tasks, and the use of the results of the literacy task in real job performance.

Functional context training. Sticht, Armstrong, Hickey, and Caylor (1987) demonstrated the integration of literacy skill with other job skill instruction in the design of a basic electricity course. Sticht et al. describe their approach as "functional context training" in that the functional context of the job is always present in the instructional situation. However, the approach is also very similar to what would be prescribed by the elaboration theory of instruction (Riegeluth & Stein, 1983).

The Air Force program just described works with trainees familiar with the basic features of the job—they have been through the traditional training course. Sticht's program is designed for true novices, who do not have any electronics experience. The key set of tasks in this program are defined as troubleshooting electronic circuits. All of the instruction, therefore, revolves around understanding and diagnosing circuits. This includes using manuals and instructional texts to gather information, doing mathematical calculations to interpret the functioning of the circuit, and constructing a mental model of the circuit to help interpret and predict the functioning of the circuit.

Since the students were novices, Sticht could not begin instruction with the complex and abstract electronic circuits that were the eventual goal of the course. Instead he began with simple circuits for objects familiar to the students, for example, a hair dryer and a flashlight. These circuits maintained the focus on the whole task and provided a familiar context to the students. It was anticipated that this latter feature would permit the students to use what they know about the appliance to better understand what is going on with the circuitry. In terms of the "given new" contract of learning (Clark & Haviland, 1977), the hair dryer and the flashlight provided the "given" context to be used in interpreting the "new" circuitry.

The functional context approach to instruction has not been evaluated yet. However, there are several analogous experimental efforts that suggest the importance of that linkage. For example, as we have already discussed, knowledge of a subject matter domain will facilitate comprehension of new text discussing concepts in that domain (Bransford & Johnson, 1972; Clark & Haviland, 1977).

Cici and McNellis (1987) presented a dramatic illustration of the importance of providing a linkage to a familiar context. They presented children with a computer displayed object. Their job was to predict where that object would move when a trial began. There were three variables determining the movement size (large goes up; small down), shape (shape 1 moves far, and shape 2 moves a short distance), and color (color 1 moves right, and color two left) of the object.

In the decontextualized condition the object was either a circle or square, and the child moved the computer cursor to the expected final position of movement. The children failed to learn this task. Performance accuracy increased only slightly across a series of over 750 trials. However, when the objects and the task took on a familiar meaning, learning progressed from a 20 percent accuracy to 90 percent accuracy across 250 trials. Task familiarity was provided by changing the cursor to a net and the objects to birds and butterflies. Thus the task was one of predicting where the bird or butterfly would fly and placing the net there to capture it.

CONCLUSION

Job and literacy skill training has not been very effective in aiding adults and the next generation they are raising. Gains in skill and gains in employment have been minimal. Nonetheless, education and training programs represent the most obvious and potentially the most powerful strategy for ending the intergenerational consequences of poverty. It is the direct path to new sources of information and new skills essential to escaping from the effects of poverty.

I have argued that the limited effects of literacy and job-skill instruction are primarily due to the inadequate model guiding the instructional design. The instructional programs must be based on an analysis of the job-skill requirements. Instruction will be most effective if it focuses on the particular tasks the individual will have to perform outside instruction, and if there is a bridge linking the new skills and knowledge to what the learner already knows. The several programs reviewed in this chapter illustrate the following principles of instructional design:

- The instruction should be based on an analysis of the specific tasks a person will have to perform after instruction is completed. There are a variety of ways of defining the tasks and analyzing the skills and knowledge required to perform the task. These approaches reflect different levels of effort and different instructional models, but they all can yield the specification of the relevant instructional requirements.
- Literacy tasks should be defined in terms of the content domain in which the literacy task is performed, the text structures the individual will have to use, the particular reading tasks, and the context of the job that signals the requirements for literacy activities, i.e., the metacognitive supports.
- The instruction must focus on the whole task rather than the skills and knowledge required for the task. This will help provide relevance for the learner, support the integration of skills, and insure that only relevant knowledge and skill training is supported. If it is simply a literacy course, then the instruction should focus on the

literacy tasks the individual will be performing as outlined in the previous point. If it is skill training, then the skill tasks should be the focus of instruction, and the literacy components of the task should be a part of that task-oriented instruction.

- The instruction on new tasks should always provide a familiar context so that the learner can use his or her knowledge base, what he or she already knows, to interpret and integrate the new skills and knowledge.

REFERENCES

Baker, M., & Hamovitch, M. (1983). *Job-oriented basic skills (JOBS) training program: An evaluation* (Tech. Rep. No. NPRDC TR 83-5). San Diego, CA: Navy Personnel Research and Development Center.

Bransford, J., & Johnson, M. (1972). Contextual prerequisites for understanding: Some investigations of comprehension and recall. *Journal of Verbal Learning and Verbal Behavior, 61,* 717-726.

Ceci, S., & McNellis, K. (1987). *Entangling knowledge and process.* Paper presented at the annual meeting of the American Educational Research Association.

Clark, H. H., & Haviland, S. (1977). Comprehension and the given-new contract. In R. O. Freedle (Ed.), *Discourse processes: Advances in research and theory* (Vol. 1, pp. 1-40). Norwood, NJ: Ablex Publishing Corp.

Derry, S., Jacobs, J., & Murphy, D. (1986-1987). The JSEP learning skills training system. *Journal of Educational Technology Systems, 15,* 273-284.

Duffy, T. (1977). Literacy training in the Navy. In J. D. Fletcher, T. Duffy, & T. Curran (Eds.), *Historical antecedents and contemporary trends in literacy and readability research in the Navy* (Tech. Rep. No. NPRDC TR 77-15). San Diego, CA: Navy Personnel Research and Development Center.

Duffy, T. M. (1985). Readability formulas: What is the use? In T. M. Duffy & R. Waller (Eds.), *Designing usable texts.* New York: Academic Press.

Duffy, T. M., Curran, T., & Sass, D. (1983). Document design for technical job tasks: An evaluation. *Human Factors, 25,* 143-160.

Duffy, T., & Hartz, C. (1984). *Evaluating the effectiveness of reading programs.* Paper presented at the annual meeting of the American Educational Research Association, New Orleans, LA.

Eisenberg, A. (1978). *Reading technical books.* Englewood Cliffs, NJ: Prentice-Hall.

General Accounting office, United States. (1977). *A need to address illiteracy problems in the military services* (Report No. FPCD-77-13). Washington, DC: Author.

Harding, S., Mogford, B., Melching, W., & Showel, M. (1981). *The development of four job-oriented basic skills (JOBS) programs* (Tech. Rep. No. NPRDC TR 81-24). San Diego, CA: Navy Personnel Research and Development Center.

Just, M., & Carpenter, P. (1987). *The psychology of reading and language comprehension.* Newton, MA: Allyn and Bacon.

Kent, W. (1973). *A longitudinal evaluation of the adult basic education program.* Falls Church, VA: Systems Development Corp.

Kirsch, I., & Guthrie, J. (1982). *Reading competencies and practices: Case studies of reading in a high technology corporation* (Tech. Rep. No. 2). Newark, DE: International Reading Association.

Kirsch, I., & Jungeblut, A. (1986). *Literacy: Profiles of America's young adults.* Princeton, NJ: Educational Testing Service.

Lesgold, A., LaJoie, S., Bunzo, M., & Eggan, G. (in press). Sherlock: A couched practice environment for an electronics troubleshooting job. In J. Larkin, R. Chebay, & C. Scheftic (Eds.), *Computer assisted instruction and intelligent tutoring systems: Establishing communications and collaboration.* Englewood, NJ: Erlbaum.

Masson, M. (1987). Remembering reading operations with and without awareness. In B. Britton & S. Glynn (Eds.), *Executive control processes in reading.* Hillsdale, NJ: Erlbaum.

Mayer, R. (1987). Instructional variables that influence cognitive processes during reading. In B. Britton & S. Glynn (Eds.), *Executive control processes in reading.* Hillsdale, NJ: Erlbaum.

Means, B., Roth, C., & Riegelhaupt, B. (1986). *Development of an integrated system to assess and enhance basic job skills* (Final Report, HumRRO FR-PRD-86-17). Alexandria, VA: Human Resources Research Organization.

Mikulecky, L. (1982). Job literacy: The relationship between school preparation and workplace actuality. *Reading Research Quarterly, 17,* 400-419.

Mikulecky, L. (1985). *Literacy task analysis: Defining and measuring occupational literacy demands.* Paper presented at the annual meeting of the American Educational Research Association, Chicago, IL.

Mikulecky, L., & Ehlinger, J. (1986). The influence of metacognitive aspects of literacy on job performance of electronics technicians. *Journal of Reading Behavior, 18,* 44-62.

Mikulecky, L., & Winchester, D. (1983). Job literacy and job performance among nurses at varying employment levels. *Adult Education Quarterly, 34,* 1-15.

Nichols, P., Porkorny, R., Jones, G., Gott, S., & Alley, W. (in press). *Evaluations of an avionics troubleshooting system* (Special Report). Brooks AFB, TX: Air Force Human Resources Laboratory.

Reigeluth, C., & Stein, F. (1983). The elaboration theory of instruction. In C. Reigeluth (Ed.), *Instructional-design theories and models: An overview of their current status.* Englewood, NJ: Erlbaum.

Sticht, T. (Ed.). (1975). *Reading for working.* Alexandria, VA: Human Resources Research Organization.

Sticht, T. (1987). *Functional context education: Workshop resource notebook.* San Diego, CA: Applied Behavioral & Cognitive Sciences, Inc.

Sticht, T., & Mikulecky, L. (1984). *Job-related basic skills: Cases and conclusions* (Information Series No. 285). Columbus, OH: The National Center for Research in Vocational Education, Ohio State University.

Sticht, T., Armstrong, W., Hickey, D., & Caylor, J. (1987). *Cast-off youth: Policy and training methods from the military experience.* New York: Praeger.

Sticht, T. G., Armijo, L., Koffman, N., Roberson, K., Weitzman, R., Chang, F., & Morocco, J. (1986). *Teachers, books, computers, and peers: Integrated communications technologies for adult literary development.* Monterey, CA: U.S. Naval Postgraduate School.

Chapter 7

Family and Community Interventions Affecting the Development of Cognitive Skills in Children

Diane Scott-Jones
University of Illinois, Urbana-Champaign

The purpose of this chapter is to examine family and community interventions aimed at enhancing children's cognitive skills and school achievement. Head Start programs, established in the mid-1960s, serve as the major example of these intervention programs. Policy makers and program developers expected to end the cycle of poverty by intervening in the lives of young children from low-income families. Improvement of the children's academic performance was considered to be the major vehicle for eliminating poverty. Minority children and families, who experience disproportionate levels of poverty, usually were the participants in Head Start and similar programs. The rationale for, and effectiveness of, these intervention programs will be explored in this chapter. Suggestions for future policies and practice will be offered.

RATIONALE FOR FAMILY AND COMMUNITY INTERVENTIONS

Assumptions regarding the cycle of poverty, early critical periods in cognitive development, and the preeminence of the family's role in children's cognitive development provided the rationale for family and community interventions. These assumptions provided answers to essential questions regarding intervention programs: Why intervention was necessary, when intervention should occur, and what institution should be changed. The arguments that provided the social science basis for intervention programs contained considerable flaws, however. The resulting intervention programs had many positive outcomes, as will be discussed in the section on the effectiveness of the programs. The programs fell far short of their goals, however, perhaps in part because of the faulty assumptions guiding their development and implementation.

Cycle of Poverty

In the rationale for family and community interventions to enhance children's cognitive skills, the complex processes that contribute to poverty in adulthood are oversimplified. The typical conceptualization is a simplistic cycle of intergenerational poverty, beginning with a low-income (usually minority) family, in which children have low genetic capacity and/or an unsupportive, unstimulating home environment, which leads to low intelligence. The children enter school with cognitive deficiencies and experience low achievement and failure. Upon ending their schooling, they experience unemployment or low-paying jobs. As adults, they form low-income families, and the cycle of poverty is repeated in the next generation. Laosa (1984, p. 53) illustrates graphically the assumed cycle of poverty underlying early childhood intervention programs.

Underlying the cycle-of-poverty conceptualization is a deterministic view of human development; it assumes that all low-income minority families will affect their children in the same manner. Further, such conceptualizations blame poor families for their subordinate position, placing the burden for change squarely on the shoulders of poor children and families. In the "unconditional war on poverty," declared in 1964 by then President Lyndon Johnson, the focus was on changing the behavior of low-income individuals; no measures were proposed to alter directly the distribution of income or to remedy structural weaknesses in the labor market (Haveman, 1977, 1987).

The role of families in their children's cognitive development, academic achievement, and later adult economic status is more complex than the typical conceptualization allows. At each point in the cycle of poverty, many factors in addition to family variables are important. If we try to detail just some of the complexities of the cycle of poverty, our description of the important elements in the life course of a child born into a poor family might proceed as follows.

We begin with a low-income family, but acknowledge that low-income parents are not a monolithic group. Important variations in income may exist among those classified as living in poverty. Further, families at the same low-income level may define themselves differently. Families' self-definitions and self-perceptions may affect the home environment they provide for their children. Among low-income families, psychological functioning and patterns of communication also vary and affect children's development (McLoyd & Wilson, 1990).

Thus, low-income families provide home environments that may vary in support of children's intellectual development. In the case of biological parents, they also contribute a broad genetic capacity for competent intellectual performance. Because many parents work outside the home, the quality of care children receive during the parents' working hours is an additional important factor in children's development.

As children approach school entry, their motivation and social skills, along with cognitive skills, will be important for the development of school skills. Poor and minority children are not always deficient in skills at school entry. For example, Ginsburg and Russell (1981) found few race or class differences in preschool children's performance on mathematics tasks, although other researchers (Saxe, Guberman, & Gearhart, 1987) have found social class differences. In addition, variability exists within racial and class groups, so that individual children may or may not exhibit the pattern of skills and deficiencies associated with group membership.

Once children enter school, their success will depend upon more than their own academic skills. Characteristics of the school (Edmonds, 1986), relationships between parents and the school, and peer relations become important. Generally, schools are organized to teach children who possess the cognitive skills, language, and knowledge base of the average middle-class white child. The typical conceptualization of the cycle of poverty omits or minimizes the role of the school. A careful analysis of school effects (Maughan, 1988), however, indicates that children's school experiences can serve as either risk or protective factors. Further, poverty affects schools directly, given that school systems rely largely on local property taxes (Flanagan, 1990). Poverty may lower the quality of children's school experiences through effects on schools, independently of effects on families.

As children move through the educational system and end their formal schooling, the level of education they attain is important but is not the sole determinant of employment status and income. The students' perception of opportunity, the actual availability of jobs, and discrimination in the workplace are important. Poor minority students may perceive that there is "job ceiling" preventing them from holding certain jobs (Ogbu, 1978). Chronic joblessness in the adolescent-to-adult transition, and resultant discouragement, lead to difficulties in fulfilling work and family roles (Bowman, 1990). Available jobs are polarized into a relatively small number of high technology jobs and a large number of low-level service jobs requiring few intellectual skills (Giroux, 1984). Because the minimum wage is low, working does not always guarantee an end to poverty (Bane & Ellwood, 1989). The current low income of young adult males is associated with decreased marriage rates, which, in turn, contributes to the increased number of children living in poverty in single-mother households (Berlin & Sum, 1988).

For those students who attain high levels of formal education, discrimination against minorities may play a role. Black college graduates are unemployed at twice the rate of whites who did not attend college. The income of a black who has attended college is only slightly higher than that of a white high school drop-out (Farley & Allen, 1987).

To summarize, the processes associated with the persistence of poverty from generation to generation are considerably more complex than assumed in the optimistic and ambitious intervention programs initiated in the 1960s. Early intervention programs "most surely cannot be considered an antidote to poverty" (Stipek, Valentine, & Zigler, 1979, p. 478). Schooling, in general, is not likely ever to be the major vehicle for reducing poverty (Slaughter, Washington, Oyemade, & Lindsey, 1988).

Underlying the intervention programs also were assumptions regarding the optimal timing of intervention in the individual's lifespan and the appropriate institution through which to intervene. Intervening early in children's lives, and changing children's families, became important aspects of intervention programs.

Early Critical Period

One rationale for early intervention is that there is an irreversible early critical period for intellectual development, when there is high plasticity or malleability in the individual. Plasticity or malleability is assumed to be substantially lowered later in the lifespan. According to this view, opportunities for intellectual growth occur mainly during early childhood.

A prominent proponent of this view was Bloom (1964, p. 88), who argued that "as much of the development takes place in the first 4 years of life as the next 13 years." From correlational analyses of 10 test scores in several major longitudinal studies, particularly the Berkeley Growth Study (Bayley, 1949), Bloom (1964) concluded that 50 percent of the intelligence measured by IQ tests at age 17 years develops by age 4 years, an additional 30 percent between 4 and 8 years, and the final 20 percent between 8 and 17 years. Bloom (1964) concluded that environmental variation is likely to have a marked effect on IQ between 1 and 5 years and little effect on the IQ after age 8 years. Bloom also believed that deficiencies at one period of development cannot be completely made up at a later period. Similarly, the effect of an excellent early experience is not likely to be "lost" at a later period.

Bloom's (1964) work, along with that of Hunt (1961), was influential in moving social scientists and policy makers away from genetic determinism in explanations of the development of intelligence. The environmental emphasis contributed to a positive climate for intervening in the lives of poor children. Bloom overemphasized the critical role of the early environment, however.

Bloom's view was based on an inappropriate interpretation of the strong positive correlation ($r = .71$) between IQ test scores at age 4 and age 17 years. As Clarke (1984) pointed out, Bloom erroneously substituted the concept "percentage of development" for "percentage of variance accounted for." Bloom asserted that the magnitude of the correlation between two sets of measurements is determined by change or lack of change in the measurements of individuals. Correlations describe the stability of rank order differences among children but do not provide information on stability or change in the test scores of individual children (Kagan, 1986). In contrast to Bloom's conclusions, longitudinal assessments of change in individuals' IQ test scores from early childhood through late adolescence indicated that a great degree of change is likely. In the Fels longitudinal study of middle-class white children, the average IQ test score change between the ages of 2.5 and 17 years was 28.5 points (McCall, Appelbaum, & Hogarty, 1973).

Correlations between children's scores at various ages do not provide valid evidence for the importance of the early period for later behavior (Colombo, 1982). It is difficult to demonstrate unequivocally that an early period of development has an effect on later cognitive development independent of the intervening experiences (Clarke, 1984). Children who have positive or negative experiences in early development tend to have similar experiences in later development. Further, "critical" stimuli have been inadequately studied. Researchers are not able to identify a critical stimulus except in a very broad sense. Similarly, the aspects of development affected during the critical period are only globally described (Colombo, 1982).

An alternative to Bloom's view of the effects of early experience is that high plasticity exists in early development, and that at least a moderate degree of plasticity remains over the lifespan. MacDonald (1986), reviewing research on cognitive development for evidence of a "sensitive period," concluded that individuals do have a heightened sensitivity or responsiveness to stimulation that occurs early in development. The more intense the stimulation, the greater the change in the individual. Plasticity decreases over the lifespan, so that more intense stimulation is required to have an effect on development. MacDonald included many different stimulus dimensions under the rubric "intensity." For example, an intervention lasting over a long period of time was viewed as having greater intensity than one lasting a shorter time.

The assumption that plasticity, although not limitless, remains throughout the lifespan leads to an optimistic perspective on intervention (Lerner, 1984). Change may be easier to effect in the early years, but the possibility for change is not lost with advancing age. Further, it is possible that some interventions should be intergenerational-developmental instead of ontogenetic-developmental (Lerner, 1984; Lerner & Hood, 1986), in cases where adults as well as children lack academic skills (Scott-Jones, 1987). Scholnick (1986) suggested that receptivity to environmental stimulation may increase during the child's development and stabilize during adulthood; compared to children, adults have a greater repertoire of responses and greater ability to choose their environments. Still another view is that, as individuals get older, they may respond to different specific features of the environment rather than merely responding less to stimulation generally (Wachs, 1986).

The notion of developmental plasticity means that individuals may change in negative as well as positive directions. Therefore, change from an early intervention may not be maintained, because later influences may offset the positive early experiences. An early intervention thus could not "inoculate" an individual against later negative influences of development. A concept such as "reinstatement" would be necessary to explain the long-term effects of an early experience (Wachs, 1986). Reinstatement refers to the periodic partial repetition of the early experience. The Follow Through programs established for children who had completed Head Start would be an example of reinstatement. An early experience may set off "naturally occurring reinstatements" in the behavior of children, parents, and teachers. Without the "reinstatement" behavior over time, the intervention would not have an effect. Similarly, Caldwell (1987) believes that a "booster" may be necessary at various points in development beyond the early intervention. Caldwell's early intervention program was followed by support during the elementary school years, so that children received some form of intervention from 6 months to 12 years of age.

To summarize, the possibility of successfully intervening may extend well past the early years. Undoubtedly, the preschool years are important in development. One cannot assume, however, that this is the only time during which an intervention might be needed or might be effective. Continuous attention to children's needs is necessary throughout the life course. Some researchers have stated emphatically that "we must discard the notion of critical periods" (Stipek et al., 1979, p. 490). A lifespan perspective on intervention is more appropriate (Lerner & Hood, 1986).

The tendency to look for the long-term effects of early experience may be motivated by reasons other than scientific evidence (Kagan, 1986). Because American society does not provide adequate resources to improve the lives of families who live in poverty, those who want benevolent change may believe that a relatively inexpensive early intervention will solve many of society's problems. If early interventions are tried and are unsuccessful, however, further efforts will be judged unnecessary, because the individuals will be assumed to be too old to benefit. Head Start and other early intervention programs are more acceptable politically than are other possible ways of reducing poverty such as directly increasing the earnings of low-income families (Washington & Oyemade, 1987).

Family Intervention

Because of the arguments that much of intellectual growth occurs before the child enters first grade (Bloom, 1964) and that the family is more influential than the school in children's school achievement (Coleman et al., 1966), intervention programs have included the family, either exclusively or in conjunction with a center-based program. In addition, research in the mid-1960s on mother–child interactions, language patterns, and teaching strategies was interpreted as evidence that these behaviors needed to be changed in poor minority mothers. This research was correlational and did not demonstrate that the maternal behaviors bore any causal relation to children's cognitive outcomes (Scott-Jones, 1984). Ogbu (1981) has argued that parental behavior does not determine their children's adult behavior; instead, parents' perceptions of possible adult roles for their children guide their childrearing strategies.

Some of the intervention programs begun in the 1960s were intended as community interventions rather than simply family interventions. Head Start, for example, was described at its inception in 1965 as a comprehensive program for children and families comprised of health, social services, and educational components. Parent involvement was mandated in the community-action philosophy driving Head Start. According to this philosophy, poor minority parents should not be merely passive recipients of public assistance but active participants in the development and implementation of intervention programs. Self-determination was the goal; parental power in institutions that provided them services and in the overall political process was a necessary condition for effective programs. An opposing view arose, however, and came to dominate Head Start and other early intervention programs. Parent involvement meant training parents "how to be parents" (Valentine & Stark, 1979, p. 297). For the most part, family interventions have been imposed on poor minority communities without the active participation of those communities.

Thus, the community-action aspect of Head Start, and of most other interventions, was not realized. The subordinate status of poor minority families and children is illustrated in the pejorative language that characterized 1960s descriptions of poor minority families. Some of these terms, for example, *disadvantaged, deprived, deficient,* are being resurrected in current discussions. These terms assume some underlying stable trait beyond poverty and minority status. These are not terms that poor minority communities would use in describing themselves. The use of these terms establishes a firm distinction between the recipients of help and the givers of help. This use of language is representative of the manner in which family interventions typically were implemented. They were imposed on poor minority communities by outsiders, with little regard for the culture and integrity of poor minority families.

Further evidence of subordinate status is that minorities were underrepresented among those developing and implementing Head Start (Washington & Oyemade, 1987). In contrast, minority children were overrepresented among Head Start enrollees. The percentage of Head Start children who were black and Hispanic was twice the percentage of black and Hispanic children, respectively, in the poverty population (Laosa, 1984; Washington, 1985).

To summarize, the family is but one of the influences on children's cognitive development and achievement. Family intervention alone is not sufficient. Some changes can be made through these programs, but wholesale change is not likely. Overselling early intervention programs may lead to excessively high expectations for widespread change. If programs fall short of these great expectations, policy makers may discontinue the programs, erroneously concluding that such programs have no value at all.

EFFECTIVENESS OF INTERVENTIONS

This section addresses the effectiveness of early intervention programs. Included are reviews of Head Start and of experimental intervention programs.

Head Start

One of the purposes of Head Start programs, begun in 1965, was to involve parents and the community in the broad goal of enhancing young children's development in the areas of cognition, socioemotional development, and health and nutrition. Head Start programs consist mainly of preschool centers, although home-based programs have been allowed since 1973. The average duration of programs is 34 weeks per year; 82% of the programs are half-day only. The majority of children enrolled in Head Start are 4 years of age; among 1986 enrollees, 40% were black, 32% white, 21% Hispanic, 4% American Indian, and 3% Asian (Washington & Oyemade, 1987).

Parental involvement was assumed to be critical to the success of all Head Start programs (Zigler, 1979). In 1969, a permanent staff position in each local site was authorized for a parent coordinator who would encourage parent involvement in Head Start. Guidelines in 1970 established parents' rights to approve the hiring of Head Start staff. The 1975 federal Head Start guidelines included four dimensions of parent involvement (Valentine & Stark, 1979; Washington & Oyemade, 1987). The first was parent participation, which included decision making about program content, working in the program in paid and volunteer positions, planning parent education, and receiving home visits from staff. The remaining dimensions were training in parenting skills, communication between staff and parents, and helping parents to influence other community institutions. Thus, both educational, individual change and political, institutional change were incorporated into the guidelines (Valentine & Stark, 1979).

Underlying the dual goals of individual and institutional change are two different views on the elimination of poverty; "individual change through education and training; and institutional change and realignment of power through self-help and collective action" (Valentine & Stark, 1979, p. 302). The former view assumes that poor mothers and their children are deficient and need to be changed. The latter view assumes that parents need to be empowered to change the schools and other institutions that perpetuate poverty; then, children's school performance will increase. Institutional change is necessary if individual children's gains are to be maintained.

Head Start has focused mainly on training parents in childrearing and "teaching" skills; less attention has been given to parents as decision makers in Head Start (Washington & Oyemade, 1987). Whether parents achieved the "maximum feasible participation" mandated by the Economic Opportunity Act of 1964 varied greatly among the Head Start sites (Valentine & Stark, 1979). In a Mississippi Head Start program, a committee of indigenous poor citizens administered each of 84 centers. In other sites, parent involvement in Head Start extended to self-help and community change. In New York City, a group of Head Start fathers studied together to pass examinations for better jobs; in central Pennsylvania, Head Start parents in a community without television reception successfully arranged for a cable system (Valentine & Stark, 1979). In some sites, Head Start was associated with the improvement of education, health, and social services in poor communities (Zigler, 1979). Further, when Head Start was endangered because of its alleged ineffectiveness, the rallying of support for the program was due to parental and community efforts as well as those of social scientists and policy makers (Condry, 1983). On balance, however, Head Start did not empower poor minority families and communities.

According to Valentine and Stark (1979), initial Head Start policy was a reflection of the parent involvement that arose spontaneously in the struggle to implement Head Start. Parental and community control were allowed only after the major political unrest of the 1960s. When the unrest subsided in poor communities, officials adopted a more limited view of parental involvement. "It is tempting to say that the political system has proved itself 'inelastic', to the extent that . . . the goal of institutional change . . . has been displaced by individual change" (Valentine & Stark, 1979, p. 308). Valentine and Stark suggest that a goal of Head Start parent involvement policy was to contain grassroots militancy.

The extent of Head Start parent involvement has not been fully documented; assessments are largely anecdotal (Washington & Oyemade, 1987). Based on interviews of parents in various Head Start sites, Robinson and Choper (1979) described parents' views of the effectiveness of Head Start. Parents believed that their children gained cognitive and social skills through Head Start. Equally important, according to parents, were changes that occurred in the parents themselves. Parents believed, not only that they become better parents and more socially involved with other parents, but that they acquired job skills, high school and sometimes college degrees, and desirable jobs in Head Start and for other employers.

In addition to parents' reports, evaluation studies of Head Start indicate the enrolled children gained cognitive skills. The substantial gains children experience, however, may not bring their performance levels up to that of their peers. Lee, Brooks-Gunn, and Schnur (1988) analyzed data for children from two Head Start sites in the 1969–1970 school year. One-year gains on cognitive measures were compared for children attending Head Start, children attending other preschools, and children not attending any program. Although children from all three groups were from low-income families, the children in Head Start had lower initial scores on almost all demographic and cognitive measures. The percentage of Black children was higher in the Head Start group than in the other preschool and no preschool comparison groups. Because Head Start does not serve all eligible children, the selection process may have favored the neediest children. After statistical controls for the initial demographic and cognitive differences among the three groups, the Head Start children still showed the greatest 1-year gains on the cognitive measures. Head Start children, however, did not close the cognitive gap. In spite of their large gains, Head Start enrollees' scores remained below those of other low-income children.

An important issue is the long-term impact of Head Start. The first major evaluation of this issue concluded that elementary school children who had attended Head Start programs did not perform better on cognitive tests than did similar children without Head Start experience (Westinghouse Learning Corporation, 1969). The conclusion that Head Start did not result in lasting gains was highly publicized and influenced public perceptions of the program. Many criticisms were leveled at the study, however (Washington & Oyemade, 1987). The evaluation focused narrowly on cognitive outcome measures, in spite of the comprehensive goals of Head Start; later, social competence replaced cognitive indicators as the primary goal for children in Head Start. The analysis did not take into account possible selection bias in the characteristics of Head Start children; as indicated in the Lee et al. (1988) analysis, children in Head Start were less advantaged than the other poor children to whom they were compared. Little attention was given to the vast differences in the content and quality of various Head Start programs; Head Start was not a single, uniformly implemented program. The evaluation did not consider the experiences of the children following Head Start; because Head Start was assumed to be a one-shot "inoculation," the quality of children's schooling and other post-Head Start experiences were not considered.

A more recent report of Head Start effectiveness (McKey, Condelli, Ganson, Barrett, McDonkey, & Plantz, 1985) was based on a meta-analysis of more than 200 studies. Many conclusions from this report, commonly known as the "Head Start Synthesis Project," were positive.

Head Start children showed short-term gains on cognitive and socio-emotional measures. In a subset of studies, Head Start children were less likely to be retained in grade or to be placed in special education classes. Head Start helped to provide health, social, and educational services to families of enrolled children; Head Start staff and parents influenced health, social service, and educational institutions to provide better services to the community, including both Head Start and non-Head Start families. The most widely discussed finding, however, was that, after 2 or 3 years, Head Start children did not maintain that cognitive and socioemotional advantage over similar children without Head Start experience. Many of the criticisms of the 1969 Westinghouse report, which was included in the metaanalysis, also apply to the Synthesis Project. In addition, the metaanalysis included some studies of low quality (Gamble & Zigler, 1989). Clearly, Head Start programs, in all their variety, resulted in at least short-term positive outcomes for children. Unfortunately, the metaanalysis provided no information about processes that might be associated with the maintenance or decline of the short-term gains that Head Start children enjoy. Process information, rather than evaluation of outcomes alone, is necessary for program development and policy formation (Gamble & Zigler, 1989). The finding that Head Start gains persisted for 2 to 3 years is distressing only if one assumes that a relatively brief early intervention will compensate for any later difficulties children encounter. Additional intervention beyond the Head Start experience may be needed.

Although Head Start did not achieve its goal of economic mobility for low-income families, the child development component of the program is widely perceived as a success (Washington & Oyemade, 1987). Head Start results in at least short-term gains, and perhaps some long-term gains, for children and their families. As a program of limited duration, Head Start has been remarkably successful.

Consortium for Longitudinal Studies

Head Start was implemented as a comprehensive service program. In contrast, other early intervention programs, smaller in scale than Head Start, were more carefully designed as experiments. Lazar and Darlington (1982; Murray, Royce, Lazar, & Darlington, 1981) reported results of pooled analyses of data from long-term follow-ups of 11 experimental or quasiexperimental preschool intervention programs. Reports of the individual projects written by the principal investigators are available in a single volume (Consortium for Longitudinal Studies, 1983) as well as in numerous individual publications. In addition to center-based programs are home-based programs, such as the Gordon Parent Education Program (Jester & Guinagh, 1983) and the Mother-Child Home Program (Levinstein, 1988; Levinstein, O'Hara, & Madden, 1983), and programs combining center- and home-based components such as the Early Training Project (Gray, Ramsey, & Klaus, 1983). At the time of follow-up, children ranged in age from 9 to 19 years; more than 90 percent of the participants were low-income black children. Typically, children were enrolled at age 3 years and older for a period of 2 years or less in curricula emphasizing cognitive development.

The most substantial finding was gains in the "real-world" phenomenon of interest—school competence. Program children were less likely than controls to be in special education programs or to be retained in grade. Compared to control groups, program children scored significantly higher on intelligence tests at the end of their programs and for up to 3 or 4 years after the program; few differences were found, however, in later follow-ups when children were between 10 and 17 years old. On standardized achievement tests, program children scored significantly better than did controls in math but not in reading achievement test scores. They were more likely to express positive achievement attitudes. The lack of strong findings of enhanced standardized test performance suggests that the skills measured by such tests were not mediating children's improved school competence. Alternatively, the convergence of program and control children on later standardized tests might have resulted from the lack of follow-up programs in the public schools (Ramey, 1982).

Clarke (1984) suggests that the programs were not directly responsible for the improved educational outcomes. Lazar and Darlington did assess possible noncognitive factors that might account for the improvements. One of the factors was a family change. For example, for those in preschool programs, mothers' vocational aspirations for their children were higher than the children's own aspirations. In addition, program parents reported greater satisfaction with their children's school work than did control parents. Although their pooled data analyses do not include explicit information on family processes, Lazar and Darlington (1982) suggest that children's participation in programs may have set in motion complex beneficial interactional patterns. Parents may have responded to children's participation with greater expectations and greater support; teachers, in turn, may have responded to positive parent and/or child behavior. Intervention programs need to incorporate measures of family processes that may mediate program effectiveness.

Findings for program outcomes were not affected by whether the programs were center- or home-based. Lazar and Darlington concluded that a variety of good early education programs lead to measurable educational benefits for poor black children. According to these authors, such programs should be expanded at the national, state, or local level.

Although they performed better than controls on measures of school competence, program children did not fare as well on occupational outcomes. Program children were more likely than controls to have jobs 3 years after high school, but there were no differences between program and control children in type of job, earnings, or hours worked (Royce, Lazar, & Darlington, 1983). Contrary to cycle-of-poverty assumptions, improved school performance did not lead to better jobs and higher incomes.

OTHER REVIEWS

Discussed in this section are four reviews smaller in scale than the Consortium for Longitudinal Studies and the Head Start evaluations. These reviews vary in conclusions regarding the relative effectiveness of intervention programs with family involvement components and programs that are center based. On balance, center-based programs with strong family involvement components are probably most desirable in terms of effects on children and on families.

Bronfenbrenner (1974) reviewed preschool programs conducted through the early 1970s. Most of the programs reviewed were center based. Home-based programs, however, appeared to result in more lasting gains for children. Bronfenbrenner pointed out self-selection may have affected results; families in home-based programs were economically better off than families of children in center-based programs. Nevertheless, Bronfenbrenner concluded that parents should receive training before a child is born, that home-based programs should occur during the first few years of the child's life, and that center-based programs should begin during the preschool years with concurrent parent programs to be continued through the primary grades. Similarly, Goodson and Hess (1978) concluded that parent involvement in early education resulted in intelligence and achievement gains, as well as improved parental attitudes toward and behavior with the child.

White, Bush, and Casto (1985) analyzed 52 reviews of early intervention programs. In the reviews, parental involvement was one of the most frequently cited variables assessed in the determination of program outcomes. The conclusion from almost all reviewers assessing parental involvement was that more parental involvement is better for children's cognitive development and academic achievement. A subsequent review of 326 studies of early intervention programs, identified mainly from the 52 reviews, indicated that programs that involved parents extensively were effective, but not more effective than those that did not involve parents (White, 1985). Effect size was used to determine whether programs involving parents were more effective than those not involving parents.

Bryant and Ramey (1987) reviewed early intervention programs they judged to be true experiments. They reviewed 17 programs, including programs that are primarily home visits and those that are center based with a focus on parents and/or child. The authors examined children's cognitive outcomes at age 2 years, 3 years, preschool, and long-term follow-up. The most effective intervention was a center-based program combined with parent training or other services to families. The least effective program was educational home visits alone. Intermediate in effectiveness was the home visit combined with medical and educational intervention, and center-based parent training. Neither the child's age at entry into the program, nor the type of curriculum, was related to cognitive outcomes in children. The programs appeared to affect children by preventing the expected decline in intellectual performance rather than by enhancing it. Bryant and Ramey emphasized the importance of incorporating programs into the parents' lifestyle and maintaining respect for the parents. For example, the authors point out that attrition rates are relatively high when the parent is required to give more than one or two hours per week to the home visit or group meeting.

Economic Analyses

A major issue in judging the efficacy of early intervention programs, in addition to whether there are long-term gains for children or changes in families, is whether such programs are cost-effective. The idea that relatively small monetary investments in programs for young children will result in great future savings is appealing. If children prepare to be productive adults, there will be lessened spending for remedial education, prisons, welfare, and other services associated with individuals living in poverty. Barnett and Escobar (1987) argued that, if the idea of early intervention as an investment is more than mere metaphor, formal economic analysis should demonstrate cost effectiveness. Barnett and Escobar reviewed the 20 economic analyses of early intervention produced over the last two decades. Only 6 of the 20 studies were judged to be methodologically sufficient.

The Perry Preschool Project (included in the Consortium for Longi tudinal Studies) was the subject of two studies; evidence from this project was judged to be the strongest of the available research. In this program, both preschool attendees and taxpayers were judged to have gained more than they lost. The costs to families, such as the value of parents' time, were included in the analyses. An economic analysis of Home Start and Head Start concluded that Home Start, because it cost less to implement, was at least as cost effective as Head Start. There were no estimates of the cost of parents' time, however, which might have biased the analysis in favor of Home Start. An analysis of the Yale Family Support Program indicated that the cost of the program was much greater than the benefits. There was an incomplete account- ing of benefits, however, and thus an underestimation of the program's benefits.

Barnett and Escobar suggested that, in future analyses, family interventions should be well represented, because of the possibility of benefits to parents and to children; they suggested a more complete analysis of increased employment and increased income of parents in addition to the focus on child outcomes. Barnett and Escobar concluded that, in spite of the popular perception that early intervention is cost effective, little evidence actually supports that perception. These au- thors asserted that various approaches to early intervention may be efficient but no judgment is possible regarding the differential econom- ic benefits of the alternative approaches.

THE FUTURE OF INTERVENTIONS:
RECOMMENDATIONS FOR POLICY AND PRACTICE

Intervention programs that aim to change poor minority children, families, and communities have resulted in some positive changes. In the future, more attention must be given to family and community control of programs; to delivery systems that do not segregate and stigmatize poor and minority children and families; to service delivery, monitoring, and evaluation that emphasize family processes over the lifespan; and to comprehensive policies for the well-being of all chil- dren, families, and communities.

Family and Community Control

An important but often neglected aspect of family intervention is the perspective of the parents being served. Cataldo (1980) questions whether program developers can deliver flexible, sensitive, and varied programs that respect parents as authorities on their own children and families. Parent programs should provide educational and social support and should not be "an attempt to re-shape homes and childrearing practices in the images emerging from rather limited research" (Cataldo, 1980, p. 184). The active involvement of parents should be encouraged, with the provision that it be voluntary and appropriate for the needs and characteristics of each family. Attention must be given to the needs and characteristics of minority families; parents, particularly mothers, should not be singled out as the only agents for change (Laosa, 1983). Families' adaptive coping strategies, not merely weaknesses, should be emphasized (Slaughter, 1988).

The representation of minorities in the development and implementation of intervention programs remains a difficult problem (Laosa, 1984; Washington & Oyemade, 1987). The input of minority scholars and minority communities is a prerequisite for successful, ethical intervention.

Segregation and Stigma

The goal of educational intervention programs, from their inception in the 1960s, has been to bring poor and minority children into the mainstream of American society. These programs, however, have segregated children at an early age. The percentage of Blacks and Hispanics enrolled in Head Start is twice the percentage of Black and Hispanic children in the poverty population (Washington & Oyemade, 1987). A rationale for targeted programs is that it is cost-efficient to provide educational services for those in greatest need. Yet, such targeted programs may subvert the overarching goal of early intervention programs. Targeted programs, in which minority communities are overrepresented but lack an active and controlling voice, suggest that poor minority families and children are the only ones in need of services. The poverty criterion is based on the erroneous assumption that all poor children have identical needs and that more affluent children do not share those needs. Potential gains in children's cognitive skills may be offset by assumptions, made by educators, policy makers, and the lay public, of unique and irremedial deficiencies in poor minority children and their families. Thus, many family and community interventions stigmatize poor and minority families.

Head Start, from its inception, has allowed up to 10 percent of enrolled children to be from families above the poverty level. That policy has not been adequate for the creation of racial, ethnic, and socioeconomic diversity. In practice, local programs have not had funds to provide services to all eligible poor children. Further, using poverty as the criterion for eligibility for Head Start is not desirable because many needy families periodically experience small increases in income and thus are not consistently served (Stipek et al., 1979). Head Start programs have had difficulty meeting the needs of poor children and simultaneously promoting economic integration (Washington & Oyemade, 1987).

Universal eligibility for Head Start and other interventions involving families could reduce the segregation and stigma accompanying such programs. Broadened eligibility is not likely to occur, however, given that Head Start serves only a fraction of currently eligible poor children. A more realistic goal might be the use of a sliding fee scale for affluent children (Stipek et al., 1979).

Preschool intervention programs might benefit from the current interest in child care legislation that would provide benefits for middle-income as well as for poor families. One possibility is to use public schools to provide year-round, full-day programs for 3- and 4-year-olds (Weintraub & Furman, 1987). If these public school programs were established, separate intervention programs for low-income children might not be necessary. Present governmental policy contains a contradiction in that tax-supported education and supervision are required for all children for most of the work day, but only from age 5 or 6 to 18 years (Scarr, 1984). The major current concern, however, is public programs for preschool children from poor families (Schweinhart & Weikart, 1988). Research and intervention have focused almost exclusively on poor Black children, prompting some researchers (e.g., Zigler, 1987) to question whether findings of positive outcomes are generalizable to other groups.

Public schools could serve an important "normalizing" or "regularizing" function for preschool programs, making them widely available to all families without the stigma of pathology, deviance, or welfare (Hobbs et al., 1984; Levine, 1978). Public schools programs would appeal to a broad range of parents if they are close to home and already serve older siblings, and if they do not charge direct fees (Kagan & Zigler, 1987). According to the National School Boards Association (1986), preschool programs will become standard in many school districts.

A number of issues would be of concern in the establishment of public preschool programs (Kagan & Zigler, 1987; Scott-Jones & Baker-Ward, 1988). Parent involvement would be needed as an integral component of these programs. The needs of working parents for full-day child care and care for very young children may not be met by public school programs; flexibility and a broad range of services would

be required. Preschool programs would need a developmental orientation, rather than one focused narrowly on cognitive skills as measured
by standardized tests. The National Black Child Development Institute (NBCDI) has questioned the wisdom of establishing public school
programs for preschool children, given that public schools have not
done an admirable job of educating older black children (Moore, 1987;
NBCDI, 1985). Public school preschool programs would need a number
of safeguards in order to be appropriate for Black children, including
regular external review by community members and child development experts (NBCDI, 1986).

One vision of the public school's role is that families would register
with the school at the time of a child's birth. An array of optional
services would be available for families and children from birth to the
preschool years. Optional half-day or full-day programs would be
available for 3- and 4-year-old children. Public schools would coordinate other existing services for children and families (Hobbs et al.,
1984: Kagan & Zigler, 1987; Levine 1978). The provision of comprehensive, developmentally appropriate strategies will require long-
range planning and commitment on the part of schools and communities (Kagan & Zigler, 1987).

Lifespan Perspective on Intervention

Intervention programs need to place less emphasis on critical periods
in development and to recognize needs in other phases of the life
course. Federal programs have been launched to serve children youn-
ger and older than those enrolled in Head Start. Parent and Child
Development Centers were established for children 3 years and youn-
ger (Washington & Oyemade, 1987). Some children who completed
Head Start programs experienced a continued intervention program,
aptly named "Follow Through," in the early elementary school years
(Becker & Gersten, 1982; Olmsted & Rubin, 1983; Seitz, Apfel, &
Rosenbaum, 1981). Levin (1977) reviewed a number of federal educational programs that did not focus on the preschool years, including the
Elementary and Secondary Education Act of 1965, Upward Bound
(tenth- and eleventh-graders), Job Corp (high school drop-outs), and
the Adult Education Act of 1966 (18-year-olds and older individuals).
Interventions need to be continued because many educational institutions are not responsive to poor minority children and because children's development, being continuous, is affected by the quality of
experiences beyond the preschool years (Stipek et al., 1979). Head
Start and other early intervention programs need to be coordinated

with other educational programs in order to have long-term effects on children (Washington & Oyemade, 1987).

The lifespan perspective requires evaluation and monitoring of intervention programs that include measures of process as well as measures of outcome at different points in time. Existing longitudinal evaluations of intervention programs do not allow any test of models that might explain the long-term effect of early experience. Early experience may have an effect independent of intervening experiences; alternatively, early experience may have an effect because it leads to positive experiences that occur after the intervention is over. If the latter situation occurs, interventions might be planned to lead systematically to the important subsequent events. Information about the type, duration, and frequency of experiences necessary to maintain the effect of the early intervention would be especially useful (Wachs, 1986).

Appropriate measures of parents' and children's behavior are needed. Measures should be meaningful to parents and children as well as to researchers (Clarke-Stewart, 1988). Open-ended questions in the language used by the participants should be developed. More structured measures should be developed only after extensive piloting comprised of talking to and listening to parents and children. Evaluations also should include a conceptualization of an "effects range" for parental behavior, that is, how much a parental behavior must change in order to have an effect on a child's development (Clarke-Stewart, 1988).

In his review of federal educational and training programs for low-income populations of varying ages, Levin (1977) concluded that the wide variety of programs had only a minimal impact on the reduction of poverty. Many factors other than individuals' competencies affect the pervasiveness of poverty in American society. Family and community interventions to enhance cognitive skills must be joined by other policy initiatives aimed at the elimination of poverty.

Comprehensive Policy

Programs of the kind described in this chapter are not sufficient to eliminate poverty. Our society needs to move toward broader, unified policies for children and families. Presently, our policies are piecemeal and crisis oriented. American society is resistant to comprehensive policies for children and families. Ironically, policies for children and families sometimes are viewed as antifamily, because the policies are presumed to usurp the right and responsibility of families to care for themselves. According to this view, policies for children and families are permissible only when children are abnormal or families are dysfunctional. Yet, one-fifth of American children live in families whose incomes fall below the poverty line and many of these are two-parent working poor families (Bane & Ellwood, 1989).

The effort to end poverty indirectly, through educating the young, must be accompanied by more direct attacks on poverty. Just as we work to enhance the academic skills of children from poor and minority families, we must also work to topple the external barriers— unresponsive schools, unending poverty, relentless racial and class bias. If we do less, we are guilty of blaming the victims of oppression in our society.

REFERENCES

Bane, M. J., & Ellwood, D. T. (1989). One fifth of the nation's children: Why are they poor? *Science, 245,* 1047-1053.

Barnett, W. S., & Escobar, C. M. (1987). The economics of early educational intervention: A review. *Review of Educational Research, 57,* 387-414.

Bayley, N. (1949). Consistency and variability in the growth of intelligence from birth to eighteen years. *Journal of Genetic Psychology, 75,* 165-196.

Becker, W. C., & Gersten, R. (1982). A follow-up of Follow Through: The later effects of the Direct Instructional model on children in fifth and sixth grades. *American Educational Research Journal, 19,* 75-92.

Berlin, G., & Sum, A. (1988). *Toward a more perfect union: Basic skills, poor families, and our economic future.* New York: Ford Foundation.

Bloom, B. (1964). *Stability and change in human characteristics.* New York: Wiley.

Bowman, P. J. (1990). The adolescent-to adult transition: Discouragement among jobless Black youth. *New Directions for Child Development, 46,* 87-106.

Bronfenbrenner, U. (1974). *Is early intervention effective? A report on longitudinal evaluations of preschool programs* (Vol. 2). Washington, DC: Office of Child Development.

Bryant, D., & Ramey, C. (1987). An analysis of the effectiveness of early intervention programs for environmentally at-risk children. In M. J. Guralnick & F. C. Bennett (Eds.), *The effectiveness of early intervention for at-risk and handicapped children* (pp. 33-78). New York: Academic Press.

Caldwell, B. M. (1987). Sustaining intervention effects: Putting malleability to the test. In J. J. Gallagher & C. T. Ramey (Eds.), *The malleability of children* (pp. 115-126). Baltimore: Paul H. Brookes.

Cataldo, C. Z. (1980). The parent as learner: Early childhood parent programs. *Educational Psychologist, 15,* 172-186.

Clarke, A. M. (1984). Early experience and cognitive development. *Review of Research in Education, 11,* 125-127.

Clarke-Stewart, K. A. (1988). Parents' effects on children's development: A decade of progress? *Journal of Applied Developmental Psychology, 9,* 41-84.

Coleman, J. S., Campbell, E. Q., Hobson, C. J., McPartland, J., Mood, A. M., Weinfield, F. D., & York, R. L. (1966). *Equality of educational opportunity.* Washington, DC: U.S. Government Printing Office.

Colombo, J. (1982). The critical period concept: Research, methodology, and theoretical issues. *Psychological Bulletin, 91,* 260-275.

Condry, S. (1983). History and background of preschool intervention programs and the consortium for longitudinal studies. In Consortium for Longitudinal Studies (Eds.), *As the twig is bent . . . lasting effects of preschool programs* (pp. 1-32). Hillsdale, NJ: Erlbaum.

Consortium for Longitudinal studies (1983). *As the twig is bent . . . lasting effects of preschool programs.* Hillsdale, NJ: Erlbaum.

Edmonds, R. (1986). Characteristics of effective schools. In U. Neisser (Ed.), *The school achievement of minority children: New perspectives.* Hillsdale, NJ: Erlbaum.

Farley, R., & Allen, W. R. (1987). *The color line and the quality of life in America.* New York: Russell Sage Foundation.

Flanagan, C. A. (1990). Families and schools in hard times. *New Directions for Child Development, 46,* 7-26.

Gamble, T. J., & Zigler, E. (1989). The Head Start Synthesis Project: A critique. *Journal of Applied Developmental Psychology, 10,* 267-274.

Ginsburg, H. P., & Russell, R. L. (1981). Social class and racial influences on early mathematical thinking. *Monographs of the Society for Research on Child Development, 46*(6, Serial No. 193).

Giroux, H. A. (1984). Public philosophy and the crisis in education. *Harvard Educational Review, 54,* 186-194.

Goodson, B., & Hess, R. (1978). The effects of parent training programs on child performance and parent behavior. In B. Brown (Ed.), *Found: Long-term gains from early intervention* (pp. 37-78). Boulder, CO: Westview Press.

Gray, S. W., Ramsey, B. K., & Klaus, R. A. (1983). The early training project, 1962-1980. In Consortium for Longitudinal studies (Eds.), *As the twig is bent . . . lasting effects of preschool programs* (pp. 33-70). Hillsdale, NJ: Erlbaum.

Haveman, R. H. (1977). Introduction: Poverty and social policy in the 1960s and 1970s—An overview and some speculations. In R. H. Haveman (Ed.), *A decade of federal antipoverty programs: Achievements, failures, and lessons* (pp. 1-19). New York: Academic Press.

Haveman, R. H. (1987). *Poverty policy and poverty research: The Great Society and the social sciences.* Madison, WI: The University of Wisconsin Press.

Hobbs, N., Dokecki, P. R., Hoover-Dempsey, K. V., Moroney, R. M., Shayne, M. W., & Weeks, K. H. (1984). *Strengthening families.* San Francisco: Jossey-Bass.

Hunt, J. McV. (1961). *Intelligence and experience.* New York: Ronald Press.

Jester, R. E., & Guinagh, B. J. (1983). The Gordon Parent Education Infant and Toddler Program. In Consortium for Longitudinal Studies (Eds.), *As the twig is bent . . . lasting effects of preschool programs* (pp. 103-132). Hillsdale, NJ: Erlbaum.

Kagan, J. (1986). Rates of change in psychological processes. *Journal of Applied Developmental Psychology, 7,* 125-130.

Kagan, S. L., & Zigler, E. F. (1987). Early schooling: A national opportunity? In S. L. Kagan & E. F. Zigler (Eds.), *Early schooling: The national debate* (pp. 215-230). New Haven, CT: Yale University Press.

Laosa, L. M. (1983). Parent education, cultural pluralism, and public policy: The uncertain connection. In R. Haskins & D. Adams (Eds.), *Parent education and public policy* (pp. 331-345). Norwood, NJ: Ablex Publishing Corp.

Laosa, L. M. (1984). Social policies toward children of diverse ethnic, racial, and language groups in the United States. In H. W. Stevenson & A. E. Siegel (Eds.), *Child development research and social policy* (Vol. 1, pp. 1-109). Chicago: University of Chicago Press.

Lazar, I., & Darlington, R. (1982). Lasting effects of early education: A report from the Consortium for Longitudinal Studies. *Monographs of the Society for Research on Child Development, 47*(2-3, Serial No. 195).

Lee, V. E., Brooks-Gunn, J., & Schnur, E. (1988). Does Head Start work? A 1-year follow-up comparison of disadvantaged children attending Head Start, no preschool, and other preschool programs. *Developmental Psychology, 24,* 210-222.

Lerner, R. M. (1984). *On the nature of human plasticity.* New York: Cambridge University Press.

Lerner, R. M., & Hood, K. E. (1986). Plasticity in development: Concepts and issues for intervention. *Journal of Applied Developmental Psychology, 7,* 139-152.

Levenstein, P. (1988). *Messages from home: The Mother-Child Home Program and the prevention of school disadvantage.* Columbus, OH: Ohio State University Press.

Levenstein, P., O'Hara, J., & Madden, J. (1983). The Mother-child Home Program of the Verbal Interaction Project. In Consortium for Longitudinal Studies (Eds.), *As the twig is bent . . . lasting effects of preschool programs* (pp. 237-264). Hillsdale, NJ: Erlbaum.

Levin, H. M. (1977). A decade of policy developments in improving education and training for low-income populations. In R. H. Haveman (Ed.), *A decade of federal antipoverty programs: Achievements, failures, and lessons* (pp. 123-188). New York: Academic Press.

Levine, J. A. (1978). *Day care and the public schools: Profiles of five communities.* Newton, MA: Education Development Center.

MacDonald, K. (1986). Early experience, relative plasticity, and cognitive development. *Journal of Applied Developmental Psychology, 7,* 101-124.

Maughan, B. (1988). School experiences as risk/protective factors. In M. Rutter (Ed.), *Studies of psychosocial risk: The power of longitudinal data* (pp. 200-220). New York: Cambridge University Press.

McCall, R. B., Applebaum, M. I., & Hogarty, P. S. (1973). Developmental changes in mental performance. *Monographs of the Society for Research in Child Development, 38*(Whole No. 150).

McKey, R., Condelli, L., Ganson, H., Barrett, B., McDonkey, C., & Plantz, M. (1985). *The impact of Head Start on children, families, and communities: Head Start Synthesis Project.* Washington, DC: U.S. Government Printing Office.

McLoyd, V. C., & Wilson, L. (1990). Maternal behavior, social support, and economic conditions as predictors of distress in children. *New Directions for Child Development, 46,* 49-70.

Moore, E. K. (1987). Child care in the public schools: Public accountability and the Black child. In S. L. Kagan & E. F. Zigler (Eds.), *Early schooling: The national debate* (pp. 83-97). New Haven, CT: Yale University Press.

Murray, H., Royce, J., Lazar, I., & Darlington, R. (1981). The Consortium for Longitudinal studies: A follow-up of participants in early childhood programs. In S. Mednick, M. Harway, & K. Finello (Eds.), *Handbook of longitudinal research* (Vol. 1, pp. 470-488). New York: Praeger.

National Black Child Development Institute. (1985). *Child care in the public schools: Incubator for inequality.* Washington, DC: Author.

National Black Child Development Institute. (1986). Growing national trend toward child care in public schools may spell disaster for Black children. *The Black Child Advocate, 13,* 7-8.

National School Boards Association. (1986). *Day care in the public schools* (Leadership Reports Vol. 1). Alexandria, VA: Author.

Ogbu, J. U. (1978). *Minority education and caste.* New York: Academic Press.

Ogbu, J. U. (1981). Origins of human competence: A cultural-ecological perspective. *Child Development, 52,* 413-429.

Olmsted, P. P., & Rubin, R. I. (1983). Parent involvement: Perspectives from the Follow Through experience. In R. Haskins & D. Adams (Eds.), *Parent education and public policy* (pp. 112-140). Norwood, NJ: Ablex.

Ramey, C. T. (1982). Commentary. *Monographs of the Society for Research on Child Development, 47,* 142-151.

Robinson, J. L., & Choper, W. B. (1979). Another perspective on program evaluation: The parents speak. In E. Zigler & J. Valentine (Eds.), *Project Head start: A legacy of the war on poverty* (pp. 467-476). New York: The Free Press.

Royce, J., Lazar, I., & Darlington, R. (1983). Minority families, early education, and later life chances. *American Journal of Orthopsychiatry, 53,* 706-719.

Saxe, G. B., Guberman, S. R., & Gearhart, M. (1987). Social processes in early number development. *Monographs of the Society for Research in Child Development, 52*(2, Serial No. 216).

Scarr, S. (1984). *Mother care/other care.* New York: Basic Books.

Scholnick, E. K. (1986). Influences on plasticity: Problems of definition. *Journal of Applied Developmental Psychology, 7,* 131-138.

Schweinhart, L. J., & Weikart, D. P. (1988). Early childhood education for at-risk four-year-olds? Yes. *American Psychologist, 43,* 665-667.

Scott-Jones, D. (1984). Family influences on cognitive development and school achievement. *Review of Research in Education, 11,* 259-304.

Scott-Jones, D. (1987). Mother-as-teacher in the families of high- and low-achieving low-income Black first-graders. *Journal of Negro Education, 56,* 87-115.

Scott-Jones, D., & Baker-Ward, L. (1987). Public education for preschoolers. *Journal of the Tennessee Association on Young Children, 29,* 10-14. (Reprinted in J. P. Bauch (Ed.), *Early Childhood Education in the Schools.* Washington, DC: National Education Association.)

Slaughter, D. T. (1988). Black children, schooling, and educational interventions. *New Directions for Child Development, 42,* 109-116.

Slaughter, D. T., Washington, V., Oyemade, U., & Lindsey, R. (1988). Head Start: A forward and backward look. *Social Policy Report, 3* (whole no. 2).

Stipek, D. J., Valentine, J., & Zigler, E. (1979). Project Head Start: A critique of theory and practice. In E. Zigler & J. Valentine (Eds.), *Project Head Start: A legacy of the war on poverty* (pp. 477-494). New York: The Free Press.

Valentine, J., & Stark, E. (1979). The social context of parent involvement in Head Start. In E. Zigler & J. Valentine (Eds.), *Project Head Start: A legacy of the war on poverty* (pp. 291-314). New York: The Free Press.

Wachs, T. D. (1986). Understanding early experience and development: The relevance of stages of inquiry. *Journal of Applied Developmental Psychology, 7,* 153-165.

Washington, V. (1985). Head Start: How appropriate for minority families in the 1980's? *American Journal of Orthopsychiatry, 55,* 577-590.

Washington, V., & Oyemade, U. J. (1987). *Project Head Start: Past, present, and future trends in the context of family needs.* New York: Garland.

Weintraub, K. S., & Furman, L. N. (1987). Child care: Quality, regulation, and research. *Social Policy Report, 2* (Whole No. 4).

Westinghouse Learning Corporation. (1969). *The impact of Head Start: An evaluation of the effects of Head Start on children's cognitive and affective development* (Report No. PB 184328). Washington, DC: Office of Economic Opportunity.

White, K. R. (1985). Efficacy of early intervention. *Journal of Special Education, 19,* 401-416.

White, K. R., Bush, D. W., & Casto, G. C. (1985). Learning from reviews of early intervention. *Journal of Special Education, 19,* 417-428.

Zigler, E. (1979). Project Head Start: Success or failure? In E. Zigler & J. Valentine (Eds.), *Project Head Start: A legacy of the war on poverty* (pp. 495-507). New York: The Free Press.

Zigler, E. F. (1987). Formal schooling for four-year-olds? No. *American Psychologist, 42,* 254-260.

Chapter 8

Illusions, Assumptions, and Generalizations

Luis M. Laosa
Educational Testing Service
Princeton, NJ

During the past 20 years the social and behavioral sciences have produced a considerable body of knowledge about the development, implementation, and evaluation of intervention programs. The field also has produced much data and theory about the factors influencing human development. At the same time, the research community has become more sophisticated about the policy-making process. As social and behavioral scientists, we therefore like to see ourselves as being well prepared to contribute significantly to solving society's problems—better prepared than the field was 20 years ago.

Although we have indeed learned a great deal, it is also true that the context in which we would apply this knowledge and expertise has changed considerably; the present societal context contrasts sharply to that of 10 to 20 years ago. There have been—and continue to be—dramatic secular transformations in American families as well as in the nation's social, economic, and political reality. How useful and appropriate are our knowledge and skills for this new and rapidly changing environment? Do we know how to translate our scientific findings to the present circumstances? Although there certainly have been significant advances in research, it is less clear that we know how to apply them effectively toward solving today's pressing social problems. My intent is not to sound a note of pessimism, but rather to stimulate a realistic discussion regarding the connection of research to policy and practice.

Whatever the level of our own optimism, however, it appears that the public has become deeply disillusioned with the ability of the social and behavioral sciences to contribute to the solution of social problems. The present pessimism contrasts sharply with the excitement and unbounded optimism of the 1960s. There were great expectations then regarding the social and behavioral sciences' potency in helping to solve problems on the national agenda. Claims made then on the basis of serious scientific work are now, more soberly, seen as exaggerated (Laosa, 1984). Reasonably, the present pessimism is partly attributed to the failure to produce applications in equal measure to those promised or expected. Although painful, let us consider it as a lesson, one worth keeping in mind as we again consider the application potential of research.

Concerns have also been raised about the perspectives, or world views, that researchers bring to bear on the problems selected for investigation. Professor Scott-Jones (this volume) rightly exhorts us to examine carefully the conceptualizations and rationales underlying our proposals for intervention. What are our implicit models—our own cognitive representations—of the social problems that we intend to help solve?

If we assume, for example, that maternal education exerts a causal influence on offspring achievement, should we not ask what the intervening links are in this causal chain? Is it not important to know and understand the mediating variables if we wish to design interventions for reducing the observed parent–child correlation in educational attainment? Putting aside the nature-nurture issue, even if we consider only environmental effects, might not there be some variables that covary with schooling attainment and which contribute to this correlation? Will increasing the parent's literacy through direct intervention necessarily make a difference in the child's development? Will an increase in parental literacy by, say, one or two grade levels, change the parent–child interaction patterns that may account for variance in the child's scholastic development? Are not the intergenerational channels of influence being eroded, in any case, by secular trends that restrict the amount (and perhaps also the quality) of time that parents can spend interacting with their children? These trends include a growing prevalence of maternal employment and of single-parent families and a financial need to spend longer hours working (Laosa, 1988a). These questions are only examples. The point is that it behooves us to articulate our assumptions about the problems that we aspire to help solve as well as the tacit models and rationales for the interventions that we would propose (Laosa, 1983).

Consider another example. Literacy intervention proposals typically assume that illiteracy is a significant source of our social problems. As Professor Scott-Jones (this volume) points out, however, by making this assumption we may well be "blaming the victim." An alternative perspective is to view the prevalence of functional illiteracy as largely a symptom and to challenge the social and behavioral sciences to uncover its causes.

The most valuable yield is likely to come from research aimed at uncovering the processes that give rise to and sustain the present educational and social inequalities. We should increase our efforts at elucidating, for example, the teaching and learning processes that occur informally and unwittingly in every family (e.g., Laosa, 1982a). There is evidence suggesting that such processes are responsive to interventions. Also needed is research that would identify the factors that contribute to scholastic success in some families in spite of unfavorable circumstances. Why do some children succeed academically while growing up in circumstances that would lead us to predict otherwise? Are there special factors in the family, in the school, or in the community that contribute to these successes? Research conducted to answer questions of this type can provide much needed information about both protective and risk factors in human development (Laosa, 1990b).

It is becoming increasingly apparent that in order to optimize validity, research should be conducted separately for different ethnocultural groups (Laosa, 1988b, 1990a). The social and educational problems facing one group are not always the same as those of another. Even when they are similar, the paths to their solution may vary. Different groups often need different intervention approaches. Sensitivity is needed to maximize the compatibility, or "match," of the intervention with the particular group. There are subtle intertwinings between developmental processes, cultural characteristics, and value structures, which we have only begun to glean (Laosa, 1979, 1983, 1990a,b). In sum, effective solutions are unlikely to be forthcoming until we acquire a better understanding of the problems themselves, the larger context in which they are embedded, and the populations we intend to help.

Although many things indeed have changed during the past 20 years, some important tensions remain unresolved. One of the underlying currents emanates from conflicting views, ambivalence, and uncertainty regarding which societal unit should be the primary target of intervention. Interventions can be aimed at one (or more) of the three basic units of society: the community, the family, or the individual. The choice can be difficult—as seen, for example, in Head Start. Originally conceived and implemented as a comprehensive community development program guided by the policy of "maximum feasible participation," Head Start rapidly abandoned this emphasis and came to focus rather narrowly on the child's IQ development (Laosa, 1982b). Subsequently Head Start again shifted its focus, this time away from the individual and toward a greater emphasis on the family (Laosa, 1984). Shifting emphases are not unique to Head Start, and they reflect broader tensions. The jostling of priorities accorded to the three units is more often a matter of politics than of substantive considerations.

Another issue still surrounded by considerable uncertainty and tension is the question of which point in the life cycle to target for intervention. It will be recalled that the policies and programs of the War on Poverty were predicated upon hopes of breaking the "cycle of poverty." A cycle, however, has many points where it might be broken. What is the optimal place for breaking into it? A staff memorandum of President Kennedy's Council of Economic Advisors, prepared in 1963 shortly before his assassination, read in part as follows: "The vicious cycle, in which poverty breeds poverty, occurs through time and transmits its effects from one generation to another. There is no beginning to the cycle, no end. There is, therefore, no one 'right' place to break into it" (cited in Moynihan, 1969, p. 9). The same uncertainty expressed in this memorandum is evident today; little progress has been made in a quarter century toward attaining consensus on the matter. Should interventions be focused on the preschool period? Elementary education? High school? Higher education? Youth training and employment programs? The special problems of adolescence? Adult literacy campaigns? On-the-job training? Education for parenthood? Parent education? The elderly? Or, to close this cycle of ambivalence, the prenatal period?

Sadly, much of the tension reflects turf issues rather than scientific considerations. Conflicts often stem from self-interests, each faction vying for a "piece of the action"—conflicting interests among the different professional areas, academic disciplines, specialties within disciplines, diverse parts of the bureaucracy, and professional versus lay communities. Objectivity at times seems clouded by guild issues, at the peril of the families we seek to serve.

Superimposed on the complexities considered thus far are those stemming from this society's ethnocultural diversity. Applied researchers and service providers in nations composed of multiple and widely varied sociocultural groups, such as the United States, face certain dilemmas that would not arise in more homogeneous societies. It is helpful to view these dilemmas in terms of the concept of population validity (Laosa, 1988b, 1990a).

Population validity refers to the *generalizability* of research findings across different populations. In this regard it is important to keep in mind that a research finding is an interpretation of data obtained from a sample representing a particular population (Messick, 1987). A measure of a construct may or may not have the same or even similar psychometric properties or patterns of relationships with other variables in different populations (Laosa, 1981). Thus, an inference may be valid for one population and not for another; an inference is valid for a particular population to the extent that it leads to correct judgments about members of that population (Messick, 1987).

To illustrate the issue, consider the recent research literature concerning the effects of classroom processes on students' development. Research during the past 15 years on the linkages between teacher behaviors in the classroom and their students' development of academic skills in the elementary grades has produced a small knowledge base concerning the dynamics of classroom processes and how such processes may affect children's learning and development. In their recent review of this literature, Brophy and Good (1986) concluded that even the most widely replicated findings on the relationships between classroom processes and students' educational development must be qualified by references to statistical interactions. Usually, these interactions involve minor elaborations of main trends, but occasionally interactions are more powerful than main effects. Such interactions suggest that the effects on children of particular instructional environments vary as a function of the child's characteristics. Some of these characteristics stem from the child's sociocultural background.

A recent study by Wong Fillmore and her colleagues (1985) illustrates the nature of such interactions. These researchers sought to determine how best to meet the educational needs of children in the United States with limited English-language proficiency. The study was designed to determine what aspects of classroom structure, teaching practices, and patterns of language use in the classroom had the strongest impact on the child's English-language development over the course of the school year. The analyses examined the oral English language development of elementary school children from two different ethnic groups—Chinese and Hispanic.[1]

---

[1] Consistent with our concern with generalizability, it should be recalled that broad sociodemographic classifications such as *Hispanic* or *Asian* may each contain varied ethnocultural groups, thus masking significant population diversity (Laosa, 1988a). Those familiar with the Hispanic population, for example, know that this category is composed of several different ethnic groups, including Chicanos (or Mexican Americans), Cuban Americans, Puerto Ricans, and other Spanish-speaking national-origin groups. Although these groups share many characteristics in common, there are also important cultural, historical, and sociodemographic differences that may limit the generalizability of research findings across them. It is therefore disappointing that a detailed ethnic breakdown of the above sample was not reported. This omission does not detract, however, from the study's value in illustrating the concept of population-by-treatment interaction, since cultural differences between Hispanics and Chinese are doubtless much greater on the average than those between detailed ethnic groups within these two broad populations.

A main effect in the data showed that children who initially had low proficiency in English made large gains in oral language development if they had been placed in classrooms where they had numerous opportunities to interact with native English-speaking peers; such peer interactions appeared to be less crucial once the children were further along in their learning of English. Further analyses revealed, however, that these results were true to a much greater extent for Hispanic than for Chinese children. Chinese children whose initial knowledge of English was limited and who were in classes in which there were many opportunities to interact with native English-speaking classmates did not show the kind of improvement in English-language skills found among the Hispanic children in such situations. Chinese children developed better in classrooms where teachers closely supervised the learning activities of students and kept them on task. Wong Fillmore et al. (1985, p. 331) concluded that "the Chinese children seemed much more directly dependent on their interactions with the teacher than was the case for the Hispanic children." It is as if the Chinese children viewed the adult authority figure as the source of knowledge, whereas the Hispanic children profited from the chance to interact with peers who were good language models. *Thus it seems that different kinds of instructional approaches work best with different sociocultural groups.*

In the realm of basic research, population generalizability remains a scientific issue. In applied work, by contrast, population generalizability emerges as an ethical issue. It is an ethical issue because in the absence of evidence regarding population generalizability, we cannot predict the outcome of a research application to a population different from that which yielded the research finding. The outcome of the application might differ from that intended—it might be ineffective and harmless or possibly harmful in a different population. Thus, an ethical question centers on whether—or under what circumstances—it is within the bounds of professional ethics to devise, recommend, or implement a service or intervention when the scientific basis lending validity to the application stems from research on sociocultural populations different from those of the intended service receivers (Laosa, 1990a).

Efforts to apply research findings to policy or practice should be predicated, therefore, on answers to these questions: Is the application directed at the same population that yielded the research findings? If not, what evidence is there to justify directing the application to members of this population (Laosa, 1988b, 1990a)?

Given the emerging evidence regarding the perils involved in generalizing research findings across populations, what is the policymaker or service provider to do in the absence of scientific information pertaining specifically to the effectiveness and appropriateness of the intervention in the context of the client's sociocultural background? Is it preferable in such circumstances to abstain from intervention in order to avoid potential or unknown risks? Should one treat the client in the same manner as one would someone from a population about which there are relevant data—and hope that the outcome will be the same in both populations? How can the level of decision making in such cases be improved (Laosa, 1988b, 1990a)?

Given the growing cultural diversity in this society, these knotty ethical issues are bound to arise with increasing frequency, and a framework for dealing with them is therefore needed. The job of creating such a framework, together with the task of resolving the other issues discussed in this chapter, evidently belongs to a future stage in *our* own development.

REFERENCES

Brophy, J., & Good, T. L. (1986). Teacher behavior and student achievement. In M. C. Wittrock (Ed.), *Handbook of research on teaching* (pp. 328-375). New York: Macmillan.

Laosa, L. M. (1979). Social competence in childhood: Toward a developmental, socioculturally relativistic paradigm. In M. W. Kent & J. E. Rolf (Eds.), *Primary prevention of psychopathology* (Vol. 3: Social competence in children, pp. 253-279). Hanover, NH: University Press of New England.

Laosa, L. M. (1981, October). *Statistical explorations of the structural organization of maternal teaching behaviors in Chicano and non-Hispanic White families*. Invited paper presented at the conference on the Influences of Home Environments on School Achievement, Wisconsin Research and Development Center for Individualized Schooling, School of Education, University of Wisconsin, Madison.

Laosa, L. M. (1982a). School, occupation, culture, and family: The impact of parental schooling on the parent-child relationship. *Journal of Educational Psychology, 74*(6), 791-827.

Laosa, L. M. (1982b). The sociocultural context of evaluation. In B. Spodek (Ed.), *Handbook of research in early childhood education* (pp. 501-520). New York: Free Press.

Laosa, L. M. (1983). Parent education, cultural pluralism, and public policy: The uncertain connection. In R. Haskins & D. Adams (Eds.), *Parent education and public policy* (pp. 331-345). Norwood, NJ: Ablex.

Laosa, L. M. (1984). Social policies toward children of diverse ethnic, racial, and language groups in the United States. In H. W. Stevenson & A. E. Siegel (Eds.), *Child development research and social policy* (Vol. 1, pp. 1-109). Chicago: University of Chicago Press.

Laosa, L. M. (1988a). Ethnicity and single parenting in the United States. In E. M. Hetherington & J. Arasteh (Eds.), *The impact of divorce, single parenting, and stepparenting on children* (pp. 23-49). Hillsdale, NJ: Erlbaum.

Laosa, L. M. (1988b). *Population generalizability and ethical dilemmas in research, policy, and practice: Preliminary considerations* (Report No. RR-88-18). Princeton, NJ: Educational Testing Service.

Laosa, L. M. (1990a). Population generalizability, cultural sensitivity, and ethical dilemmas. In C. B. Fisher & W. W. Tryon (Eds.), *Ethics in applied developmental psychology* (pp. 227-251). Norwood, NJ: Ablex.

Laosa, L. M. (1990b). Psychosocial stress, coping, and development of Hispanic immigrant children. In F. C. Serafica et al. (Eds.), *Mental health of ethnic minorities* (pp. 38-65). New York: Praeger.

Messick, S. (1987). *Validity* (Report No. RR-87-40). Princeton, NJ: Educational Testing Service.

Moynihan, D. P. (1969). The professors and the poor. In D. P. Moynihan (Ed.), *On understanding poverty: Perspectives from the social sciences* (pp. 3-35). New York: Basic.

Wong Fillmore, L., Ammon, P., McLaughlin, B., & Ammon, M.S. (1985). *Learning English through bilingual instruction: Final report submitted to the National Institute of Education.* Berkeley and Santa Cruz: University of California.

Part II

Intergenerational Intervention Programs

Chapter 9

Introduction to Part II: Intergenerational Intervention Programs

Micheal J. Beeler

Intergenerational interventions are a new genre of educational intervention. They differ from the programs of Part I in that they attempt to increase the cognitive skills of both parents and children, rather than of either alone.

In Chapter 10, Nickse summarizes the theoretical work that has led to the development of intergenerational interventions. Then she describes the Family Learning Center, an intergenerational literacy project located at, and sponsored by, Boston University. The project was initiated under sponsorship of the U.S. Department of Education as part of President Reagan's National Adult Literacy Initiative.

The purpose of this project, as Nickse states, is to (a) provide multicultural urban adults with free literacy and language instruction; (b) evaluate the efficacy of this approach; and (c) identify tools and methods of instruction that facilitate family literacy. The three approaches that have been implemented at the Family Learning Center since 1983 are discussed. The outcomes reported are optimistic in terms of participant retention rate and family participation.

In Chapter 11, Heberle provides a description of both the Parent and Child Education Project (PACE) and the context in Kentucky that has supported an intergenerational intervention. The goal of PACE is to interrupt an existing intergenerational cycle of undereducation by providing basic adult education, enhancing parenting skills, and better preparing children for academic success. This unique program requires that the parent and preschool child come to school together. The parents participating in this project are without high school diplomas, and their children are 3 to 4 years old.

The first cohort of families to participate in the PACE program are reported to have benefitted in a variety of ways. In regard to parents, rates of program retention and GED completion, in comparison with other adult education programs, has been interpreted as success. The children who participated are reported to have improved their "measurable developmental skills" by an average of 28 percent. This evidence for optimism has brought international attention to the program and has resulted in legislative support in the form of future funding.

In Chapter 12, Askov, Maclay, and Bixler posit that the negative influence of low-literate parents can be so detrimental that any positive effects of compensatory education programs may be defeated. For this reason the authors support a "whole family" approach to education, and have developed computer assisted instruction (CAI) courseware to be used with adult beginning readers. The courseware consists of 28 disks of instruction that require 20 hours of interaction.

Developed as the Penn State Adult Literacy Courseware Project, this curriculum has now been completed by 52 low-literate parents (and a control group of 24) whose children are enrolled in Chapter 1 remedial reading programs. The effect that this program has on children is indirect, as the children are not required to participate in any way. The goal of this program has been to upgrade the literacy skills of parents enabling them to help their children. The results of this project are discussed in terms of parental reading test scores and teachers' comments regarding the subsequent classroom behavior of the participants' children.

Chapter 13 is a commentary on the preceeding three intergenerational programs that highlights some of the substantial difficulties these programs, and others like them, are up against. Park discusses the variability in the scope of these programs and the strong theoretical rationale for intergenerational interventions. However, Park very pointedly brings up the issue alluded to by Laosa (this volume) regarding the need to identify "channels" of intergenerational transmission. Park says, "If the research base is so strong, why are hard results so difficult to come by?" Noting the optimistic results of the three programs, Park recommends cautious interpretation and turns to a discussion of the difficulty of achieving objective measures of reading skill.

Noting the developmental nature of reading, Park provides a concise explication for the need to increase overall cognitive abilities, as opposed to a more simplistic view which suggests that merely increasing low-level reading skills is a sufficient goal. In summary, Park suggests that these programs have raised more questions than they have been able to answer.

Concrete and well-defined methods for the improvement of intergenerational programs are not available. However, it is clear that, in the future, intergenerational intervention programs must acknowledge the social nature and transmission of cognition and language, and be designed with the importance of context and content for learning clearly in mind. A major task in designing any intergenerational intervention will continue to be the development of a learning environment that will be effective simultaneously for multiple age groups and subcultures. Unfortunately, what will constitute an effective learning environment, and for whom, has not been well established. What has been well established is that well-read and educated parents provide a more "literacy-enriched" environment for their children, and their children typically achieve greater academic success. How the long-term benefits of a literate childrearing environment are to be achieved by intervention on low-literate parents is not known.

A second obstacle in educational interventions is designing a program that permits the most objective measurement of known dependent measures. If scientific validity and reliability cannot be achieved, skepticism and patchwork funding will continue to be the rule in this field. Another serious issue that each of the intergenerational projects discusses is program recruitment and retention. If programs are to attract volunteer participants they must offer something tangible in return. In Part III, Simmons suggests that by emphasizing the connection between education and the activities deemed meaningful by participants, we can project the hope for tangible return.

Chapter 10

Family and Intergenerational Literacy Practices at the Family Learning Center: One Voice of Experience

Ruth S. Nickse
Nickse Associates
Brookline, MA

Little research exists on the transmission of literate behaviors from native speaking adults to their children using low reading and writing skilled adults as study subjects. However, theorists and observers in the field of adult literacy suggest the importance of programs designed to support intergenerational literacy (Nickse, 1990; Sticht, 1983; Harmon, 1987; Sticht & McDonald, 1989). Research on the characteristics of such adults and descriptions of the impact of minimally literate, English speaking environments on children in families in the United States are rare. Studies of the interactive effects of adults with low literacy on the literacy behavior and school achievement of their children are also hard to find. The difficulty of this kind of research cannot be minimized. Yet there is a compelling need for it if effective family and intergenerational literacy programs are to be successfully designed.

Evidence of the importance of social and linguistic context on emergent literacy in the acquisition of reading and writing concepts is reviewed by Mason and Allen (1986). This thorough summary includes some references to home environments and to specific actions literate parents take to promote their children's literacy. While this review and others provides a context for studies of the origins of literacy, the orientation is generally on the development of children's literacy with the children themselves as subjects. Observations are usually conducted in middle- or upper-class, English-speaking homes with literate parents who, almost automatically, but with considerable variation, one might guess, maintain "literate home environments." In a carefully performed study on eight families (Teale & Sulzbury, 1986), parents were chosen specifically because they already read to their children, which is the standard used in subject selection.

The fact that there are variations in how parents read stories to children is noted by Lancy (1988), who further explores the nature of these in recently reported work. Some adults read to children in ways that are more helpful than others. Adult readers who are effective models for children use elaborated strategies when assisting children to read, giving clues and asking questions. Less effective adult models are reductionist, providing less support for children's reading attempts. These include taking away clues by covering the illustrations, and emphasizing phonics rules. This study has implications about who reads to children and how they do it—Lancey believes that effective strategies can be taught to those interested in learning. But the point is that these working class adult subjects can and do read, albeit with some reluctance and with greater or lesser effectiveness.

Heath's ethnographic work (1982, 1983) gives us insights into home styles that are culturally different, literate in ways which differ from the school literacy expected by teachers in particular elementary schools. This work makes clear the limiting effects on the school success experienced by children in these communities.

If we believe evidence from several complementary lines of current research which points to the importance of parents in supporting children's literacy, then adult basic education (ABE) programs designed with an intergenerational and family focus are overdue. The data support the impact of positive parental roles on schools and schooling (Cochran & Henderson, 1986); in families and communities in preparing children to read (Heath, 1980, 1983); and in encouraging school achievement (Clark, 1983). The observation that parents are the "first teachers" of their children abounds in the literature; mothers' educational level is considered a major variable in children's school achievement; and reading to children is a single most important step in contributing to school success in reading (Anderson et al., 1985). Results from the National Assessment of Educational Progress (NAEP) studies (Applebee et al., 1987) adds more data in support of the importance of a positive home environment. This conclusion seems inescapable.

However, millions of barely literate parents are "at risk"—unable to achieve personal goals related to literacy. They recognize its importance and suffer guilt and anxiety because they are unable to act as reading models for children. Other adults are oblivious to their role as literacy models, lacking both the skills for involvement and the knowledge of its importance (Nickse & Englander, 1985). Their inability is costly to their children and to society—contributing to school failure, high dropout rates, teen pregnancy, the cycle of illiteracy, and lives truncated by dashed aspirations and lost opportunities. Their failure is our failure.

A review of research (Nickse et al., 1988) identifies at least four areas in which parents may have an impact on children's literacy achievement. These are (a) in providing supportive home environments for literate behaviors, (b) in sharing reading activities, (c) in acting as literate role models, and (d) in encouraging positive aspirations and attitudes about the importance of education.

A contribution based on a literature review of English language family literacy for nonnative speakers criticizes current perceptions about English as a second language (ESL) families, and concludes that prevailing notions about parent involvement in literacy endeavors are based on hidden assumptions not verified by research. These assumptions constitute a deficit hypothesis, blaming family factors for schooling problems (Nash, 1987). Generalizations about the supposed barrenness of literacy materials and practices is wrong, claims Nash, because studies have often found that many ESL families value literacy and also provide print-rich environments for their children. Population and cultural differences thus contribute to the complexity of this issue and point to the need for more specific research.

CONTEXT FOR RESEARCH

To encourage investigation into the development of family literacy, Boston University opened The Family Learning Center in 1988–89, an adult basic education storefront site sponsored by the University for three purposes: (a) to provide free literacy and language instruction for urban adults from multicultural backgrounds and to support literate behaviors in home environments, (b) to collect research data on the effectiveness of this approach, and (c) to develop materials and methods to facilitate family literacy. The Center provided field site opportunities for undergraduate and graduate students interested in working in adult basic education and English as a second language. An eclectic, meaning-based and holistic approach to the teaching of literacy to adults was used.

The earlier work began in 1983 at the request of the U.S. Department of Education as part of the Reagan National Initiative in Adult Literacy, and employed and trained students as tutors using Federal College Work-Study funds to pay them (Nickse, 1984; Nickse & Englander, 1986). The staff included a professional Director and teachers working with the faculty member who founded the Center. The Center was supported by public and private grants and contracts and was subject to all of the uncertainties in funding and scarcities in resources that characterize adult basic education programs across the nation. Additional problems arose from vagaries in the recruitment and retention of adult, voluntary participants. The mechanics of administering an ABE site in this fashion were therefore as difficult for us in an academic setting as for others who deliver services through public agencies.

However, since action research can continue to some degree in a university context for short periods whether particular programs are funded or not funded, we had an opportunity for observation and some reflection and program revision, a luxury our service-driven colleagues at many ABE sites do not enjoy. Although incrementally accrued through somewhat painful experience, we can add a modest contribution to the fascinating topic; the improvement of intergenerational literacy through the provision of services to families.

Materials and Methods

The search for effective practices to promote intergenerational literacy is an evolving odyssey. Three methods employing a variety of materials were used since the work began in 1983–84. Each method was an attempt to organize a literacy instructional program for adults (not all of whom were parents) wishing to improve their own reading and writing skills. Each also involved some kind of support to aid parents in improving the literacy of their children or the children with whom they interact. This focus was maintained with dogged determinism regardless of the emphasis or interest of the Center's funders. Each method had some research validity and yielded significant information. Each practice had advantages and disadvantages and each enjoyed, more or less, "success." None to date has been entirely effective depending, of course, on definitions of "success," which necessarily changed as a function of the constraints imposed by the various funding sources. This work was underway prior to the development of both public and private funds now available for family literacy programs.

1. *Television mediated storybook reading with one-to-one tutorial.* Our first efforts, in collaboration with the Boston Public Li-

brary, involved the use of the critically acclaimed *Reading Rainbow* television series and its accompanying original collection of about 20 children's books (Nickse & Englander, 1985). About 20 native-speaking adults were recruited who agreed to read children's literature to prepare to read it to children, and also to be tutored in reading both personal interest and job-related materials. More than half of the participants were parents or others who interacted with children in some capacity; grandmothers with custodial care, aunts and uncles who read to small relatives—and some adults who "borrowed" neighbor's children to read to them. Library and community buildings were used as sites. Tutors showed the half-hour videotapes to adults, discussed the particular children's books which were highlighted, and then coached the adults in reading aloud. The books, selected by the adults with the tutors' help, were within their own skill range and were thought to be of interest to them and the children. When adults felt proficient enough, they took these books home to read to and with children. Additional activities related to the texts were demonstrated by the tutors, and adults were encouraged to perform these activities at home (Staryos & Winig, 1986).

Tutors made audio tapes for home use as checks for text accuracy and to provide a framework for a form of "shadow reading." Adult/child reading partners could play these tapes and follow along, fingers underlining the text. A master vocabulary list of all words in the 20 children's books was assembled as a sight vocabulary: a high proportion of the words matched such lists indicated as essential for adult new readers. Tutors used this word bank to make vocabulary cards for practice in sight recognition and sentence construction and for use in writing language experience stores.

This programmatic variation on adult literacy service delivery (in effect a pilot study), was not funded—so rigorous evaluation was not possible. Informally we learned that books that have appeal for adult new readers (to be used at home in shared reading with their children) need to have themes that each can relate to from personal experience. Stories from the *Reading Rainbow* collection about daily life events, whether happy or sad, appealed to both adults and children while the fantasy and nonsense stories had little appeal for adult new readers. Shared stories opened the opportunity for discussions on attitudes about books and reading, about school problems experienced by the adults when they were young, and about current school successes (and failures) of their children who were affected by the program.

The *Reading Rainbow* television tapes which modeled effective story reading were not as powerful or popular as a medium of literacy instruction as might have been expected, given the frequency of TV

viewing reported for adult populations in general. Program participants, having committed a precious two hours a week for literacy
instruction wanted to practice reading with books—and "not watch
TV." However, television occupied a great deal of time in many homes.
One learner reported she owned six sets! Further, although TV may be
"educational," few learners reported viewing it with that intent or
perception—entertainment was the primary use of TV in these homes.
This finding has implications for the structuring of story lines and the
addition of literacy models in popular family oriented "soaps." Charac-
ters should be portrayed as readers and should support reading, schooling, and education on a sustained basis through their characteriza-
tions. Public attitudes about the value of reading and writing can be
shaped—the experience of the *Electric Company* and *Sesame Street* are
excellent examples. As an aside, the adult audience for these programs
has been estimated in the millions, with many adults watching without children present.

   2. A family intervention/prevention approach. With a grant
from the U.S. Department of Education, Office of Education Research
and Improvement, we next began a collaboration with the Boston
Public Schools, as well as continued to use the Boston Public Library
system as tutoring sites. The purpose of this funded research was to
study the effects of a family approach with a targeted population—low
reading skilled parents with children in school who had already been
identified as "at risk" and were currently in Chapter 1 school remedial
reading programs. This orientation evolved as a result of the prior
year's work—we wanted to target the adult study population and to
include the schools in a research partnership. The grant provided
funds to hire a school-based coordinator to act as liaison to our ABE
project and to recruit low literate parents of the 1,600 children in
Chapter 1 elementary remedial reading programs in a nearby school
district.

   Recruitment of adult learners was difficult for a variety of reasons—
many adults felt unable to make a commitment to improve their own
skills while also reading to their children on a regular basis. Eventually a study population of adults was identified, and a more formal
procedure for data collection was initiated.

   In this approach literacy tutors used a variety of instructional techniques and materials to improve adult literacy and to encourage adult
participation in literacy events with children at home. This instructional model for adult participants, while still individual and tutorial,
was concentrated mainly in library sites where a great many children's books were available. Individual tutoring sessions were enhanced by two "literacy socials" for parents—where refreshments,

encouragement, and information about reading and the possible roles of parents in improving literacy were highlighted. Children's books were given away, a critical element in attracting adults with children in any family or intergenerational literacy program.

Briefly, adults who participated in this program ($n = 30$) had low reading skills (1st- to 5th-grade level on a standardized test), had positive attitudes towards books and reading, and said they were willing to read with their children. About a third were nonnative speakers. There was no typical pattern for participation and no consistent pattern of attendance or planned inclusion of children in tutoring.

The interventions combined tutorial instruction of adults by college students using a four-step model (Rosenshine, 1984) consisting of (a) supervised observation/consultation, (b) modeling of literacy behaviors by tutors, (c) coaching of parents, and (d) special family events focused on improvement of family literacy. When tutors reported that parents were not reading to children, an expanded list of literacy related activities was suggested by tutors which seemed to fit better both the skills and lifestyles of the learners. Tutors regularly discussed reading to and with children as a part of the adult tutoring sessions, and also suggested other activities which included, for example, asking about school work, talking with children, and taking field trips with families. Adults enjoyed talking about their children—sharing information about them with tutors.

Adults were tested on a variety of formal and informal measures using the Adult Basic Learning Examination (ABLE). Pre- and post-test scores were gathered after 30, 40, and 50 hours following weekly two-hour tutoring sessions over a period of 4 to 8 months. Adults who completed 50 hours of tutoring showed more gains than those who attended fewer hours. Retention of adults in the program was almost 75 percent, confirming a finding (Heatherington et al., 1984) that adults in tutoring with children in school tend to stay in literacy programs longer than those without. The national figure for dropout from ABE programs is between 30–50 percent (Balmuth, 1986). A detailed description of the study and results of the adult sample are reported in a special issue on Adult Literacy reported in the *Journal of Reading* (Nickse et al., 1988). The effects on the reading achievement of children in the study follow (Nickse & Paratore, 1988).

Chapter I teachers were asked whether children in the experimental group (those with parents in the adult literacy program) and the control group (no parents in the literacy program) had improvement in reading ability that was "noticeable," for example, in reading group discussion, oral reading fluency, word recognition, reading comprehension, attitudes, and general behavior toward reading. Judgments were made on informal observations noted on a three-point scale. A t-test was used to measure the achievement gain of each group—the difference between the groups was not significant. The one child who was identified as having made "unusual" gains in reading was a youngster in the experimental group who, at year's end, was moved from Chapter I to a regular classroom. His parents, both involved in the literacy program, had maximum tutoring (75 hours each), but in addition, consistently reported reading to and with their son, as well as initiating other suggested literacy events in the home.

Conclusions and recommendations of this study follow. Collaboration with the public school facilitated enrollment of adults into this adult literacy program; an intergenerational approach focused on expanding the variety of literacy events in the home was more successful in increasing literate behaviors in parents, especially in homes where storybook reading had rarely occurred. This finding suggests that parents may model literacy events, like shared book reading, only when they themselves are successful at it. For measurable progress with adult new readers, doubling the hours of direct instruction of parents (to four from two hours weekly) is desirable; further, the study advises, tutors working in family or intergenerational instruction need to be professionally prepared, or work under the direct supervision of professionals to achieve more than the most modest of gains, for teaching adult beginning readers is often a complex and difficult task, needing exceptional sensitivity and skill. While noting that adult retention in literacy program was high, the study concludes that for children to achieve measurable gains in family reading projects, increased and longer-term adult instruction in combination with greater emphasis, more frequent modeling, and more specific intervention in the incidence of literacy events in home settings, need to occur (Nickse & Paratore, 1988).

3. The family learning center—a dedicated site. In 1987–88, with a full-time ABE/ESL program open 63 hours a week in a specially renovated storefront site complete with a children's library area, we radically changed the administrative and programmatic structure of the program. With a new computer laboratory, space for teaching adults and for training college work-study literacy tutors and our first volunteer tutors, we had to reconceptualize, both philosophically and practically, what the "family learning center" agenda might be. This was not an easy task, for many reasons noted later in this chapter.

Small ABE and ESL classes taught by professional teachers were added to individual tutoring by college work-study students in recognition that professional teachers must take the primary responsibility for teaching reading and writing to adults. Computers for word processing expanded the instructional techniques to include the writing of dialogue journals and language experience stories, some of which were collected and published by the Boston Public Library for circulation to other branch libraries (Writings, 1988). The computer laboratory permitted "family computer mornings" when children, accompanied by adults, played with computers with their parents.

An expanded set of "special family literacy events," sponsored in collaboration with the Boston Public Library, greatly enlarged the opportunities to supplement more traditional learning. The Saturday morning series featured authors and illustrators of children's books, storytellers, and poets. An expanded book collection for lending to adults and children and collections of contemporary magazines helped to organized a "literate environment" which taught indirectly, by example. Direct intervention, that is, the "coaching" of adults to use specific books for reading to children and follow-up activities to prompt this behavior was not an instructional objective for adult learners in 1987–88: the appropriateness of direct versus indirect intervention with particular adult learners was under discussion.

Unfortunately, we had no research money to collect data on the school achievement of children who used the Center's services. However, the dedicated site attracted more than 80 families in 10 months to its services, confirming that family literacy was a marketable concept for adult learners. Further, the Family Learning Center itself was closed in August 1988, due to a lack of funding. Its full-time program with its emphasis on the improvement of family and intergenerational literacy was terminated, bringing to a close almost five years of work on this topic. Despite this premature closure, some observations can be shared which may be of value to others interested in new forms of adult literacy services.

IMPLICATIONS FOR PRACTICE AND RESEARCH

Although the administrative structure, the college-student literacy tutors, the sites used, and the population of adult learners changed almost constantly, and we had little money to do formal research, we reached some conclusions about practice in family and intergenerational literacy. These involve matters concerned with (a) program design, recruitment, retention, and motivation of adult learners, (b) funding, (c) staff training, and (d) doing research and evaluation under variable conditions.

Program Administration/Design of Curriculum/Staffing

Family and intergenerational literacy work is not without difficulty both in conceptualization and in practice. There is tension between providing learner-centered ABE and ESL literacy services to adults, filling "slots" to satisfy funders, and implementing an intergenerational instructional model. For example, how is the intergenerational component best facilitated—should it be integral to the curriculum and taught directly as part of a parenting strand, or should it be transmitted by example, through the Center's "literate environment" and special activities? As is common in ABE, what is best depends on the characteristics of the particular learners and their patterns of participation. This was a problem during 1987–88 as the population of the Center changed frequently. Targeting particular populations and then retaining them for sufficient time to study effects proved difficult.

Training of staff, whether professional or not, is more complex with a focus on a family literacy agenda, since some understanding of children and their learning is necessary. The participation of an early childhood specialist working with the Center is important, yet we could not afford this. When working with a multicultural population and planning a family and intergenerational approach, special care needs to be taken to recognize cultural differences. Finally, and not insignificantly, the setting for literacy instruction needs to be arranged attractively for adults and children.

Recruitment/Motivation/Retention of Adult Learners

Adult participants who came to the Center posed very different problems for recruitment, instruction, and retention. For example, to recruit only parents or adults who care for children in order to control the subjects either for instruction or for research is exclusionary and is ill-advised for a community-based program seeking to establish itself with open-entry recruitment for both ABE and ESL populations. ESL adults seemed more motivated—they both responded in greater numbers and attended instruction more regularly. Often, the ESL audience was literate in its own language and has a literate home environment appropriate for its culture. Yet, some second language speakers have little or no literacy in their home language: we could only speculate on the nature of their home literacy environment in support of their children's school success in English.

ABE adults were difficult to recruit and had more irregular attendance in general. Their motivation seemed more complex, and the less able were often a challenge to teach. They must be willing to support the idea and the intent of a family and intergenerational agenda. To demonstrate any lasting effect, they must have children in their care. Thus, the concept of family literacy has to be "sold" to participants. However, the opportunity to bring children to the Center validated the adults as learners and parents. Offering child care to parents who came for instruction included tutors/volunteers who were available to read to, or talk with, children. Simple "babysitting" is a missed opportunity. Children's attendance was, like their parents, also erratic—so appropriate staffing was a problem.

Research/Evaluation

Research studies in family and intergenerational literacy with adult subjects who are less-able readers are scanty and findings often contradictory. Little is known about adult learners and their ability to transfer cognitive skills to their children (Sticht, 1983). Lack of the most basic information about this affects the program design for any family learning center wishing to implement practice based on action research. Further, it is difficult to plan formal research studies in adult literacy centers for any number of other reasons. For example, adult learners are "test shy;" getting information on their performance is difficult under the best of circumstances. Reading tests are generally inadequate measures, and the relationship of reading test scores to cognitive abilities of adults is not well described. Adults' attendance is erratic and unreliable because their lives are busy and responsible— this makes their progress in learning slow, and difficult to assess, particularly in 12-month grant periods! Sensitive measures and methods are needed to track learner gains, and these must be broadly defined (Charnley & Jones, 1979).

The social context in which adult learners live is often chaotic, with economic, housing, health, and child care needs more important than learning in their daily life. How then, and what, should we incorporate into a family literacy curriculum? How do we enlist families in research studies without further burdening them? Finally, if we knew how to do this, and could do it, what are the ethical issues involved in attempting to change family life behaviors, even for a "good cause," such as school success for children and improved opportunities for their parents?

Perhaps some answers to these and other complex questions will emerge from work underway; chiefly, the evaluation of the federal program called Even Start.

Communication between family literacy programs should be encouraged—this conference is a highlight for those of us privileged to attend and signals the need for further gatherings. The Federal Task Force on Family Literacy should be convened on a regular basis with key players in attendance from across agencies interested in family literacy. A national conference on this topic may be indicated in consideration of its importance.

Policy Implications and Funding

If we are to make progress to increase family literacy, clear priorities are essential. Federal and state policies which stress immediate goals, such as workplace literacy for adults, are welcome but shortsighted; many of tomorrow's workers are already failing their first-grade reading tests. Comprehensive policies and funding which target adults and children's literacy improvement seem imperative. However, policy initiatives must include provisions for funding which (a) pay for ABE/ESL programs serving adults *and* children, and (b) supports research. More and better coordinated funding is essential.

At the Federal level, although the Even Start bill has been funded, there are no monies targeted for ABE intergenerational work: the Office of Bilingual Educational Minority Language Affairs (OBLEMLA) supports a limited number of programs for ESL families. In Massachusetts the new ABE State Plan targets mothers with children, but no special state funding is yet available. In any case, funding for operations and research is not usually available from one source, making life difficult for service providers, including university-based researchers operating ABE/ESL centers. Collaborations between ABE/ESL, Chapter 1 and Head Start programs in support of family literacy should be encouraged by Federal and state policymakers whenever possible.

Finally, politicians should increase the funding support (not the rhetoric), for increased literacy for all ages. To do less is to reap consequences that are already well recognized, at an unacceptable price to individuals, families, communities, and society as a whole. Family literacy is an untested idea which holds much promise. The work reported here helped to justify the Even Start legislation, and to set the stage for other projects, notably the PACE project in Kentucky and the nationwide Kenan Trust Family Literacy programs.

REFERENCES

Anderson, R. et al. (1985). *Becoming a nation of readers: The report of the Commission on Reading.* Washington, DC: The National Institute of Education, the United States Department of Education.

Applebee, A., Langer, J., & Mullis, I. (1987). *Learning to be literate in America: Reading, writing and reasoning.* Princeton, NJ: National Assessment of Educational Progress, Educational Testing Service.

Balmuth, M. (1986). *Essential characteristics of adult literacy programs: A review and analysis of the research.* Unpublished paper. New York: The Adult Beginning Reader Project, Kingsboro Community College, CUNY.

Charnley, A. H., & Jones, H. A. (1979). *The concept of success in adult literacy.* Cambridge, England: Huntington Publishers.

Clark, R. (1983). *Family Life and School Achievement: Why Poor Black Children Succeed or Fail.* Chicago, IL: University of Chicago Press.

Cochran, M., & Henderson, C. (1986). *Family Matters: Evaluation of the Parental Empowerment Program* (NIE Contract #400-76-0150). Ithaca, NY: Comparative Ecology of Human Development Project, Cornell University.

Harmon, D. (1987). *Illiteracy: A National Dilemma.* Cambridge Book Company, New York, NY.

Heath, S. B. (1980). The functions and uses of literacy. *Journal of Communication, 30.*

Heath, S. B. (1982). *What no bedtime story means: Narrative skills at home and school.* Language in Society.

Heath, S. (1983). *Ways with words: Language, life and work in communities and classrooms.* Cambridge: Cambridge University Press.

Heatherington, B. S., Boser, J., & Satter, T. (1984). Characteristics of adult beginning readers who persisted in a volunteer tutoring program. *Lifelong Learning: The Adult Years, 7*(5), 20-22, 28.

Lancy, D. (1988). *Parents' strategies for reading to and with their children.* Paper Presentation, AERA, New Orleans, LA.

Mason, J. M., & Allen, J. (1986). A review of emergent literacy with implications for research and practice in reading. In E. Z. Rothkopf (Ed.), *Review of research in education* (13th ed.). Washington, DC: American Education Research Association.

Nash, A. (1987). *English family literacy: An annotated bibliography.* Boston, MA: English Family Literacy Project, University of Massachusetts/Boston.

Nickse, R. (1984). *The college work-study adult literacy project: A survey.* Washington, DC: The National Association of Student Employment Administrators, U.S. Department of Education.

Nickse, R. S. (1990). *Family and intergenerational literacy programs: An update of "the noises of literacy"* (ERIC ED. IN 342). Columbus, OH: Center on Education and Training for Employment, ERIC Clearinghouse on Adult, Career, and Vocational Education.

Nickse, R., & Englander, N. (1985). At risk parents: Collaborations for literacy. *Equity and Choice* (Vol. VI, No. 3). Boston, MA: Institute for Responsive Education, 11-18. (ERIC ED EJ 368 680).

Nickse, R., & Englander, N. (1986). *Administrator's handbook, Collaborations for literacy: An intergenerational reading project.* Boston, MA: Trustees of Boston University.

Nickse, R. S., & Paratore, J. (1988). *An exploratory study into the effects of an intergenerational approach to literacy* (Final Report). Washington, DC: U.S. Department of Education, Office of Educational Research and Improvement, Contract No. G008610963.

Nickse, R. S., Speicher, A. M., & Bucheck, P. C. (1988). An intergenerational adult literacy project: A family intervention and prevention model. *Journal of Reading, 31*(7), 634-642.

Rosenshine, B., & Stevens, R. (1984). Classroom instruction in reading. In P. D. Pearson (Ed.), *Handbook of reading research* (pp. 745-798). New York: Longman.

Staryos, M., & Winig, L. (1986). *Tutor's handbook: Collaborations for literacy: An intergenerational reading project*. Boston, MA: Trustees of Boston University.

Sticht, T. (1983). *Literacy and human resources development at work: Investing in the education of adults to improve the educability of children*. Alexandria, VA: Human Resources Research Organization.

Sticht, T., & McDonald, B. (1989). *Making the Nation Smarter: The intergenerational transfer of cognitive ability*. San Diego, CA: Applied Behavioral and Cognitive Sciences, Inc. (ERIC ED 309 279).

Teale, W.H. (1986). Home Background and Young Children's Literacy Development. In W. H. Teale & E. Sulzby (Eds.), *Emergent literacy: Writing and reading* (pp. 176-206). Norwood, NJ: Ablex.

Writings by adult learners. (1988). *It's never easy*. Boston, MA: Boston Public Library.

Chapter 11

Pace: Parent and Child Education in Kentucky

Jeanne Heberle
Workforce Development Cabinet
Office of Adult and Technical Education

BACKGROUND

The Kentucky Department of Education and the Kentucky General Assembly created Kentucky's Parent and Child Education program, or PACE, in 1986 to address the problems of undereducation and poverty affecting a significant proportion of the state's population. The program, based on a widely accepted theory of the factors related to the generational cycle of academic and vocational performance, seeks to solve these problems by addressing family characteristics that contribute to a pattern of undereducation and unemployment. PACE seeks to raise parents' educational levels, to improve children's learning skills, to increase parents' educational expectations for their children, and to develop positive relations between home and school. PACE is a family support program that focuses on family literacy.

The PACE program began with six pilots in 1986. Six were added in 1987, and the program was expanded to 18 classrooms by the 1988 General Assembly. In 1989, two classrooms were added as a pilot implementation of the JOBS portion of the federal Family Support Act. In 1990, the General Assembly expanded the program to a total of 33 classrooms in 30 counties and districts.

PACE was initiated because of acute needs within Kentucky. When the program was established, the state ranked 50th in the nation in the percentage of adults with high school credentials and had one in four children under the age of five living in poverty, which is above the national average. Kentucky was experiencing economic decline and above-average unemployment. Not easily measured, and therefore the hardest to define, assess, and change, is an attitude problem. The undereducated and underemployed in Kentucky do not typically look to education as a means for personal or vocational improvement. Kentucky's legislative leaders, painfully aware of economic decline in the state and already prepared to address educational reform, saw in the PACE plan an innovative, promising attempt to solve a significant part of the state's educational and economic problems.

PROGRAM GOALS

In a public school setting, PACE provides a variety of services designed to address the characteristics of the family environment that contribute to the cycle of undereducation. Parents receive adult basic education, a family support program, and support for parental skills conducive to children's personal success and achievement. Children are given a high-quality early childhood program to mediate the effects of the existing family environment. Parents and children take part in joint learning activities to strengthen and extend the learning relationship between them.

PACE brings parents and children to a public school to:

1. Raise the educational level of the parents of preschool children through instruction in basic skills.
2. Enhance parental skills through family support activities.
3. Increase developmental skills of preschool children to prepare them for academic and personal success.
4. Enable parents to become familiar with and comfortable in the public school setting.
5. Provide a role model for the child of parental interest in education.
6. Enhance the relationship of the parent and child through planned structured interaction.
7. Demonstrate to parents their power to affect their child's ability to learn.
8. Encourage early identification and treatment of physical or mental handicaps that may inhibit the child's learning ability.

9. Encourage identification and treatment of any handicapping condition in the adults that may inhibit their ability to care for themselves and their children.

MEASURABLE OBJECTIVES

The following are objectives of the PACE program:

1. Seventy percent of parents in the program will achieve a GED diploma and/or raise skills by two grade levels and/or enroll in further educational or job training programs.
2. Children's performance on appropriate developmental measures will improve.

ADMINISTRATIVE DESIGN

Once the competitive grants are awarded to eligible districts, the state agency retains authority over the curricula, the training, some areas of the budget, and such reporting requirements as enrollment, attendance, participant information, and finances. Following guidelines from the state agency, the districts hire, supervise, and evaluate the PACE staff. The state agency evaluates the programs yearly.

A citizen and professional task force advises the staff on policies. Members helped design the district selection process, the training program, and proposed research and evaluation designs.

In most districts the centers are located in space in the public elementary school. A few are in nearby mobile units, and a few are in neighboring churches or buildings. Each PACE unit has one classroom for the adults and one for the children, usually close to each other.

PROGRAM, CURRICULUM, TRAINING AND MONITORING

Parents and children arrive at school together, usually on school transportation. After breakfast, the parents go to adult education classes and the children to early childhood classes for two hours. At the end of that period, parents come into the children's room for an hour to be their teachers. With the classroom teacher as a facilitator, they use the curricular materials in activities with their children. The children and parents go to lunch. While children take naps, the parents spend an hour with the team of teachers working on family, vocational, and life skills. The parents and children attend three full school days a week. The staff is hired for four days. The fourth day is for preparation, home visits, and recruitment. (Many school districts hire the staff for a fifth day as substitutes or homebound teachers in other programs.)

PACE adopted the High/Scope Educational Foundation curriculum for the children. This program has been recognized through the National Diffusion Network. The curriculum is an open-framework model derived from Piagetian theory. The classroom program emphasizes decision making and active learning and reflects the needs and interests of the children being served. The teacher serves as a guide, facilitator, and supporter of focused learning activities.

For adult education, the Comprehensive Adult Student Assessment System (CASAS), also an NDN program, has been adopted.

During parents' time in the classroom, the parents and children follow a general routine that is consistent with the High/Scope curriculum. They plan a play activity, they do it, and they talk about what they did. These activities range across computer, math, language, art, and social activities, all in the context of play. Emphasis is placed on shared control and responsibility for learning.

During parents' time while children nap, parents and staff members work together, using the PACE Family Resource Curriculum. The curriculum, developed by the national Family Resource Coalition in cooperation with PACE staff members and participants, acknowledges the adult's role as individual, parent, family and community member, citizen, student, and potential and actual employee.

PACE uses the materials developed by High/Scope. Each early childhood classroom is fully equipped and arranged to allow for self-directed, hands-on activities that foster each child's abilities. Adult education materials are selected to coordinate with the CASAS system. At parents' time in the classroom, several curricula are available. Experts have developed curricula in family support, emergent literacy, family math, and family computer skills and trained the PACE staff in their use.

Each site has one adult educator, one early childhood teacher, and one teaching assistant. Teachers and teaching assistants are employees of the local school system and receive compensation equal to that of district employees. The teaching staff is selected at the local level. Adult education teachers and early childhood education teachers must have college degrees, and teaching assistants must have high school diplomas. All teachers work four days a week in the PACE program. The fourth day is spent planning, visiting homes, and recruiting.

PACE staff members receive at least 15 days of training the first year of program implementation and at least 10 days of training in subsequent years. After each training session, the trainer visits each classroom at least once for observation and feedback. The curriculum and training in the PACE program are interdependent because the methods and materials used by teacher trainers are planned as demonstrations for teachers to use with parents and ultimately for parents to use within families.

Training in adult education, family support, and early childhood education is given simultaneously to all PACE staff members to promote team efforts in teaching and program planning.

The state agency, using published and self-designed instruments and reporting forms, periodically monitors and evaluates program performance.

RECRUITMENT

Recruitment is done with the assistance and cooperation of informal and formal organizations. Among the informal methods are word of mouth and contacts with community leaders. Brochures are posted in logical places. Slide presentations, videos, and other visual materials are available for community meetings. Recruiters participate in local events such as fairs and parades. More formal contacts occur with all local educational, social, religious, and health service agencies.

There are difficulties with recruitment. Many undereducated adults are not as personally dissatisfied as anticipated, and if they are, they may not see education as a way out. Their experience in public school may have been very negative. Many have not experienced or witnessed immediate benefits from education. They were either hired without an education or laid off because of lack of work in the community. Because of lack of work, those who did get an education left the community, and families, painfully aware of that, are not necessarily supportive. In general, husbands are not enthusiastic about changes in family routines. As awareness of the obstacles increased, recruitment became a much more important element of the design.

COSTS

Cost benefits can only be identified speculatively, based on such existing research as the High/Scope Foundation study on the cost benefits of high-quality early childhood education and various studies indicating

Table 11.1. Sample Budget

Personnel	2 teachers, 1 assistant, salary and fringe	$40,000
Training		3,000
Equipment	Start-up	4,000
Materials and Supplies		500
Other	Rent, 2% indirect costs, janitor, transportation, insurance, recruitment	1,500
Total Cost		$50,000
Cost per student/user	Based on 30 individuals each year	$ 1,666

the cost benefits of successful adult education programs. Such studies indicate the obvious investment value of PACE when it achieves its goals. It is equally speculative to establish an accurate cost per partici-pant, since PACE is an open entry/exit program with varying enroll-ments across the districts.

Table 11.1 provides a sample budget with an estimated cost per participant.

DEMOGRAPHICS

The participating population tends to be white, female, and between 20 and 35 years of age. Fewer than half the participants receive Aid to Families with Dependent Children (AFDC), and fewer than half are from single-parent homes. The participating rural districts have few minorities in the population. These facts show PACE to be representa-tive of Kentucky, which is fourth in the nation for married-couple households and has a minority population of 7.1 percent blacks and 0.9 percent Hispanics.

Kentucky's demographics of poverty and undereducation created abundant opportunities to pilot a statewide family literacy program. In 162 of the 175 school districts, 20 percent of the children are on the free and reduced price lunch program. The PACE grants, awarded using a blind readers system, were fairly equally distributed across the state. All participating districts but three are rural. All are characterized by higher than average unemployment. Eleven of the 30 districts partici-pating are in the Fifth Congressional District, acknowledged to be the poorest in the United States. The three urban districts are in the greater Cincinnati area of Northern Kentucky.

RECOGNITION AND DISSEMINATION

The PACE program has received outstanding recognition. It won a 1988 award for Innovations in State and Local Government from the Ford Foundation and Harvard University's John F. Kennedy School of Government. The Harvard Family Research Project is conducting a major case study. The program won a Five-Star Award from the Kentucky Community Education Association in 1989. The Kentucky Chamber of Commerce listed PACE as its first funding priority in its recommendations to the 1990 General Assembly for education reform and economic development. PACE won the 1991 Council of State Governments innovation award. Information requests have come from 40 states and 3 foreign countries. PACE staff members have been asked to consult and make presentations at numerous state and national conferences. The Kenan Charitable Trust established the Kenan Family Literacy Project to fund, research, and disseminate programs nationwide. The program was adopted by the Bureau of Indian Affairs for use in public and tribal schools on Indian reservations beginning in the fall of 1990.

It is featured in *First Teachers: A Family Literacy Handbook for Parents, Policy-makers, and Literacy Providers,* published by the Barbara Bush Foundation for Family Literacy. It has been featured by PBS/ABC television, and in the *New York Times,* the *Phi Delta Kappan, Modern Maturity,* and numerous conference proceedings and journal articles, including the *Yale Law* and *Policy Review.*

OUTCOMES

A number of studies of the PACE program conducted between 1987 and 1989 have demonstrated its effectiveness in the areas of adult and child achievement and adult aspirations for children. These studies include program evaluations done or commissioned by PACE. Two early studies were conducted in 1987 by researchers in two different departments at the University of Kentucky. A PhD dissertation was completed in 1989. A comprehensive review of the program was conducted by the Department of Education's Office of Research and Planning (Hibpshman 1989). Three results of program performance were identified:

1. The program is effective in changing parent's attitudes about education.

A dissertation on the program (Kim, 1989) included pre- and postprogram interviews with a sample of adult participants. The results of these interviews indicated that significant changes had occurred in the parents' expectations about their children's ultimate educational outcomes. As shown by Table 11.2, the proportion of parents who expected that their children would graduate from high school and attempt some sort of postsecondary education increased after their participation in PACE.

2. The program is effective in raising the parents' literacy levels.

A basic tenet of PACE is that poorly education parents tend to produce poorly educated children, because of the children's modeling of parental behavior. This theory sees attainment of a high school credential by the parent as a means of reversing the negative effect of parental devaluation of education. The PACE program was successful in obtaining educational credentials for a substantial proportion of its population, as seen in Table 11.3 (Kim, 1989). Note that the PACE program was more than twice as effective as traditional adult basic education programs in causing its participants to obtain a GED.

Table 11.2. PACE Participants' Educational Expectations for Their Children

I expect my child (children) to finish . . .

	Enrollment		Conclusion	
	Freq.	%	Freq.	%
Grade School	105	28.68	16	11.76
High School	162	44.26	78	57.35
Vocational School	28	7.65	8	5.88
Two-year College	37	10.11	13	9.56
Four-year College	34	9.30	21	15.45
Total responses	366			136
N	166			82

Table 11.3. Two-by-Two Contingency Table of PACE and ABE Participants Who Obtained GEDs.

Obtained GED	PACE	ABE	Total
Yes	28(36.84%)	9(15.25%)	37(27.21%)
No	49(63.64%)	50(84.75%)	99(72.79%)
Total	77	59	136
($p \S$ .01)			

Table 11.4.   Paired-Comparisons T-test of TABE Gain Scores.

	Mean Increase	Std Error of Mean	T	PR¶ [T]
Reading	1.3109	0.2229	10.66	0.0001
Math	1.7140	0.1632	10.55	0.0001
Language	1.2734	0.1566	8.13	0.0001
Averaged grade	1.7343	0.1348	12.86	0.0001

In addition to having participants obtain GEDs, the program has also been successful in raising the literacy levels of its population as measured by other standards. Analysis of data showed that 70 percent or more of the program participants either obtained GEDs or raised their academic skills by two or more grade levels (Kim, 1987). Table 11.4 shows that PACE parents demonstrated more than chance gains in educational levels in math, reading, and language (Kim, 1989).

3. The program is effective in developing children's learning skills.
    An analysis of the Child Observation Record (COR) periodically administered assessments done in 1988 showed an overall 28 percent improvement in children's scores. The Child Observation Record, a user-validated, criterion-referenced instrument used to collect data, was developed by the High/Scope Educational Research Foundation in 1987 and contains nine subtests that include Using Language, Representing Experiences, Classification, Seriation, Number Concepts, Spatial Relations, Temporal Relations, Movement, and Social and Emotional Development. COR assessment data collected during the three years of program operation showed positive gains for all the children.

Another dissertation proposal using PACE as the subject has been approved and is underway. Janet Klein, studying under Dr. Margot Ely at New York University, is doing a qualitative, ethnographic study that will include analysis of observations and interviews. Ms. Klein expects to complete the dissertation in 1991.

OUTLOOK

Three major problems of program administration have been addressed and are improving. Early separation, child care for children too young to attend, and transportation from isolated areas had posed outcome and recruitment and retention problems.

It was assumed that when a parent received a GED diploma, that person was no longer eligible for the program and the parent and child exited. This problem has been dealt with in several ways. Entering parents who pretest as able to pass the GED are counseled either to enter and postpone taking the test or to go to another adult learning center for immediate test preparation. Parents who advance quickly are encouraged to remain. Since the curriculum is individualized, appropriately motivating and advanced activities are offered. This obviously increases the cost per participant, but is considered to be nonetheless cost-effective in the long run.

The program now has funds to offer participants who demonstrate willingness to attend if child care and transportation aid are available.

Two major programmatic issues have and will continue to receive priority. The organization of both the family support and the adult education segments are being continually improved. We now offer family support curriculum more closely correlated with the goals of the program, and a stronger adult education program that helps adult educators recognize the diversity of adult learning styles, differing functional levels and the need for an introduction to the world of work.

Even more difficult to address than the above are effective follow-through services for graduates of the program. In areas of high unemployment and scarce child-centered services, satisfactory employment and good child care are difficult to find. It is often easy to become discouraged in the job-seeking process. Possible partnership agreements are being explored with what local employers there are and with schools and other agencies.

The 1990 Kentucky General Assembly reenacted the PACE legislation and doubled the appropriation to $1,800,000 for each year of the biennium. A small amount of the funds are set aside for training, research and evaluation, and supplemental parent aid. Beginning in September 1990 there will be 33 classes in 30 school districts throughout the state.

The 1990 Kentucky Education Reform Act requires family resource centers to be placed in every elementary school with 20 percent of its population receiving free lunches within the next five years. It also calls for health and social services, child care, school-age child care, and a PACE program to be included in each center. The potential for community collaboration in sustained support of families participating in PACE seems unlimited.

In addition, the PACE program is positioned to be an effective resource for implementing the federal Family Support Act, which Kentucky is phasing in. PACE is considered an especially humane and attractive choice for eligible families who will eventually be mandated to enter education and training programs in order to receive benefits.

The most significant issue for PACE is the need for an appropriate research design. It appeals to a broad spectrum of political and social policy makers. National concern about illiteracy, poverty, and the critical need for a better educated work force has accelerated state and national dissemination despite the lack of validation.

CONCLUSION

The Kentucky family literacy model, PACE, is a unique effort to solve the widely recognized problem of the generational cycle of undereducation, unemployment, and poverty. The family and the school, two major socializing forces, are where the problem originates. Recognizing the interdependency of those forces, PACE introduced the innovation of influencing them simultaneously in one program in the public school.

Efforts to evaluate and research the outcomes of the program indicate it is effective in reaching both its measurable objectives and its long-range goals. Over the four years, PACE has been modified as a result of evaluation and research, but the major elements remain. The Kenan Family Literacy Project, which is PACE's most significant replication, operated by the National Center for Family Literacy in Louisville, KY, is in its third year. Research for that project validates the need for all three elements of the program for desired outcome achievement (Hayes, 1990). Further research is in progress, and a comprehensive, appropriate design and funds for implementation are being sought.

State and national recognition and interest in the program reflect the joint demands of humane education and welfare reform in the face of a severe work-force crisis. The appeal of PACE is its unique approach for providing comprehensive and sustained help for families to enable them to replace patterns of dependency with those of self-sufficiency.

BIBLIOGRAPHY

Books and Pamphlets

Adolescent pregnancy in the south: Breaking the cycle (p. 31). (1989, May). Washington, DC: Southern Regional Project on Infant Mortality.
Family literacy: Abstracts of family literacy programs (pp. 6-7). (1990, March). Washington, DC: U. S. Department of Education.

Family support, education and involvement: A guide for state action (pp. 12, 38). (1989, November). Washington, DC: Council of Chief State School Officers.

First teachers: A family literacy handbook for parents, policy-makers, and literacy providers (pp. 5-8, 54, 64). (1989). Washington, DC: Barbara Bush Foundation for Family Literary.

Franklin, M. R. (1989). *Intergenerational literacy projects: What works*. Little Rock, AK: International Reading Association Institute on Intergenerational Literacy.

Goodman, I. F., & Brady, J. P. (1988). *The challenge of coordination: Head Start's relationship to state-funded preschool initiatives* (pp. 25-26). Newton, MA: Education Development Center, Inc.

Harvard Family Research Project. (1988). *Pioneering states: Innovative family support and education programs.* (pp. 5-8). Cambridge, MA: Harvard Graduate School of Education.

Hayes, A. (1990). Research validates need for family literacy programs. In *Special report on family literacy* (pp. 5-6). Louisville, KY: National Center for Family Literacy and Project Literacy U.S.

Heberle, J., & T. L. Hibpshman (1989). *The Kentucky parent and child education program and the plan for research.* Frankfort, KY: Kentucky Department of Education.

Helping families grow strong: New directions in public policy. (1990). Papers from the Colloquium on Public Policy and Family Support. Washington, DC: Center for the Study of Social Policy.

Hibpshman, T. P. (1989). *A review of the Parent and Child Education (PACE) program.* Frankfort, KY: Kentucky Department of Education, Office of Research and Planning.

Hibpshman, T. P. (1989). *An explanatory model for family literacy programs.* Frankfort, KY: Kentucky Department of Education, Office of Research and Planning.

Kentucky Parent and Child Education (Fact Sheet). (1989). Frankfort, KY: Kentucky Department of Education.

Kentucky Parent and Child Education Program (1990). Frankfort, KY: Kentucky Department of Education.

Kim, Y. K. (1987). *Parent and child program evaluation report.* Lexington, KY: University of Kentucky, Human Development Institute.

Kim, Y. K. (1989). *Evaluation study of Kentucky's Pilot Adult Basic Educational Program.* Lexington, KY: University of Kentucky, Human Development Institute.

McAfee, O. (1989, July). *Prekindergarten curriculum: Implications for state policy* (pp. 38-39). Charleston, WV.: Appalachia Educational Laboratory.

Paul, D. L., Moreton, R. E. (1990). *Tomorrow's innovations today: Exemplary alternative education programs* (pp. 77-78, 250). Fort Lauderdale, FL: Nova University Center for the Advancement of Education.

Profiles in innovations: Selected nominees in the 1988 Ford Foundation/ Harvard University's Innovations in State and Local Government Awards

Program. (1988). Cambridge, MA: Harvard University, John F. Kennedy School of Government.

Smith, S., Blank, S. & Bond, J. T. (1990). *One program, two generations: A report of the Forum on Children and the Family Support Act* (p. 10). New York: Foundation for Child Development in Partnership with the National Center for Children in Poverty.

Teachout, W., & Nedostup, R. (1989). *Innovations in State and Local Government Awards Program: Update 1989* (pp. 13-14). Cambridge, MA: Harvard University, John F. Kennedy School of Government.

Townley, K. (1987) *Parent and Child Program.* Lexington, KY: University of Kentucky, Department of Home Economics.

Articles

Bush, B. (1989, October). Literacy: Our shared goal. *The Reading Teacher, 43,* 10-12.

Cohen, D. (1990, May 9). Parents as partners: Helping families build a foundation for learning. *Education Week, 9,* 13-20.

Friendly rivals join to fight illiteracy. (1989, February-March). *Modern Maturity,* p. 96.

Harper, S. (1989, May-July). We changed the world: Parent and Child Education Literacy Project. *Special Report,* p. 64.

Hausman, B., & Parsons, K. (1989, May). PACE: Breaking the cycle of intergenerational illiteracy. *Equity and Choice, 5,* 54-61.

Kentucky Parent and Child Education Program. (1989, October). (S. L. Kagan, guest ed., Early care and education: Reflecting on options and opportunities.) *Phi Delta Kappan, 71,* 140-41.

Layson, R. (1990, February). Bureau of Indian affairs adopts Kentucky's PACE program. *The Link, 9,* 8-9.

Lewin, T. (1988, March 8). Family support centers aim to mend two generations. *The New York Times,* p. 1.

Nickse, R. S. (1990, February). Family literacy programs: Ideas for action. *Adult Learning, 1,* 9-13, 28-29.

Noe, R. (1989, Spring/Summer). Accelerating the 'PACE' against illiteracy: Parent and child education. *Yale Law & Policy Review, 7,* 442-48.

Jenkins, E. D. (1987, January). How do schools in the region fare in helping parents care for children? *The Link, 5,* (Policy Briefs) 2-3.

Shanahan, E. (1988, October). Breaking the 'cycle of undereducation.' In Tales of ten governments that show what innovation is all about. *Governing, 2,* 40.

Teltsch, K. (1988, October 4). Literacy project in Kentucky wins $100,000 prize. *The New York Times,* p. A20.

Waldrip, C. (1989, October). PACE: When parents, preschoolers learn together. *Kentucky Journal, 1,* 16.

Chapter 12

An Intergenerational Study of the Impact of Computer-Assisted Instruction with Low-Literate Parents

Eunice N. Askov
Connie M. Maclay,
and Brett Bixler
Institute for the Study of Adult Literacy
The Pennsylvania State University

Many researchers (Karnes, Teska, Hodgins, & Badger 1970; Laosa, 1982; Sticht, 1983; Wagner, 1987) point to the intergenerational effects of illiteracy. Children whose parents do not read—or who read only marginally—lack the role model provided by a literate parent. They also lack early exposure to reading by not having stories read to them by a parent. It has been well documented that children who are read to as preschoolers do better in school than those with no exposure to reading before entering school (McCormick & Mason, 1986). Home support is clearly related to children's educational achievement (Applebee, Langer, & Mullis, 1988).

Furthermore, functionally illiterate parents are unable to help their children with school work. Because they may be embarrassed and insecure about their own literacy skills, they may brush off their children when they seek assistance. The children may interpret this behavior to mean that the parents think school is not important. In some cases parents have had very bad school experiences and, in fact, are negative as well as fearful about school—the place where they experienced failure. These attitudes are usually passed on to their children.

Often parent intervention programs ignore that parents may be low-literate and as a result unable to help their children. For example, Landerholm and Karr (1988) do not even mention parents' literacy level as a consideration in designing parent involvement programs. Nor does a recent publication from the U. S. Department of Education entitled *Becoming a Nation of Readers: What Parents Can Do* (Binkley, 1988) even consider how low-literate parents can help their children. In surveying informational materials routinely sent home by Chapter I teachers—some of which instructed parents in how to help their children—Askov (1984) discovered that many of these materials were of a high readability level, too difficult for the low-literate parents of the children being served in compensatory education programs. Instead of helping low-literate parents break the cycle of illiteracy by helping their children in any way they can, we inadvertently perpetuate it by giving the parents materials that they cannot read.

Chapter I programs, on the other hand, have made great strides in the past 20 years in providing compensatory education for children. However, the enormous influence of the family can lessen or even defeat program effects. These children's parents lacked access to the special instruction that they may have needed in school. Therefore, to have the greatest impact, a "whole family" approach to education makes sense as the best approach to teaching children. In response to this concern, the Penn State Adult Literacy Courseware project was begun.

DESCRIPTION OF THE COURSEWARE

Computer-assisted instruction (CAI) courseware was developed during the 1984–1986 fiscal years with funding from the Pennsylvania Department of Education, Chapter I, and Section 310 Adult Basic Education Special Projects (Askov, Maclay, & Bixler, 1987; Maclay & Askov, 1987). This courseware uses a "whole word" approach with some word building activities in teaching 1,000 high-frequency and functional words to adult beginning readers. The goal is expanded word recognition for adult nonreaders. The courseware, which delivers the instructional program and records student responses, is interactive, branching, and responsive to the user's answers and needs. The courseware runs on an Apple IIe microcomputer with two disk drives, a color monitor, a printer, and a speech synthesizer (Echo GP).

The courseware begins with a module on computer usage that is especially designed to acquaint the student with the speech synthesizer, the commands, and the letter/number keys. Reading vocabulary is divided into two categories: picturable words (Module 2) and nonpicturable words (Module 3). These two categories are further divided into lessons of 10 words. Picturable words are introduced with a graphic, while nonpicturable words are introduced with short selections of a variety of topics. The words are taught in context using the speech synthesizer with multiple choice and completion exercises to practice recognition of the target words. Games are used to reinforce the identification of new words.

The student is pretested before each lesson with 90 percent set as mastery level. If mastery is not attained, the student is directed to the instruction and games to help him or her learn the target words. The student is posttested upon completion of the lesson and/or games. Five forms of each test exist. The courseware uses branching to permit review and reinforcement. An elaborate record-keeping system records and analyzes responses, number of attempts, and response time. A file editor disk allows the instructor to monitor the student's progress.

Module 4 teaches 140 words commonly found on application forms of all types. The student practices this vocabulary by completing an application form with his or her own data, which may be printed as a reference. Module 5 teaches 170 words which are based on high-frequency phonograms. This module gives practice in word building with consonants being added before 16 common word patterns (such as *ake*). Module 6 (a word processing module) allows the student to use the words he or she is learning in writing activities. It is recommended that this module be used concurrently with the other modules. In addition, Modules 3 and 6 can be customized by the teacher to include his or her own words and sentences.

RESEARCH STUDY

The courseware was disseminated to cooperating Intermediate Units in Pennsylvania. These Units, in turn, made it available to the Chapter I reading programs of the school districts which they served. By a variety of methods, the Chapter I teachers contacted parents of children currently receiving Chapter I services. These parents were invited to participate in the program. Of those who were contacted, 92 eventually were tested for reading level/skill. They had to score below a fourth grade reading level to qualify for the experimental program. Of these, 52 completed the required 20 hours of instructional time (which usually took about 3 months) and were given all of the evaluation measures. The others who are not reported in this study were either unable to complete the required 20 hours or were not tested on all of the measures. A variety of demographic data was kept on the parents. Although giving such information was purely voluntary, most of the parents agreed. We are, therefore, able to more clearly define our experimental group.

Our sample was comprised of 37 mothers and 19 fathers. The range of ages was from 29 to 52, with 35.6 being the mean age and 33 being the median age. Of the sample, 68% were Caucasian, 21% were black, and the remaining 11% were of other racial backgrounds. Of these parents, 38% lived in urban settings and 62% lived in rural settings. English was the home language in 75% of the homes. Of those reporting a language other than English as the home language, Spanish was the predominant second language. Eleven percent of the parents reported having visual problems, and 4% reported auditory problems. Only 9% reported having any previous computer experience.

Of our sample 30% had graduated from high school, 22% had completed only the 11th grade, 13% had completed only the 10th grade, 3% had completed only the 9th grade, and 32% had dropped out of school prior to completing the 9th grade. Of these parents, 51% had been in some type of regular program/classroom in school, while 49% had been in a special education program. When asked why they had left school, 22% cited economic reasons, 14% cited pregnancy or marriage as the reason, 36% said they were frustrated by school, and the remaining 28% cited a variety of other reasons.

When asked why they had been interested in this program, 71% said they simply wanted to learn how to read or to improve their reading, 18% said they wanted to help their child/children, 3% said they were interested in the computer, 5% said they wanted to learn more English, and 3% cited other reasons for enrolling in the program. Most (86%) had never attended any other adult basic education or literacy programs. The parent literacy program was clearly attracting a new constituency to an adult education program, even though their expressed reason for attending (for 71% of the parents) involved self-improvement rather than helping their children.

After interviews for the descriptive information the parents were pretested for reading skill/level. This testing involved the *Slosson Oral Reading Test* (SORT), two sections of the *Baltimore County Design* (BCD), and the *Bader Reading and Language Inventory*. These informal measures were selected over standardized reading tests for adults because they were considered more sensitive to change and more valid in measuring what was being taught. Satisfactory reliability coefficients for these measures had been established in earlier pilot studies.

After assessment the parents began to use the courseware. They first used Module 1, which introduced them to the formats, activities, and the voice used throughout the courseware. They were then either allowed to choose a lesson or were assigned to a lesson by the teacher. The teachers were encouraged to use the courseware for approximately 80 percent of the instructional time and to supplement that with additional activities that emphasized the transfer of vocabulary and skills learned on the computer to everyday reading and writing tasks. Extensive records of student responses and response time were kept on the student data disks. Each teacher was instructed to posttest the parent after 20 hours of instructional time. The posttesting used the same instruments as in the pretesting phase.

In addition to the experimental group, data were also kept on a control group. This group consisted of 24 parents who were interested in, and eligible for, using the courseware but, because of scheduling problems, transportation, and child care, were unable to participate at this time. This group, although smaller than the experimental group, allowed us to make some comparison statements concerning the effectiveness of the courseware.

EVALUATION OF IMPACT ON PARENTS

The mean pre/posttest scores for both groups are shown in Table 12.1. The pretest and posttest scores of both groups were analyzed using analysis of variance for repeated measures. This type of test allows a

Table 12.1.   Parents' Pre- and Posttest Reading Scores

	N	Pre/M	SD	Post/M	SD
		SORT			
Exp. Group	52	3.26	2.00	3.93	2.05
Control Group	24	2.74	1.92	2.67	1.85
		BCD-E2 (Words in Isolation)			
	N	Pre/M	SD	Post/M	SD
Exp. Group	52	18.48	5.73	22.33	3.85
Control Group	24	17.13	5.04	16.88	4.79
		BCD-E3 (Words in Functional Setting)			
	N	Pre/M	SD	Post/M	SD
Exp. Group	52	20.13	5.35	22.67	3.15
Control Group	24	16.00	6.22	16.13	5.95
		Bader			
	N	Bader Pre/M	SD	Post/M	SD
Exp. Group	52	2.33	1.80	3.63	1.76
Control Group	24	2.04	1.73	1.79	1.91

researcher to look at the interaction between time of measurement and treatment. It is used to decide whether the difference between the means of the pretest and posttest scores of the experimental group is significantly greater or less than the difference for the control group. With an alpha value set at .05, we found significant differences between the pre–posttest scores for the experimental group with all four measures. The experimental group had gained more than one year in reading level in only 20 hours of instructional time; traditional programs usually take a minimum of 50 to 80 hours to make comparable gains.

EVALUATION OF IMPACT ON CHILDREN

Although no direct involvement by the students was mandated, it was hypothesized that a parent's interest in learning to read should have a positive effect on the child. Therefore, pretest and posttest data for these children were compared with pretest and posttest data from other children in the Chapter I programs in Pennsylvania. While the gains made from pretest to posttest were significant ($p \leq .05$), they were not significantly different from the gains made by other Chapter I children in Pennsylvania.

In addition, we hypothesized that attendance patterns of the children might change as a result of the parents' involvement in school. Attendance data were collected for the 3 months prior to the parents' involvement in the program and the 3 months immediately after the parents became involved in the program. Although no statistical comparison was done with a control group, the change in percentage of days attending school for the experimental group is quite interesting. Prior to the parental involvement in the program, these children were in school an average of 88 days out of 100; after parental involvement, they were in school 95 days out of 100. In view of the correlation between attendance and achievement, this statistically significant ($p \leq .05$) change from 88% to 95% in attendance is an important change.

The greatest changes were evident in teacher's observational comments. Since in most cases the same teacher taught the parent and child, the teacher was able to observe changes in the child after the parent enrolled in the parent literacy program. Anecdotal records kept by the teachers indicated positive, and sometimes dramatic, changes in the children.

MODELS FOR USE

With a variety of sites, teachers, and adult students, it was inevitable that the ways of using the courseware would also vary. Some methods were more successful than others. Although the success of a particular model may have been influenced by the specific location or individual, some generalizations can be drawn from the experiences of these teachers in 46 sites in Pennsylvania. The models for use fell into four categories: (a) single parent, (b) both parents, (c) single parent and child/children, and (d) both parents and child/children.

In most sites a single parent came for instruction without having any children present. This model had the advantage of scheduling flexibility and freedom for the parent. Parents were able to vary the length of their instructional time more easily when no children were present. (The teacher in this case had to be attuned to the parent's needs in terms of child care.) In most of the sites where a single parent came in for instruction, they were trained to use the courseware on equipment that was set up in a room in the school. In this way, he or she could come in during the day (while the child was in school) and use the courseware at his or her convenience. The times were mutually arranged so that the teacher had some free time immediately before or after the parent had used the courseware, which allowed them to discuss the lesson and do any supplemental activities the teacher had planned.

In some of the sites both parents came for instruction, but without any children being involved. Here again, the teacher was attuned to child care needs. This situation was generally less flexible in terms of scheduling; since one or both of the parents probably had a work schedule, these sessions were usually scheduled in the late afternoon or evening. The location of these sites varied—the child's school, the teacher's home, a local library, a local church. The major advantage to this situation is that each parent had a support person. Generally it was useful for the parents to work together unless they were on very different reading levels. In this case, allowing one parent to work with the computer while the second parent worked with the teacher was the easiest model. In cases where the teacher was able to adjust his or her schedule to meet both parents, parents were able to attend more sessions.

In some of the sites, a single parent came for instruction and brought his or her child along. In these cases, the child was allowed to be involved with the parent in working on the computer rather than with the follow-up/supplemental activities. As with the two parent model, the parent/child model had the advantage of a built-in support person. Additionally, working with his or her parent appeared to send strong messages to the child about the importance of education. These children were more apt to change their attendance patterns and their apparent attitude toward school. The major disadvantage was that scheduling became more difficult. Participants at these sites generally met in the evenings and at the teacher's home.

In a few cases both of the parents and the child/children were involved with the courseware. This model, which also had the advantage of a built-in support group, appeared to be sending the strongest messages to the children. They were able to see a tangible example of the value of education in both of their parents' lives. These children showed the most marked changes in attitude and behavior in school. Changes were apparent in children of high school age as well as children of elementary school age. Clearly, the disadvantage to this model was the complexity in scheduling. This plan appeared to work best in cases where the computer was located in the teacher's or the student's home. When this was the case, the amount of instructional time could be more flexible and could more easily meet the scheduling needs of the individuals.

Although the models involving children in the instructional experience proved very successful, it must be pointed out that this is not always true. In some cases the parent was very uncomfortable having his or her child present. Many parents had tried to hide the fact that they read poorly, so admitting their poor reading skills to their child was difficult. In these examples, the teacher had to be willing to follow the needs of the adult student in planning a program. In fact, it was found that initially, the teacher should allow the student to make the decision concerning the model with which he or she was most comfortable.

CONCLUSION

The teachers involved in this project were very excited and pleased with the accomplishments of the parents, who showed changes in both attitude and achievement. Long-term research and follow-up data collection to determine rate and maintenance of learning growth, although deemed important, was not possible given funding constraints. Nevertheless, the teachers have continued to use the courseware on their own.

Getting started was not easy. Very few of the teachers had past experiences working with adults. Many had little or no experience with computers. Most of them were very hesitant to attempt the task of recruiting parents to work in the program. Aware of these problems, the staff offered workshops to all of the teachers and included help in recruitment. The assistance of adult literacy councils and adult basic education programs was enlisted for recruitment, also having the effect of putting the Chapter I teachers in contact with the adult education network in the community. Most of the workshop time, however, was spent in "hands-on" experience with the courseware. The sessions were well attended and highly valued by the teachers.

But something else important has happened. Participating parents are beginning to bring their friends to the program. Although most of the test sites now serve only one, two, or three parents, new parents have been identified who want to begin working with the courseware as soon as possible. A grass-roots parent network seems to be forming to combat one of the continuing difficulties faced by many teachers— that of recruiting parents who cannot read and are often fearful and embarrassed to admit this. It appears that recruitment becomes less of a problem as the program becomes better known in the community. Use of computers offer a "face-saving" and modern way to learn to read and write, attracting new parents to the program once they hear about the use of computers from other parents who were involved.

The intergenerational aspects of illiteracy have often been cited. Children of parents who have low-level literacy skills have numerous educational and emotional disadvantages. The intent of this inter-generational project was to intervene with the parents—to upgrade their literacy skills—so that they could help their children. Feeling better about their literacy skills gave the parents in our program the confidence and skills to attempt to help their children.

One of the important results of the intergenerational literacy proj-ect was described by one of the parents when she said: "I never read to my kid. I'm not quite ready yet. But now, I think I'll try it real soon."

REFERENCES

Applebee, A. N., Langer, J. A., & Mullis, I. V. S. (1988). *Who reads best? Factors related to reading achievement in grades 3, 7, and 11.* Princeton, NJ: Educational Testing Service.

Askov, E. N. (1984, April). *Can the parents of your remedial readers read? How can you help them?* Paper presented at the annual Bloomsburg Univer-sity Reading Conference, Bloomsburg, PA.

Askov, E. N., Maclay, C. M., & Bixler, B. (1987). *Penn State Adult Literacy Courseware: Impact on parents and children (final report).* University Park, PA: Institute for the Study of Adult Literacy, Penn State Univer-sity.

Binkley, M. R. (1988). *Becoming a nation of readers: what parents can do.* Washington, DC: Office of Educational Research and Improvement, U.S. Department of Education.

Karnes, M., Teska, J., Hodgins, A., & Badger, E. (1970). Educational interven-tion at home by mothers of disadvantaged infants. *Child Development, 41,* 925.

Landerholm, E., & Karr, J. A. (1988). Designing parent involvement program activities to deal with parents' needs. *Lifelong Learning, 11* (5), 11-13, 19.

Laosa, L. M. (1982). School occupation, culture, and family: The impact of parental schooling on the parent-child relationship. *Journal of Educational Psychology, 74* (6), 791-827.

Maclay, C. M., & Askov, E. N. (1987). Computer-aided instruction for Mom and Dad. *Issues in Science and Technology, 4* (1), 88-92.

McCormick, C., & Mason, J. (1986). Intervention procedures for increasing preschool children's interest in and knowledge about reading. In W. Teale & E. Sulzby (Eds.)., *Emergent literacy: Writing and reading* (pp. 90-115). Norwood, NJ: Ablex Publishing Corp.

Sticht, T. G. (1983). *Literacy and human resources development at work: Investing in the education of adults to improve the educability of children.* Alexandria, VA: Human Resources Research Organization.

Wagner, D. A. (1987). *Intergenerational literacy: Effects of parental literacy and attitudes on children's reading achievement in Morocco.* Paper presented at the Biennial Meeting of the Society for Research on Child Development, Baltimore, MD.

Chapter 13

Commentary on Three Programs for the Intergenerational Transfer of Cognition

Rosemarie J. Park
University of Minnesota

In this commentary I will try to analyze the three programs presented. The programs seem to be representative of the parent–child literacy projects around the country. As such, this commentary deals with some of the strengths, but also some of the very real difficulties, programs have in documenting gains made by parents and then passed on to their children. These difficulties are more than apparent to those who deal on a daily basis with parent–child literacy programs.

ALL PROGRAMS HAVE BROAD GOALS

All three projects encompass fairly broad goals in terms of improving parents' educational level in order to improve their childrens' abilities. The Penn State program probably is the narrowest in its goals, since it deals mainly with parents' reading skills and serves those with skill levels below grade four. The Kentucky PACE program is broader in scope and includes work both with parents and their preschool children. The curriculum covers both parenting and developmental skills for children and academic work with their parents. The Boston Family Learning Center involves a range of basic reading skills for parents who read below a fifth-grade level and opportunities for parents and children to work together on Saturday mornings on a voluntary basis. No direct teaching of parents with their children, or of children by themselves, is involved as in the Kentucky project.

ALL PROGRAMS HAVE
A STRONG THEORETICAL BASE

The rationale for each program cites a theoretical research base that suggest illiterate parents tend to produce illiterate children. This contention is supported by extensive local demographic research in Kentucky, and is documented in the original proposal for this conference by Sticht (Sticht, 1983; Hess & Holloway, 1979). The chapter by Ruth Nickse (this volume) particularly gives a detailed research rationale for just why improving the educational skills of parents should improve children's academic ability. If the research base is so strong, why are hard results so difficult to come by? All three programs present case studies of why, as Sticht has suggested, there is no hard research evidence on the "extent to which adults can be educated to improve their own cognitive ability and how the new competence of the parents can be transferred to the children" (Sticht, 1988). An overall analysis of the three programs with information currently available is given in Table 13.1. An analysis of these programs suggest a range of difficulties in achieving positive results particularly in improving academic skill levels.

THE DIFFICULTY OF GETTING RESULTS
IN A SHORT SPACE OF TIME

The hours spent working with adults in these programs varies between 20 hours in the Penn State project, and 30 to 50 hours at the Family Learning Center, to a projected 7½ hours three days a week at PACE (2½ hours spent on adult academic work). All previous research seems to show that cognitive achievement for adults is not a rapid process. It takes somewhere between 80 to 100 hours of teaching to improve reading scores one grade level. Despite this, the most carefully controlled study at Penn State seems to have achieved a 1.3 grade level improvement in 20 hours of instruction. Reading comprehension gains range in the other studies from -.2 to 1 grade level in Boston and one grade level per 75 hours of instructions gained in PACE programs.

Table 13.1. Summary of Three Parent–Child Literacy Programs

Type of Program	Curric. & Lit. Skills	Adults	Hours Compl.	Children	Test Gains — Rdg. Comp.	Test Gains — Voc.	Findings — Plus	Findings — Minus
1. Family Learning Center. Boston	Family Learning Center for parents (open on Sat a.m. for parents and children)	0–5 yr Decoding vocabulary building reading listening comprehens	N = 30 Parents Chap. 1 children Asian 23 His 23 Bl. 37 Wh. 17 (40% ESL)	30 hrs 40 hrs 50 hrs	44 59% primary Chap. 1	Rdg. Comp. 1.0 .7 .5	Voc. .8 .5 −.2	Higher retention rate Good research base	Changed levels on ABLE post No data on children Few preschool children Conclusions need to be hinged to research
2. Penn State Adult Literacy Courseware Report	C.A.I. parent Literacy Sites No involvement by children mandated	0–4 yr Whole word approaches Beg. reading software	N = 52 (As. Hisp) 10% Bl. 21% Wh. 67% (ESL 25%) M19 F37	20 hrs	Chap. 1	SORT .67 BCD words 3.85 Bader 1.3 yr		Use of Control Children's attendance improved	No data on children Adult standard tests not used
3. PACE Project Kentucky	Programs in economically disadvantaged countries	4–8 yr GED Flexible reading parenting & parent-child interaction		2½ hrs 3 × per week	Presch only	TABE GED 70% got GED 1 grade level gain per 75 hrs		Conceptually good 28% children improved developmental skills	No research data available beyond broad description

MEASURES OF LITERACY

One reason for caution in interpreting results is that reading is a complex skill. Is it possible to develop a complex skill in a short time? If one reviews the Sticht model of reading that accompanies these conference materials, reading is viewed as a skill that develops within the context of an internal language environment. Once oracy is achieved, reading and writing develop as part of a complex interaction between an external environment that includes written and spoken information, and a cognitive and metacognitive skill base. Reading is not simply the ability to translate the graphic symbols into spoken language. "Reading" a page of technical information does not mean the reader will automatically "understand" it. That is, the reader needs the appropriate knowledge base in order to interpret the information on the page. This point is made in early research on auding and reading by Sticht (1974). Adults read about where they understand. Advanced cognitive development cannot take place by oracy alone. Hence, to raise cognitive ability takes more than a quick fix of decoding skills. Some impact can be made on a knowledge base in 75 hours, but is 20 hours a feasible length for a program?

It is difficult to make comparisons in reading gains, since these programs target adults at different stages of reading skill. Reading theorists suggest a "stage" model of reading acquisition (Chall, 1983). Initial stages of reading that involve "decoding" the printed word may involve different processes and have little impact on the cognitive knowledge base of the adult until more cognitively complex material can be read and assimilated. Teaching parents to decode may then have less influence on their children in the short term. Programs that teach context skills involved in higher levels of reading may have more overall impact. Longitudinal data from all three programs may provide an interesting set of comparisons.

DIFFICULTIES IN THE OBJECTIVE
MEASUREMENT OF READING SKILLS

Much of the difficulty involved in measuring academic gains in adult programs is due to the inherent problems in developing an objective measure of adult reading achievement. There is an initial problem of the content validity of the tests. Most adult programs, with the exception of GED classes (here Kentucky has an advantage), do not teach what the tests measure. Parenting skills programs are hardly likely to raise the general vocabulary skills that are measured on the TABE, for example. This lack of congruance, together with the Standard Error of Measurement on both the TABE and the ABLE, make negative gain scores not uncommon, as the Boston program found out.

Adult tests reflect the fact that there is a huge variability in adult reading performance. Even the latest and more sophisticated editions of the ABLE and the TABE have SEMs that negate any gain scores of less than a year. Take a raw score on the ABLE Level One reading comprehension subtest of 30. The SEM is 2.5 for this test. A raw score of 30 translates to a grade equivalent score of 3.7. Add the two points close to the standard deviation (scores do not deal in fractions), and the grade equivalent is 4.1. Subtract 2 points from 30, and the grade equivalent becomes 3.3. Thus the swing of the SEM for this particular score is 3.3 to 4.1. Using + or − 2.5 the range of scores would be more than a year (Karlsen & Gardner, 1986). Similarly, taking level M of the TABE, Form 6, a score of 17 plus or minus one SEM gives a range of 3.1 to 4.5 grade. It should also be noted that scores will be within one SEM only 68 percent of the time (CTB/McGraw Hill, 1987, p. 22). This problem is graphically illustrated by Figure 13.1, taken from the TABE technical report above. Note that the SEM swings dramatically upward at the upper and lower ends of a normal curve, thus making it

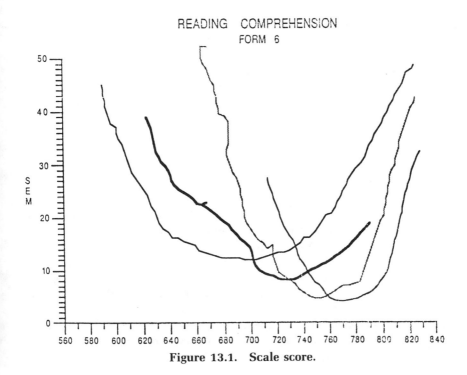

Figure 13.1.   Scale score.

obvious why regression towards the mean is such a strong factor to be reckoned with in testing adults.

Given the fact that two of the studies targeted the lowest adult readers where regression effects are bound to be greatest, one might well expect adults to make at least 1 year of progress on technicalities alone.

THE DIFFICULTY OF ADMINISTERING TESTS UNIFORMLY

Most adult programs have difficulty administering standardized tests. Part of the reason for this may be that many teachers distrust such tests and are inexperienced in administering them. For example, teachers in the Kentucky PACE project had to be cautioned to time their administration of the TABE as the instructions demand. A similar slip led to the different levels of the ABLE being administered as pre and post-tests in Boston. In addition, teachers and volunteers dislike testing people who enter adult programs voluntarily and are very hard to retain in programs. Teachers are literally afraid of scaring clients away.

Most adults stay relatively short periods of time in programs, often less than 3 months. Given the length of stay in programs it is difficult to image that solid cognitive gains can be made by adults let alone be transferred to children. Evidence that gains are being made academically is elusive. The three programs here rightly look for evidence that programs are having positive effects beyond academic gain scores. The PACE program, for example, can point to a 70 percent rate of adults who achieved a GED.

LOOKING BEYOND COGNITIVE GAINS

The "literacy variable" is incredibly difficult to isolate. Certainly it is influenced by a number of socioeconomic and sociocultural variables such as poverty level status (Hunter & Harmon, 1979) and mother's educational level (Sticht, 1988). Common to class and educational level is an attitude towards education as a positive value that reinforces children's achievement in school. The Penn State study reports increased school attendance among children of parents attending literacy classes. The Boston project reports on the increased retention rate for adults in their program (73%). Given normal drop-out rates of above 50 percent, this is a real achievement.

Most of the research used to back the intervention programs in the 1960s, including the much discussed Perry Preschool Project cited in the background material for this conference, assumes that intervention is most effective for preschool children. The Boston project is interesting in that it includes parents with children of a range of ages, 59 percent of which are primary age, the rest above. The Penn State children are also older. Only the PACE program limited enrollment to parents of preschool children. One future project would be to combine data to see if there are differential effects on preschool or perhaps adolescent children. None of the studies have really looked for differential effects with various populations. For example, the Boston project has a heavy ESL population (40%), Penn State has 25 percent ESL. These populations really should be treated separately.

SUMMARY

In summary this report covers three projects in a new and exciting area. All three raise more questions than they answer. How effective are adult literacy programs in improving cognitive skills of parents or children? In all honesty, no hard data exists to demonstrate they do. Part of this is the fault of measurement techniques that need to become more reliable and to be adaptable to the variety of curricula taught in adult programs. Certainly, more sophistication has to be developed by teachers in literacy programs so that tests are administered and interpreted correctly. Perhaps in the meantime we must document secondary, but no less important data. Improvement in children's attendance records, and parent's GEDs, are very tangible results. The ultimate need is for good longitudinal data that depends on solving the bugaboo of erratic and short attendance by adults in literacy programs. Certainly, helping their children in school is a marvelous hook for getting parents involving in literacy programs.

REFERENCES

Chall, J. (1983). *Stages of reading development.* New York: McGraw-Hill.
Hess & Holloway (1979). *The Intergenerational Transmission of Literacy* (Report). Washington, DC: U.S. National Institute of Education.
Hunter, C., & Harmon, D. (1979). *Illiteracy in America.* New York: McGraw Hill.
Karlson, B., & Gardner, E. (1986). *ABLE norms booklet.* Chicago: The Psychological Corporation, Harcourt Brace Jovanovich.

Sticht, T. (1974). *Auding and reading.* Alexandria, VA: HumRRO.

Sticht, T. (1983). *Literacy and Human Resource at work: Investing in the education of adults to improve the educability of children* (HumRRO Professional Paper 2-83). Alexandria, VA: Human Resources Research Organization.

Sticht, T. (1988). *The intergenerational transfer of cognitive skills: Knowledge synthesis with policy, practice, and research recommendations.* (unpublished manuscript). San Diego: Applied Behavioral and Cognitive Sciences Inc.

TABE Technical Report, Forms 5 & 6 (1987). Monterey, CA: GTB/McGraw Hill.

Part III

Policy, Practice, and Research Issues in the ITCS

Chapter 14

Introduction to Part III

Micheal J. Beeler

Issues surrounding the intergenerational transfer of cognitive skills touch every sphere of life. This is illustrated in Cole and Serpell's view of the theoretical issues surrounding the intergenerational transfer of cognitive skills (Chapter 15). The issues they bring up include the segregation of child-rearing practices from other life activities, the need for better educational planning, and the need to recruit adults for the enterprise of preparing subsequent generations for the challenges of life. It is interesting to note that, while these issues are not new, they pose new problems and call for new insights, due largely to our rapidly changing environment and social structure.

Chapter 16, by Orasanu, deals specifically with research design and methodology issues. The bind that develops in this field of research is particularly thorny. It involves satisfying concerns of scientific validity and ethical practice simultaneously. Orasanu points out the lack of generalizability of learning effects across subcultures and age groups. Her suggestion is that the focus of research should be on understanding processes.

Chapter 17, by Armijo, addresses issues of assessment. The fact that programs as old as the Perry Preschool Project and Head Start are still being evaluated 20 years later speaks to the difficulty of assessment in the education arena. Among the issues that have been hotly debated are: (a) Is "objective" measurement possible? (b) How much change in behavior is sufficient for claiming success? (c) Can current assessment techniques be translated into practical and useful methods in the future?

In Chapter 18 Simmons addresses some issues surrounding delivery systems. The central issue that Simmons discusses is cultural diversity. He suggests that interventions must satisfy, rather than compete with, the needs of the disadvantaged. Simmons correctly points out the need for institutional changes at several levels if intergenerational intervention programs are to be implemented successfully in the future.

Chapter 19 by Hartman is instructive to those who must look to legislative bodies for funding. In his chapter Hartman suggests several features that can enhance the prospect of political support for a particular program. In summary, Hartman concludes that, if more social programs are to be implemented, a broader consensus for action is necessary and can be best achieved through the cooperation of policy-makers, researchers, and practitioners.

Finally, in Chapter 20, Wagner focuses on some of the unifying themes that emerged during the conference on the intergenerational transfer of cognitive skills. His comments are directed toward social mobility and the motivation for educational interventions, including the purposes or goals that drive these educational interventions. Wagner also poses a set of research questions that he feels remain neglected. In particular, Wagner directs attention to the special problems that result from cultural diversity. In conclusion, he views the prospect of specialists intervening in the intergenerational transfer of cognitive skills for the common social good very appealing.

Identifying individual aspects or components of a broader issue has several advantages and has been very much a part of our investigation. Typically in America, solutions to problems are sought by analysis. The authors of the chapters in Part III do a scholarly job in analyzing particular aspects of the intergenerational transfer of cognitive skills.

Two important issues that deserve comment (that did not benefit from this analysis) are "social capital" (Coleman & Hoffer, 1987) and the fundamental structure of our economic and social support systems here in America.

Social capital is a concept developed by (Coleman & Hoffer, 1987) that he describes as (a) existing within the relations between persons, and (b) facilitating productive activity. Examples of social capital are motivation to succeed and trust within a social group. Coleman has developed the concept of social capital to help understand the benefit and superior academic success of parochial school children who reside in religious communities. One significant aspects of social capital is closure within social networks. Closure refers to congruency between the norms and sanctions of a community. This concept of social capital can be useful in future policy development and can help us understand the shortcomings of many of the social programs launched during the War on Poverty.

Efforts directed toward the intergenerational transfer of cognitive skills must avoid falling into the political realm of social welfare, as did many of the educational interventions developed during the War on Poverty. Only by avoiding this dangerous pitfall will researchers address the most relevant questions in the most objective fashion: will practitioners be able to expand their usefulness, and will policymakers meet the needs of their culturally diverse constituencies?

REFERENCE

Coleman, J., & Hoffer, T. (1987). *Public and private high schools*. New York: Basic Books.

Chapter 15

Conceptual and Theoretical Issues In the ITCS

Robert Serpell
Michael Cole
University of California, San Diego

At the Conference on the Intergenerational Transfer of Cognitive Skills (ITCS), a working group on conceptual and theoretical issues expressed dissatisfaction with the way in which child-rearing practices had somehow been isolated conceptually from the ensemble of culture and with the notion of cultural disadvantage. Historically the motivation for intervention programs has arisen from several different public policy concerns, including a desire to overtake the Soviet Union in the space race, putting out the fires of the civil rights protests, and competing with Japan in the international computer market. Each of these phases has tended to focus the discussion in somewhat different ways.

A number of different reasons were articulated by the group for wishing to modify the socialization and/or education offered to children: some more child-centered, such as promoting personal fulfillment, a wider range of personal choices, and more of a learning atmosphere throughout the individual's life-span; others more socially focused, such as preparation for citizenship, flexibility on the job market, manning new jobs in the economy and promoting the American way of life. Each of these long-term goals could be used as a justification for the desire to prepare children to perform better in school.

After some debate it was concluded that an interventionist concern with intergenerational transmission is grounded in some relatively uncontroversial premises, that:

- Some intergenerational transfer occurs.
- The chances are that the family environment is involved in this transmission process (it remains, however, a question for research to determine in exactly what ways it is involved).
- Parents have a moral right to participate in decisions about child-rearing (although the origins and limitations on that moral priority remain a matter for debate).
- Some of the socialization/educational goals enumerated earlier are so important that the educational community feels an obligation to advocate them even to the extent of pleading guilty to Ivan Illich's charge of "wanting to manipulate people for their own salvation." The underlying faith of those who adopt such an advocacy or "conscientization" role is that open-ended discourse will eventually discover a consensus.
- In support of that faith, the group noted a prevalence across most sections of American society of high aspirations phrased in terms of so-called "mainstream" values.
- Somewhat less evenly distributed is a commitment to the ideology of education as a means of fulfilling those aspirations. Part of the resistance to that ideology centers on the question of how education is defined. If it is taken to mean what is currently offered by your neighborhood school, then many families are skeptical of its capacity to help their child achieve his or her goals. But there remains for many a residual belief that the right kind of education could in principle provide a crucial stepping-stone to the good life.

An essential precondition for any intervention program, the group agreed, is an understanding (or at least a theory) of what is already being transferred between generations. Values and attitudes appeared to several of us to be an important part of the subcultural traditions which differentiate between the groups with a record of more and less successful participation in the educational system. There are also differences in functional value of specific cognitive skills and subroutines in relation to the particular ecological niche occupied by different social groups. Neither individuals nor groups, however, are static in this ecological system, and educational intervention has the potential to mobilize reciprocal influences between generations. Young women and young members of minority ethnic communities can and do sometimes redefine for their parents what is functional for them in society.

The theoretical status of the notion of higher-order cognitive skills was debated somewhat inconclusively. It was noted that, in the framework of cognitive science, this notion lays claim to greater specificity than the ability factors of earlier multifactorial theories of intelligence. The defining criteria for what is higher-order, however, appeared somewhat elusive, and it was even suggested that the hierarchal metaphor might itself be a source of confusion. Two features of what had been called higher-order skills appeared to the group to be of particular importance in relation to the problem of relevance in education: nonalgorithmic openness and purposive orchestration. A relevant and effective education would certainly wish the literacy and numeracy it imparts to have these properties.

A connection was noted with the concept of task analysis in the design of training curriculum. In the professions of law and medicine it has been argued that training can only be loosely related to its field of application, since the problem domains are not definable in advance. Training is therefore best organized around principles and cases.

The discussion then shifted to the question of how to define the problem domains which the children of traditionally disadvantaged groups should be prepared to cope with. Who is to make such decisions? Political and ethnical criteria assign priority to the adult members of the disempowered community. Every cultural group has a stock (or "bank") of indigenous beliefs, knowledge, skills, and values which should be documented, made visible, and mobilized as educational resources. In some cases, however, the goals set by those adults for their children lie beyond the frontiers of the cultural world whose parameters they themselves understand. (Alice Paul gave us the example of a Native American community wishing to see some of its youth trained as doctors. Such problems are, of course, abundant in the societies of Third World nations, such as Zambia, where decisions about educational curricula are taken by members of a small elite whose own education was received through a largely alien and potentially alienating colonial culture.)

The challenge for educational planning posed by this paradox is how to use indigenous cultural resources in a curriculum which will broaden horizons and open up new possibilities. One set of research questions concerns the possibility that cultures vary in their preferred modes of intergenerational transmission of knowledge and skills, and the relations between such culturally distinctive modes of transmission on the one hand, and on the other hand the demands of certain curriculum-content domains. Another set of questions concerns the articulation of strategies for recruiting adult members of the community to participate (be it as parents, as school teachers, or in other social roles) in the enterprise of preparing the next generation to cope with the challenges of the life ahead of them. The specifics of such participation (including such parameters as language) will need to be matched to the dynamics of each particular sociocultural group's relations with the so-called mainstream of American society.

Drawing on the parallels between individual and social development, on the proposition that cognition is socially distributed and on the notion of orchestration of cognitive skills, the group agreed that a productive way of defining the goal of intervention in the domain of ITCS might be as follows: that there is a kind of conversation which a disempowered community could be holding among its members and with other sections of the wider society which would be socioculturally of a higher order than what has been going on in the past. This conference may have identified some of the ingredients for such a genuinely progressive conversation.

Chapter 16

Research Design and Methodology Issues in the ITCS

Judith Orasanu[1]
U.S. Army Research Institute for
the Behavorial and Social Sciences

Research design and methodology recommendations made apart from specific research questions suffer from being so general that they are tantamount to saying, "Do it right," where "right" reflects accepted science as found in methods and design textbooks. To avoid this problem, our working group felt that it was necessary to establish central research questions that would constrain design and methodology issues. The two central questions we specified were:

- How do families affect their children's cognitive and academic development?
- What kinds of intervention strategies involving both parents and children are most effective in fostering the intellectual and social development needed for school success (given schools as they presently exist)?

Both questions must be answered for families from different sociocultural backgrounds and in diverse educational environments.

These two questions represent two distinct types of research, both of which are needed if significant progress is to be made in improving family literacy. The first question exemplifies the need for *basic* re-

---

[1] Now affiliated with NASA-Ames Research Center.

search on fundamental processes in parent–child interaction through which cognitive development and academic socialization take place. But this effort must be informed by theories of child development and further contextualized by understanding of adult development and learning. The second question highlights the need for *applied* social-policy research on the effects of various types of intervention programs. While the methodology and design issues discussed in this chapter pertain mainly to applied intervention research, we feel it is important to include basic research, because it yields the theories and knowledge base that serve as the foundation or backdrop against which interventions are designed.

For example, recent basic research efforts have expanded our conceptions of intelligence to include "practical intelligence" (Wagner, this volume) and notions of tacit learning. Basic research has also defined the nature of reading comprehension (Orasanu, 1986) and "higher order cognitive skills" (Chipman, Vol. II). Together with new theories of cognitive development such as Vygotsky's (Gavelick, Vol. II), these basic research efforts can help designers of ITCS intervention programs to specify both their goals (what kinds of cognitive skills should be targets of intervention programs) and strategies for developing those skills.

However, a major problem was identified during the conference that must be addressed, a further reason for raising basic research issues in this chapter. The problem is that most scientific theories of child development and parent–child interaction patterns (with a few important exceptions, e.g. Laosa) are based on research conducted with white middle-class children and their families. Laosa (this volume) pointed out the critical need to establish the cultural validity of theories and findings by replicating studies in diverse cultural settings. For example, among white middle-class American families, the best predictor of a child's school achievement is the mother's I.Q. However, among Asian students in American schools, the best predictor is the mother's expectation for her child's achievement (Spitz, this volume).

Cross-cultural research by Cole and his colleagues (Cole & Scribner, 1974), Serpell (1976), and Wagner (1978) among others, has shown how culture bound are fundamental scientific concepts, such as perception, memory, and intelligence. Research in the United States on, for example, language use and participation patterns among diverse subcultural groups demonstrates the variety of normal question and reply sequences between adults and children or oral narrative structures among Native American, Hawaiian, Eskimo, and rural black children (Cazden, John, & Hymes, 1972; Heath, 1983; Michaels & Collins, 1984; Schieffelin, 1979).

Some people may question the need for more basic research. They are impatient to get on with building interventions to help children they see sliding behind in academic and economic opportunity. The problem is that program design is always based on theories, whether explicit or implicit, and sometimes those theories are inappropriate or wrong.

Conference discussions highlighted several critical gaps in the basic research literature that need to be filled if full understanding of intergenerational transfer of cognitive skills is to be achieved, and if successful intervention programs are to be designed. These concern:

- *The nature and mechanisms of adult learning and cognitive development, especially among low-literate or nonliterate adults.* Most research to date has focused on higher level academic learning among literate adults, although some has addressed functional literacy in the workplace (Mikulecky, 1986; Sticht, 1989). Better understanding is needed of the roles of motivation, self-concept, and culture-specific attitudes toward schooling and occupational opportunities on adult learning.
- *The roles of values, attitudes, and belief systems in cognitive and intellectual development within families.* While books have been written on the sociology of poverty and academic failure, few scientific studies have examined the family within the broader context of the larger community and society to understand the effects of cultural values, aspirations, and expectations on literacy practices and understandings (but see Reder, Vol. II). Ginsberg and Bempechat (Vol. II) and their colleagues have shown how some parents' beliefs about the sources of intellectual ability influence their children's academic success, but more needs to be known about how these successes (and failures) are brought about. What behaviors are driven by beliefs? How do a parent's beliefs influence their child's self-concept and efforts? What factors lead to change in adult attitudes and beliefs?
- *Individual differences in learning and ability,* focusing, not on IQ differences, but on differences in social learning strategies, such as learning by imitation, caretaker teaching strategies, tacit learning from one's environment (R. C. Wagner, Vol. II), and the active role of the child in parent–child interaction patterns.

Each of these three issues needs to be addressed in diverse cultural groups to broaden our theories and to provide a more valid foundation for designing intervention programs.

Obstacles to Policy-Relevant Research

We now turn to issues pertaining to method and design in applied policy-relevant intervention research. Contemplating such efforts immediately highlights the incredible difficulty of doing research that will yield meaningful and scientifically valid findings. Two major impediments stand out. Both concern ethical issues involved in conducting intervention research, the first having to do with the tension between requirements of scientific design and provision of services; the second deals with "ownership" of the research and the ethics of intervention.

The first issue pits the requirements of scientific design against the legitimate needs of families for participation in literacy programs. The ideal scientific design would randomly assign families to treatment conditions in order to study effects of program participation, ruling out other factors. Doing so means that some participants would not have access to program that could make a significant difference to their children's intellectual development. Just this dilemma frequently faces medical researchers conducting clinical trials of a new drug that could save many lives.

Several solutions might be considered. One is to design studies so that all conditions receive some form of treatment, providing all participants with an opportunity to benefit in some way. This solution also avoids the problem of segregating or stigmatizing the families who are participating in a program. This solution may also partially reduce expectation effects on outcomes. In educational/developmental research it is difficult to create "placebo" conditions (inert treatments such as sugar pills that look like the real thing to both subjects and experimenters) because of the social nature of the interventions.

A second alternative is to offer participation in the intervention to all families in a community, allowing them to self-select into the study. While this alternative reduces the consequences of segregation, it complicates interpretation of results. Multiple regression analyses after the fact, coupled with close observation of the interventions, can yield findings whose generality must be supplemented with alternative methods. A third method is to enlist a large pool of potential participants and use a lottery system to select a subset who will actually participate.

The second ethical issue concerns who "owns" the research. Who decides what kinds of educational treatments will be available? Who decides what kinds of outcome measures are important? Who decides who can participate? At the ITCS conference (and elsewhere), concerns were raised about researchers descending on a community with *their* ideas about how to improve schools or kids, with little concern for the needs or concerns of the families involved. Both on ethical and on practical grounds, the families' needs, values, and goals must be taken into account. While researchers may bring their knowledge of theory and ideas about how to improve family literacy, there is little chance of bringing about significant change, or even of getting significant participation, if the efforts are not sensitive to the families' goals and values.

One solution is to involve the parents as collaborators in the programs. Previous efforts to study classroom teaching have involved teachers as collaborators with remarkable success (e.g., Au et al., 1986; Gitomer, personal communication, February 12, 1990). The teachers provided insights about classroom events and about the students that would have remained inaccessible to the researchers. As full partners in the design of classroom interventions, they were eager participants, instead of resisting or sabotaging implementation of experimenter-designed programs. A similar approach may work well with parents. That does not mean that parents would be expected to design experiments. It does mean involving them in plans for intervention programs and working toward their goals, while satisfying criteria for scientific rigor.

Involving parents in the project, and building on community social networks, may also help to overcome another major impediment to successful intervention research: family participation. For an adult who has experienced failure in school and who may distrust educational authority figures, any new program may be seen as just another opportunity to fail. We heard from the service providers at the conference how difficult it is to enlist adults' participation and to keep them coming back.

Nickse (this volume) pointed out that the longer an adult participated in her literacy program and the more intense the participation, the greater the gains. She observed that the most potent motivator was the parent's desire to help her or his child in school. For adults without children, perhaps an adopt-a-kid-for-literacy approach would work.

A fourth impediment to conducting intervention research is the problem of obtaining valid, reliable measures of progress, especially from adult participants. Adults who might be targets of intervention programs are often test-shy, reflecting previous academic failure. As Sticht (1989) observed, standardized reading test scores are probably not appropriate measures, in any case. Innovative measures will need to be devised for assessing progress and for communicating it to the participants.

The two impediments just discussed—both obtaining continued

adult participation, and developing appropriate meaningful measures of participant progress—feed into a broader issue having to do with the time-frame of the studies and the sizes of effects. The time requirements built into any intervention must be adequate for effects to occur. Too many studies expect effects in too short a time period. In the past, researchers have gone into a school or community, trained the instructors, given them a few months to put the instruction into practice, come back 3 or 4 months later, and expected to see increases in children's IQ scores. While this may sound like a caricature, it characterizes many published studies. Time is needed prior to undertaking a study to develop a workable plan up front, to gather input from the community, and to prepare the trainers or others in the community who will actually be implementing the intervention; time for effects to be enacted; and time to evaluate both the implementation and outcomes in formative and summative fashions.

Unlike many previous school-based interventions, ITCS interventions will be expected to have two tiers of effects, one on the parents and one on the children. Effects on the children will be both direct and indirect. Direct effects will reflect participation in the interventions themselves, to the extent they involve manipulations directed at the child. Indirect effects will be mediated by changes in parents' behaviors, resulting from participation and changes in their literacy practices and achievements, as well as self-concept or attitude changes. These changes take time to become established as behavior patterns. Thus, changes in adult behavior and indirect effects on children will become manifest more slowly than the direct effects on children. Significant changes in children's behaviors can't be expected in the short term, because of their dependence on changes in their parents' behavior. Hence, the problem of keeping families in the programs over a relatively long period of time becomes a critical issue.

Likewise, designing dependent measures that are appropriate to the time frame of the studies will be critical. As Datta (this volume) has pointed out, the size of the effects should be interpreted in light of the complexity of the variables and the time scale of the project. For example, the following dependent variables might be appropriate for the following study durations:

- Short-term (3 mos.): Participation rates—adults and children.
- Mid-term (3 mos.–1 yr.): Children's school behaviors. Parents' interaction patterns with children.
- Longer mid-term (1 yr.–3 yrs.): Parents' literacy achievement and behaviors; attitudes and self-concept. Children's literacy behaviors and achievement; school achievement; self-concept.

- Long-term (3 yrs. plus): Years of school completed, grades, drop out rates, pregnancy rates, job preparation and employment. As a rule of thumb, smaller effects might be judged to be significant for longer term studies, given that more factors can influence these outcomes and the problem of attrition becomes more pressing.

Park (this volume) has pointed out the problem of determining how much involvement is needed to bring about effects on participants of various ages, given different rates of learning and social factors that may impede or facilitate progress. However, a more significant issue may be determining how to maintain effects over the long haul, as was discovered in evaluations of Head Start. Impressive gains in IQ and school achievement in the early school years were followed by gradual erosion of those gains (relative to control groups) as Head Start children progressed into the middle and upper grades. This phenomenon suggests that different factors affect continued cognitive and social development beyond early advances. What those factors are, and how they operate, clearly need to be better understood. This problem has prompted efforts to involve parents in literacy activities so they can help their children continue to grow over the years. But more needs to be known about how to help parents help their children. Clearly, one of the major issues that ITCS intervention programs must address is how to create community contexts that will support continued growth on the part of both parents and their children. Such sustainment is critical if a program is to make a significant difference in the long run.

Many impediments (scientific, social, and political) stand in the way of designing interventions that will be effective in enhancing the literacy and cognitive skills within families. However, lessons can be learned form previous efforts, especially from Follow Through (see House, Glass, McLean, & Walker, 1978). Two primary points stand out. First, a centrally planned and controlled grand design applied to all participating sites is probably doomed to failure. Problems of assuring uniformity of implementation might well intimidate the most intrepid researcher.

Developing a single intervention approach and a single yardstick by which to measure program effectiveness has proven difficult in the past and should give the next generation of researchers pause. A minimal set of program and evaluation requirements should be established, and then local experts should be allowed to tailor their efforts to local needs. Such guidelines might include the following requirements: adult and child coparticipation; a minimum amount of time for program involvement and duration; parent/community collaboration in local program design; and certain uniform dependent measures, including amount of participation time (hours), and behavioral, test, and attitude measures.

The second lesson, which complements the first, is that variety is needed in approaches used by local programs to meet the needs of families participating in them and to be responsive to culturally diverse adult/child interaction patterns. A blanket approach will not do. Different trajectories can lead to the same end point, and researchers must allow for such diversity, despite the fact that such an approach might not fit their idea of a tidy research design.

METHOD AND DESIGN DESIDERATA

While the previous sections of this chapter have focused on impediments and difficulties that will surely be encountered in attempts at intergenerational intervention programs, the remainder will address design and methodology guidelines. These can only be specified as somewhat global desiderata that will contribute to scientifically valid and practically useful knowledge.

First of all, multiple methods are needed for studies of varying scale, ranging from longitudinal studies replicated among many subcultural groups to small case studies and embedded experiments to test specific hypotheses. Analytic techniques might include LISREL modeling of the longitudinal studies or microethnographies of family or classroom interactions.

Traditional experimental methods (e.g., compare instructional method A with method B) are inadequate to the task of understanding how effects are brought about. An emphasis must be placed on understanding the *process* driving the effects. A process focus is necessary to understand outcomes, especially when programs or experiments are replicated with various cultural groups. Without an understanding of underlying mechanisms, outcomes (whether similar or different) cannot be interpreted, nor can successful programs be reproduced in new sites. A focus on underlying process also increases the likelihood of identifying phenomena common to diverse groups.

A process-oriented approach should include determining how participants (parents, teachers, community members) interpret and define the intervention, their attitudes toward the intervention, and their beliefs about potential outcomes. Observations carried out in homes or other program sites (community centers, schools) will provide information on the degree and manner of program implementation: What is actually being taught? How? By whom?

The possibility of reactivity, that is, behavior changing as a result of being observed, can be reduced by using participant observers who are members of the community. They can function naturally in the environment and can provide informed interpretations of events because of their familiarity with the participants, culture, and situations.

Finally, two issues relate specifically to design of studies. First, what is the unit of analysis? Most studies of child development have focused exclusively on the child. Future studies must also consider the family, the community, or the program. The unit of analysis must be appropriate to the focus of the intervention: at what level is the intervention targeted—the parent, the family, the community? The unit must be appropriate to the goals of the study. It would not make sense to study parent–child interaction patterns as a function of state-by-state variations in funding levels for school enrichment programs.

Second, variables may serve equally well as independent, moderating, and outcome measures, depending on the design. Factors such as parent literacy levels and practices, or parents' beliefs, attitudes, and expectations for their children, could be outcomes of interventions, but they could also be independent or moderator variables affecting their children's literacy activities or school achievement. Given the emphasis recommended here on understanding the process by which effects are brought about, variables must be treated flexibly.

The goal of the studies of ITCS is dual: to design and implement programs that will foster literacy and cognitive development in families, both among adults and children, while also generating scientific theories and data that will enable successful duplication of effective programs in new sites. This dual goal will yield culture-specific understandings of communities' and families' literacy practices, beliefs, values, and aspirations, while also seeking broader scientific principles that hold for all groups. Current scientific thinking suggests that general theories can best be achieved via specific cases. The guidelines offered above seek to channel researchers in that direction.

One more desideratum emerged from our working group. Provisions should be made for data sharing among participants in the various basic and applied research efforts studying ITCS. A community of scholars would be able to learn from each other, sharing progress and problems, and would contribute to initiation of syntheses and meta-analyses, where appropriate.

A final word of caution. While we fervently hope that improved levels of literacy among adults and their children will lead to greater personal fulfillment, raise levels of employment, and lead to more skilled jobs, there is a danger of expecting individual changes in literacy to result in broad societal changes. Public alarm is raised over declining productivity in American industry. In the same breath, sagging levels of literacy are mentioned, as though the latter are causing the former. The danger lurks in drawing conclusions about causality from correlations. As outcome measures used in studies of intervention programs become more distant, the danger of unfounded interpretations increases. Little ambiguity may exist when outcomes consist of reading test scores, school grades, graduation rates, or GED achievement. Understanding causal relations become more fragile the further from observed behavior the study goes—for example, to teenage pregnancy rates, school attendance, or drug use. Most elusive are effects on ultimate employment, poverty levels, or GNP measures. In fact, comparative studies across cultures (Resnick & Resnick, 1977) have found that as a country's economy improves, so does its literacy. The danger lurks in blaming low literacy levels for failures in society which in fact may themselves be causes for low literacy. Our hope is to see both literacy levels and societal productivity increase together.

REFERENCES

Au, K. H., Crowell, D. C., Jordan, C., Sloat, K. C. M., Speidel, G. E., Klein, T. W., & Tharp, R. G. (1986). Development and implementation of KEEP reading program. In J. Orasanu (Ed.), *Reading comprehension: From research to practice*. Hillsdale, NJ: Erlbaum.

Cazden, C., John, V., & Hymes, D. (1972). *Function of language in the classroom*. New York: Teachers College Press.

Cole, M., & Scribner, S. (1974). *Culture and thought*. New York: John Wiley.

Heath, S. B. (1983). *Ways with words*. New York: Cambridge University Press.

House, E. R., Glass, G. V., McLean, L. D., & Walker, D. F. (1978). No simple answer: Critique of the Follow Through evaluation. *Harvard Education Review, 48* (2), 128-160.

Michaels, S., & Collins, J. (1984). Oral discourse styles: Classroom interaction and the acquisition of literacy. In D. Tannen (Ed.), *Coherence in spoken and written discourse* (pp. 219-244). Norwood, NJ: Ablex Publishing Corp.

Mikulecky, L. (1986). Effective literacy training programs for adults in business and municipal employment. In J. Orasanu (Ed.), *Reading comprehension: From research to practice*. Hillsdale, NJ: Erlbaum.

Orasanu, J. (Ed.) (1986). *Reading comprehension: From research to practice*. Hillsdale, NJ: Erlbaum.

Resnick, D. P., & Resnick, L. B. (1977). The nature of literacy: An historical exploration. *Harvard Education Review, 47* (3), 370-385.

Schieffelin, B.B. (1979). Getting it together: An ethnographic approach to the study of the development of communicative competence. In E. Ochs & B. B. Schieffelin (Eds.), *Developmental pragmatics*. New York: Academic Press.

Serpell, R. (1976 . *Culture's influence on behavior*. London: Methuen.

Sticht, T. G. (1989). Assessing literacy skills and gains in job-oriented literacy training programs. In *Literacy and the marketplace: Improving the literacy of low-income single mothers*. New York: The Rockefeller Foundation.

Wagner, D. A. (1978). Memories of Morocco: The influence of age, schooling and environment on memory. *Cognitive Psychology, 10*, 1-28.

Chapter 17

Assessment of Intergenerational Transfer of Cognitive Skills: The Distant Target

Louis A. Armijo
CACI, Inc.

The assessment and measurement working groups focused on the assessment and measurement of intervention programs designed to affect the intergenerational transfer of cognitive skills. As working groups we could not approach specifics of the desired assessment process independent of the specific theory of change developed and the design of the program to be implemented. The working groups therefore dealt with basic issues of what are assumed to be long-term research efforts, given the subject. The two major categories of focus were general structure of the assessment and specific areas that should be measured and assessed.

GENERAL OBSERVATIONS ON ASSESSMENT

When observing a simple, nontechnical culture, where one is not blinded by the trappings of a so-called "highly advanced" technological civilization, the transfer of cognitive skills across generations seems obvious. In hunter/gatherer cultures, young boys learn hunting and tracking by observing and direct instruction from experienced hunters. They learn the entire culture, values, attitudes, and ways of behavior through much the same process: observation, direct instruction, and indirect instruction (such as games) (Cole & Scribner, 1974).

But in our highly diverse, multicultural, multiethnic society it becomes very difficult to determine in detail what are the major effects on a child's cognitive development. We see, in our diverse society, that what seems to have a major effect on one group appears to have little, if any, effect on another. Though, for example, the literacy of the mother is highly correlated with literacy of the child, the correlation levels appear to vary significantly across ethnic, cultural, and economic groupings.

GENETIC DIFFERENCES

Without denying that genetic differences exist, the genetic similarities are greater than the differences. Normally, all humans learn language. All human groups have produced rules, whether formal or informal, which govern the interactions of people and allow us to live in societies. The universality of language and culture, for a creature with so few instincts, can be credited to the basic intelligence of the human race. The variations in language and culture can be viewed as a clear example of the innate malleability of the human species. It is on these assumptions of innate intelligence and malleability of man that the various social sciences base their attempts to influence and change patterns of behavior so as to maximize human potential and growth.

ENVIRONMENTAL DIFFERENCES

We do know that the environment influencing the mental development of a child is a complex interaction of many factors. A child raised in an inner city slum is more likely to drop out of school. Children raised in environments where skills such as reading are neither valued or practiced, would not be expected to be academic achievers (Sticht, this volume). But a nontrivial number of people raised in the poorest, most disadvantaged environments do achieve a great deal more than one could assume from their backgrounds. Bempechat (Volume II) notes that the work on the school achievement of Asian-American children that Herb Ginsburg, Eliott Mordkowitz, and she are working on examines the degree to which immigrant status and a Confucian ethic may influence the socialization practices of Asian-American parents such that they foster motivational and attitudinal tendencies that contribute to high achievement. For example, in studies of fifth and sixth graders, they are testing the hypothesis that, relative to Caucasian children, Asian-American children are less vulnerable to learned helplessness, have a positive view of the value of objective evaluation, and perceive their parents to be intimately involved with their school progress. Preliminary findings are in support of this hypothesis. This leads to the question, what are the primary environmental factors influencing the intergenerational transfer of cognitive skills?

But as with any attempts at human intervention, especially those based on "yet to be confirmed theory," the researchers/practitioners must be able to gather enough information to support or disapprove the theory or the way the theory was applied. In his chapter, Sticht (this volume) notes that, despite the fact that over 20 years have passed since large amounts of funding and research were focused on youth and adult intervention programs, remarkably little hard evidence exists today concerning their success or failure. Researchers summing up the progress of the last two decades uniformly cite the need for more carefully planned and executed research in the area. This chapter will focus on assessment and measurement issues as they apply to the general concept of intervention programs affecting intergenerational transfer of cognitive skills.

ASSESSMENT AND MEASUREMENT ISSUES

Assessment and measurement can be a very simple or complex task, depending on what is to be done. In the case of making some sort of manipulation affecting the intergenerational transfer of cognitive skills, the assessment and measurement issues become extremely complex. In some respects it may be a near impossible task.

If we assume that effects of an intervention program would be self-sustaining, that is, that the children's children will be positively affected, then it would be necessary to assess several generations. Following families for generations in an open and mobile society such as ours is an extremely difficult task.

The specifics of what is to be assessed and measured, and how and when it is to be done, depend greatly on the specifics of the general theory of change that is developed and the design of the intervention developed to achieve the change.

The assessment of interventions programs can be described by simple algorithms where each of the factors can be assigned a value (Keppel, 1973).

If X Then Y

If one thing is done, then one other thing is changed: This is the simplest of all designs. For an intervention program where one can expect immediate results, such a simple design is possible. In this case we are concerned that one thing is done properly, and then we can measure the variable of interest.

If X and A and B and C Then Y

Here we assume that, if multiple changes are made, then the one goal is achieved. This type of design is used if only one factor is of interest. In this design, even if there are multiple factors affected by the intervention, only one is of interest. Such an assessment approach ignores all other outcomes. If, for example, an intervention program improved a child's reading ability, but no other factor changed, such as school performance, drop-out rate, and so on, then this approach to assessment would never reveal the very limited scope of the success, thereby allowing people to assume that other variables commonly linked to reading had been affected.

If X Then A and B and C and D and . . .

In this design only one intervention factor was used or is of interest. This one intervention is expected to have multiple outcomes. An example of such a powerful intervention would be supplying a reasonable diet to a village suffering from chronic malnutrition. One could measure more than simply the fact that the people lived.

If W and X and Y Then A and B and C . . .

This is probably the most realistic example of an intervention program. One has to look, not only at the variables that were manipulated, but also the intervening variables. A particular intervention strategy may have a very different outcome, depending on the mix and strength of the various intervening variables.

In the assessment of an intervention program dealing with intergenerational transfer of cognitive skills, there are numerous factors that must be considered and assigned a value. The following is a list of some of those factors.

I = the intervention
E = ethnic/cultural grouping
O = economic status
L = literacy of parents
F = one or two parent household
G = age of child at intervention
N = number of siblings
X = other programs/interventions
T = length of intervention
d = drop out likelihood
a = attitude to education
e = level of educational achievement
f = academic performance
g = antisocial behavior
h = positive self-image
i = SES achievement
j = standardized test performance
k = problem-solving capacity.

One difficulty with long-term research covering generations is that practically every factor must be considered a variable. Nothing can be viewed as a constant. Even such factors as ethnic and cultural groupings become fuzzy through intermarriage.

During the general sessions and working groups it became clear that we must focus, not only on the desired goal, "positive changes in children," but also on what is done, the treatment.

1. Was the treatment properly implemented? If the treatment was not properly implemented, the theory of intervention may be perfectly correct but the research is not successful.
2. Did the treatment create the desired change in the primary change agents (parent/schools)? To determine if a treatment created the desired change in the primary change agents should require fairly complex, long term, and in-depth assessments.
3. Did the change transfer to the children? It is necessary to assess that a change did occur, was of significant magnitude, and continues to exist.

As was mentioned in the working group, we may well make a change that is extinguished because of other variables not considered, or because the intervention did not have a significant enough impact.

All the factors discussed at this conference as important to transfer or development of cognitive skills exist in degrees. A treatment may move things in the desired direction but not enough.

DESCRIPTION OF THE ASSESSMENT PROBLEM

In long-term studies it is not a simple matter to prove that some intervention was the prime cause of some positive result. Rather it is necessary to assess subjects within the context of relevant community and cultural environments.

It will be necessary to take into account the effect of various other intervention programs on the children of subject families. It may be possible for example to have a synergistic effect between interventions, positively affecting the overall performance of the subject children. Or a specific child-directed program may have a strong short-term effect on all children participating (and many intervention programs have had), hiding the longer term positive effects of the intergenerational intervention.

The assessment of any intergenerational intervention program should address following points:

A. Does the intervention program appear to have positive effects on the children? (A positive effect would be noted if one or more of the outcomes occur.)
1. Children of subject families have a lower drop-out rate.
2. Children of subject families have a more positive attitude towards education.
3. Children of subject families perform better in academic pursuits than their SES counterparts in the same geographical area over an extended period of time.
4. Children of subject families achieve a higher level of education than their SES counterparts.
5. Children of subject families have a lower incident of antisocial/ self-destructive behavior.
6. Children of subject families maintain a more positive self-image over an extended period of time than their SES counterparts.
7. Children of subject families have children that are higher achievers than their SES counterparts.
8. Children of subject families perform better in standardized tests than their SES counterparts.
9. Children of subject families are more active problem solvers than their SES counterparts.
B. Is the change relatively permanent? We will want to know if there

is a significant likelihood that such change can be transferred over to a second generation without continuous intervention. A self-sustaining effect would clearly be the most desirable outcome. If an effect is shown to be self-sustaining across generations, that in itself would be justification for large-scale implementation of a program causing such an effect.

CONCLUSION

The measurement and assessment of any intervention program affecting the intergenerational transfer of cognitive skills will be, at best, a difficult task. But without such data the value of an intervention research project becomes trivial. A well-executed assessment, combined with good program implementation, will add significantly to our sum of knowledge and possibly help us eliminate long-established patterns of poverty and failure in segments of our population.

REFERENCES

Bempechat, J. (1992). *The intergenerational transfer of motivational skills.* In T. Sticht, B. McDonald, & M. Beeler, (Eds.) *The intergenerational transfer of cognitive skills. Volume II: Theory and research in cognitive science.* Norwood, NJ: Ablex Publishing Corp.

Cole, M., & Scribner, S. (1974). *Culture & thought.* New York: John Wiley & Sons, Inc.

Keppel, G. (1973). *Design and analysis, a researcher's handbook.* Englewood Cliffs, NJ: Prentice-Hall.

Chapter 18

Delivery Systems Issues for ITCS

Warren Simmons
Prince George's County Public Schools

This chapter considers issues involved in setting up programs for the intergenerational transfer of cognitive skills. While the focus is on programs for literacy development, the points made are relevant to programs to improve mathematics and other cognitive skills.

The success of intergenerational cognitive skills programs depends on the development of instructional models (i.e., delivery systems) based on current knowledge about: (a) learning and thinking; (b) similarities and differences in the attitudes and performance of adults, youth and children with skill deficiencies; and (c) educationally relevant aspects of the home, community and school experiences of individuals with comparatively low levels of literacy and/or other cognitive skills.

National surveys of literacy reveal consistently that the reading and writing skills of the poor and members of minority groups lag behind increasing demands for literacy in mainstream society (Kirsch & Jungeblut, 1986; Applebee et al., 1988). We must be mindful of the fact, however, that achieving mainstream literacy standards is only one of a number of difficulties faced by the poor and a significant number of racial and ethnic minorities. Under- and unemployment, along with inadequate housing, health, and childcare are a few of the many problems which compete with literacy for attention.

The struggle to acquire literacy, then, coincides with efforts to achieve higher standards of living and, in many cases, to learn a new language and culture. An effective literacy delivery system for individuals pressed by a variety of concerns must support, if not address directly, the economic and social aspirations of individuals in conjunction with reading and writing. Stated differently, literacy programs for the disadvantaged must complement, rather than compete with, the myriad needs of its audience.

Delivery systems are the means for providing services, training, and instruction to individuals. This chapter examines critical implementation and instructional design issues concerning the development of effective intergenerational cognitive skills programs.

As discussed in Part II, intergenerational literacy programs provide educational and other types of training and services to a mixed-age and ability audience which may consist of parents and their children, adults and unrelated children, or youth and adults. The audience for such programs, based on evidence cited previously, is likely to comprise individuals from low-income and/or subcultural groups (e.g., blacks, Hispanics, Native Americans).

The responsibility for creating a literate citizenry has rested traditionally with three types of institutions: (a) formal educational institutions (i.e., public and private elementary, secondary and postsecondary institutions); (b) community, religious, and advocacy groups (e.g., the Urban Coalition, ASPIRA, Literacy Volunteers of America); and (c) private industry and organized labor.

FORMAL EDUCATIONAL INSTITUTIONS

The continuing failure of large numbers of minorities and the poor to acquire "mainstream" literacy skills attests to weaknesses in the nation's first line of defense against illiteracy, formal educational institutions. The decade of the 1980s has been replete with school reform recommendations aimed at improving the performance of the general school population. In the early part of the decade, these recommendations concentrated on raising standards, expanding testing and evaluation, and strengthening school curricula by focusing on the "new Basics" (see National Commission on Excellence, 1983). Recent calls for school reform have gone beyond curriculum content and school climate issues to address the very organization and management of schools at the district and school building level (see The Carnegie Foundation for the Advancement of Teaching, 1988).

Calls for restructuring public elementary and secondary schools have largely been made with general, rather than minority, populations in mind, and in relation to a kindergarten through 12th-grade scheme. Obviously, the adoption of intergenerational models by formal schools will require structural adjustments along with changes in instructional methods and activities, and curriculum objectives and content.

Curriculum objectives and content

Formal educational institutions transmit socially valued skills and knowledge. Acculturation, along with intellectual and academic development, is a primary goal of schooling. Most school curricula promote beliefs, skills, and knowledge needed to participate in mainstream American culture which has its origins in the beliefs and practices of this country's white, Anglo-Saxon, male Founding Fathers. The paucity of attention devoted to American subcultural and foreign frames of reference in school curricula poses significant educational problems for individuals from subcultural or immigrant groups and their teachers. Recent research and discussion about academic estrangement among low-income and minority youth indicate that this phenomenon is generated by school curricula and instructional grouping practices which encourage teachers and students alike to view academic achievement as a dominant culture attribute (e.g., Fordham & Ogbu, 1986; Rist, 1973).

Curricula that fail to incorporate the contributions and perspectives of women, blacks, Hispanics, and Asian-Americans foster false dichotomies between mainstream culture and educational achievement, on the one hand, and subcultural group membership and less-valued pursuits (e.g., sports, music) on the other. Anglo-centric school curricula also limit the extent to which the prior knowledge of nonmainstream students can be used to advance their learning and development of critical thinking and problem-solving skills.

The academic alienation of women and minorities is a high price to pay to preserve Anglo-male dominance of American life. The social and cognitive distance engendered by the exclusion of minority group perspectives in school curricula has largely been ignored by the recent school reform movement. This oversight has hampered attempts to improve school performance (cf. Stedman, 1987). The realization of this problem is leading many schools to explore ways of infusing diverse cultural viewpoints into the content and organization of instruction. As a result, some schools are moving away from the topical approach to multicultural education, often referred to as the three f's—foods, festivals, and famous persons—and adopting a conceptual approach which applies nonmainstream perspectives throughout the various academic content areas and in the organization of instruction (cf. Banks, 1988).

Multicultural curricula and instructional practices should be a primary development principle for intergenerational literacy programs. The content and design of services must encompass mainstream and minority outlooks and build connections between literacy and meaningful activities. The Kamehameha Early Education Project (Tharp, 1982), the Minorities Math and Science K-6 Project, and the Middle-College School for at-risk youth are innovative examples of programs that: (a) incorporate educationally relevant aspects of minority students' experience into the content and organization of instruction, (b) offset or accommodate competing social, health, and economic concerns by providing counseling and other services, and (c) maintain the achievement of mainstream educational objectives as their central goal (for a description of these projects, see The Carnegie Foundation for the Advance of Teaching, 1988; Cole & Griffin, 1987; Chu-Clewell et al., 1987).

Instructional Organization and Methods

The Anglo-centric character of most school curricula is a problem that schools from Stanford University to the local elementary school are striving to address. Perhaps the greatest challenge for formal institutions posed by intergenerational programs is the adoption of instructional activities for mixed-age and ability groups. Secondary and elementary schools, to a lesser extent, traditionally have offered instructional programs tailored ostensibly to meet interests and needs of students. At the elementary school level this is represented most often by within-class ability grouping for subjects like math and reading, and the operation of separate programs for the gifted, students with limited-English proficiency, students with basic skill deficiencies, and students with learning disabilities and physical handicaps. High schools often provide instructional tracks for students with different abilities and interests which usually consist of an honors and/or academic program, a general program, and a vocational instructional line. Age-grouping is also an explicit part of the tracking and ability-grouping scheme, that is, children of similar age, ability, and interests usually receive instruction together.

These practices have continued despite a dearth of evidence regarding educational benefits of ability-grouping, particularly for students with academic deficiencies (see, Oakes, 1985; Cicourel & Mehan, 1985; Cusick & Wheeler, 1988), and in the face of rising equity concerns. In addition to grouping students by age and ability, tracking and ability-grouping also sorts students by race, ethnicity, and social class (Oakes, 1985; Raywid, 1985). Moreover, standardized test performance rather than student/parental preferences usually guides decisions about track placement, raising questions about whether tracking reflects student needs and preferences as opposed to institutional beliefs about the potential of certain students.

The extensive use of age- and ability-grouping in formal institutions limits their feasibility as sites for intergenerational educational programs. These practices can be altered by school boards and administrators with support from parent organizations. A shift in policy of this magnitude, however, will require a major change in beliefs about learning held by parents and school officials. Parents and school officials must be exposed to emerging models of development and intelligence represented by the works of Vygotsky, Sternberg, Gardner, and others (see chapters by Gavelek and R. Wagner in Vol. II) and their implications for education. The thinking of many educators is still guided by theories of intelligence which view ability as being general and largely immutable. Thus, our schools provide intellectually enriching experiences for those with high ability, and a knowledge of the basics for those with "demonstrated" low-ability. This arrangement is little more than an additional manifestation of the self-fulfilling prophecy.

The Middle-College, a high school for at-risk youth located on the campus of Queens Community College, exemplifies an alternative educational model in keeping with intergenerational concerns. The Middle-College program is integrated, wherever possible, with the larger campus program. Middle-College students interact with students from the larger campus in the college library, dining facilities, and may enroll in college-level courses when warranted. The community college faculty often provide instruction and guidance to the program. As a result, Middle-College students are exposed to and bound by the requirements of college life in a program with features designed to meet their unique needs.

Postsecondary-secondary program integration, business-school partnerships, and coordinated services between school and community organizations allow students of different ages, with different abilities, and from different backgrounds to support each others learning and aspirations. These kinds of alliances, though, depend on the cooperation of parent groups and school officials, businessmen and community leaders; but more importantly, their belief in a common goal and model for its attainment. To achieve unity of purpose of direction, school board members, parent organizations, school superintendents, State education officials, and business and community leaders must have guided exposure to current educational theories and research findings and their implications for school restructuring and instructional design. Traditional efforts to promote dialogues between researchers and educators has focused on classroom teachers and school principals who generally have little control over curricular and instructional policy. Creating change on a wider scale will require greater communication between researchers, state and local school administrators, and leaders of business and community organizations.

Curricular Objectives and Content

Age- and ability-grouping in schools have been reinforced by the prevalence of basic skills curricula designed to teach skills and knowledge in hierarchically organized sequences that begin with lower-order skills and facts and proceed to cover successively more sophisticated information and processes. This particular approach has been criticized for:

- emphasizing abstract skills and knowledge
- neglecting the interdependence between lower- and higher-level skills/knowledge
- stressing rote learning and skill development at the expense of knowledge expansion and the development of critical thinking skills
- ignoring work, home, and community applications for skills and knowledge, and for
- fostering two-tiered educational programs—one enrichment-based and the other grounded in basic skills (Simmons, 1987; Cole & Griffin, 1987; Cusick & Wheeler 1988; Oakes, 1985).

Basic skills curricula employing drill-and-practice workbooks are even less appealing to and successful with adults than with children (Darkenwalk, 1986; Mezirow, Darkenwalk, & Knox, 1975). The integration of intergenerational programs into formal institutions should speed the adoption of curricula that consolidate basic and higher-level skill/knowledge instruction and which use work, community, and civic life as contexts for learning.

COMMUNITY ORGANIZATIONS

Formal educational institutions should play a leading role in the intergenerational literacy effort. They possess the facilities, staff, organization, and fiscal resources needed to insure stable operations. The disadvantages inherent in formal institutions, in addition to ones already mentioned, are their lack of ties to communities where the educationally disadvantaged reside, and the distrust held by many of the people in these communities toward formal institutions (cf. Comer, 1980). Moreover, formal institutions are often unaware of and unable to meet the myriad social and economic concerns felt by the educationally disadvantaged. Literacy instruction cannot be expected to "take" if other pressing needs are ignored. Community organizations can and should play a vital role in the intergenerational literacy process. Their location and flexible scheduling eases burdens associated with travel and time conflicts. In addition, their staff is more likely to be knowledgeable about the conditions of life for people for which literacy is only one among a number of challenges. This knowledge enables community-based educators to do a better job of making instruction reality-centered rather than abstract. Furthermore, community-based organizations frequently deal with the "whole" individual, providing social, economic, and educational services. For example, "The Door," located in New York's Chelsea, provides educational training, counseling, and health services for its clients. Formal institutions are usually more restricted in their areas of responsibility.

The location and whole-life approach of many community organizations makes a compelling argument for their choice as sites for intergenerational programs. The comprehensiveness of the services offered by community organizations coupled with their reliance on "soft" monies (corporate, government, and individual contributions), though, often leaves them unable to retain staff, program offerings, and facilities over long periods of time. Community-based organizations are often in the throes of fund-raising efforts to insure their year-to-year survival, even as they provide services for their clients. The funding uncertainties faced by community organizations curtail ability to plan and operate programs on a long-term basis. Dependence on funding from an ever-changing mix of sponsors, moreover, leaves these programs vulnerable to redirection based on the pursuits of "this year's" funder.

CONCLUSION

Formal institutions and community organizations possess weaknesses which make the successful operation of intergenerational literacy programs by each alone unlikely.

When combined, these institutions and organizations can enhance their respective strengths and offset their respective weaknesses. For example, Playing To Win (PTW), a community computer center located in New York's East Harlem, leases its facilities to public schools, health organizations, and other formal institutions. The monies acquired provide a small but stable source of support for PTW's broader programs. PTW's availability to schools and other institutions, in turn, extends their hours of operation and ties to the community. This kind of arrangement should be encouraged as a putative model for intergenerational literacy programs linking community organizations and formal educational institutions. One of the missing elements in this arrangement, however, is the participation of the educational research community. The estrangement between schools and community organizations is only exceeded by the gulf between researchers and everyone else. In the past, there have been few incentives or mechanisms to encourage interaction between researchers, public schools, and community organizations. In addition, the researcher's status as "expert" discouraged dialogue and cooperative efforts. Cut-backs in federal and private funding for basic research has sharpened researchers' interests in more applied areas of work. Concomitantly, the 1980s reform era has spurred searches for new educational strategies and models by school and business leaders resurrecting their interest in research and the rehabilitation of "Ivory Tower" social scientists. Collaboration between researchers, educators, and community leaders, however, remains a process fraught with mutual distrust and awkwardness. It occurs most successfully when guidelines are provided identifying roles and strategies for engagement.

The Follow Through Academic Learning Time Project sponsored in 1983 by the National Institute of Education is an excellent example of how researcher-educator-community collaboration can be facilitated. The request-for-proposals (RFP) for the project called for a school-based endeavor employing strategies developed and tested in collaboration with researchers. The RFP, then, required schools, over a three-year period, to work with researchers to: (a) identify a model for increasing academic learning time (the models had to be described in the proposal), (b) use the model to design staff development and instructional activities in accord with the model, and (c) implement the activities and test their impact on key variables.

The Follow-Through Academic Learning Time RFP resulted in five separate school-district/research institution collaborations that generated a variety of models, five school-based demonstration projects involving researchers, teachers, school administrators, and parents, and a wealth of findings regarding the success of various approaches.

Federal and/or private funding programs on intergenerational literacy would do well to follow the NIE model. This would reduce shortcomings associated with previous Federal educational programs such Chapter I and Title VII, which have been criticized for lacking evaluation data and sound conceptual continuity between the models offered by research, and the practices and beliefs existent in schools and community groups.

Finally, an intergenerational literacy program model should also comprise strategies for informing and soliciting aid from policy makers to insure a close match between program appropriation levels and regulations, and the needs of clients and providers.

REFERENCES

Applebee, A. N., Langer, J. A., & Mullis, I. V. S. (1988). Who reads best: Factors related to reading achievement in grades 3, 7 and 11. *National assessment of educational progress* (Report No. 17-R-01). Princeton, NJ: Educational Testing Service.

Banks, J. A. (1988). *Multiethnic education: Theory and practice.* Newton, MA: Allyn & Bacon, Inc.

The Carnegie Foundation for the Advancement of Teaching. (1988). *An imperiled generation: Saving urban schools.* Lawrenceville, NJ: Princeton University Press.

Chu Clewell, B. C., Thorpe, M. E., & Anderson, B. T. (1987). *Intervention programs in mathematics, science, and computer science for minority and female students in grades 4 through 8.* Princeton, NJ: Educational Testing Service.

Cicourel, A. V., & Mehan, H. (1985). Universal development, strategy practices and status attainment. *Research in social stratification.* (Vol. 4, pp. 3-27).

Cole, M., & Griffin, P. (1987). *Contextual factors in education: Improving science and mathematics education for minorities and women.* Madison, WI: Wisconsin Center for Education Research.

Comer, J. P. (1980). *School power: Implications of an intervention project.* New York: Free Press.

Cusick, P. A., & Wheeler, C. W. (1988, February). Educational morality and organizational reform. *American Journal of Education,* pp. 231-255.

Darkenwalk, G. (1986). *Effective approaches to teaching basic skills to adults: A research synthesis.* Washington, DC: Office of Higher Education and Adult Learning, Office of Educational Research and Improvement, United States Department of Education.

Fordham, S., & Ogbu, J. U. (1986). Black student's school success: Coping with the "burden of acting white." *Urban Review, 18,* (3, 176-206).

Kirsch, I. S., & Jungeblut, A. (1986). Literacy: Profiles of America's young adults. *National Assessment of Educational Progress* (Report No. 16-PL-02). Princeton, NJ: Educational Testing Service.

Mezirow, J., Darkenwald, G. G., & Knox, A. B. (1975). *Last gamble on education: Dynamics of adult basic education.* Washington, DC: Adult Education Association.

The National Commission on Excellence in Education. (1983). *A nation at risk: The imperatives for educational reform.* Washington, DC: U. S. Government Printing Office.

Oakes, J. (1985). *Keeping track: How school structure inequality.* New Haven, CT: Yale University Press.

Raywid, M. A. (1985). Family choice arrangements in public school: A review of the literature. *Review of Educational Research, 55,* (4, 435-467).

Rist, R. (1973). *The urban school: A factory for failure.* Cambridge, MA: MIT Press.

Simmons, W. (1987). Beyond basic skills: Literacy and technology for minority schools. In R. D. Pea & K. Sheingold (Eds.), *Mirrors of minds: Patterns of experience in educational computing* (pp. 86-100) Norwood, NJ: Ablex Publishing Corp.

Stedman, L. C. (1987, November). It's time we changed the effective schools formula. *Phi Delta Kappan,* pp. 215-223.

Tharp, R. G. (1982). The effective instruction of comprehension: Results and description of the Kamehaneha Early Education Program. *Reading Research Quarterly, 17,* (4, 501-527).

Chapter 19

Policy Issues and the Intergenerational Transfer of Cognitive Ability

Andrew Hartman
Staff Director of Committee on Education and Labor

Each generation, born without a reservoir of knowledge and values, provides both an opportunity and a threat to our society. It is the task of the preceding generation(s) to create an environment, or set of opportunities, which ensure the transfer of knowledge and skills to the next. It is the purpose of this chapter to describe the policy relevance of research and practice that has the goal of understanding and improving this intergenerational transfer of cognitive skills.

At first blush, the intergenerational transfer of cognitive abilities sounds too esoteric to be a matter of serious concern to policymakers mired in the here and now of the "real world." However, if we restate the phrase in other words—the education of a new generation of American citizens, for example—its policy implications become very clear. Some of our greatest leaders, such as Thomas Jefferson and Lyndon Johnson have argued that our style of government and quality of life depends on the successful education, or transfer of skills, to a new generation.

Twenty-five years ago there was much interest among policymakers in breaking the intergenerational cycle of poverty that existed in segments of American society. Part of the intellectual underpinning of the programs that constituted the War On Poverty was the idea that there was also an intergenerational cycle of ignorance which paralleled, and indeed led to, the cycle of poverty. Many of the programs of this era, Head Start for example, were based on this belief and attempted to improve the learning opportunities of young children.

During the past 6 years there has been a renewed interest in improving the intellectual development of our young children. For while the War on Poverty had some successes, it by no means eradicated the poverty or ignorance it set out to eliminate. In 1983, the report *A Nation At Risk* cited the economic, military, and social dangers inherent in the low level of cognitive skills the commission had found in America's youth. This concern has already found its way into the policy realm as part of major trade legislation. In an effort to improve the nation's competitive position in relation to other countries, a major portion of the 1988 trade bill is devoted to programs addressing the educational needs of children, youth, and adults. Congress evidently believes our trade deficit is related to a cognitive deficit.

LEVELS OF ANALYSIS
AND POLICY IMPLICATIONS

Participants at the 3-day meeting on the intergenerational transfer of cognitive skills represented diverse professional backgrounds. There were researchers with a great deal of expertise in basic cognitive science, social scientists who are more involved in applied cognitive research, persons who design and operate programs that put the concept of intergenerational transfer into practice, and policy people whose job it is to develop public policy that improves the opportunities for intellectual growth and development.

There is a policy interest in the advancement of both basic and applied cognitive research. This is a fast-developing field with important implications for the fields of education, computer science, industry, and the military. The federal government, state governments, foundations, and private sources have provided a great deal of funding for work in this area. Probably most, if not all, of the researchers represented at the meeting have received federal support at some point.

During the course of the meetings, several features of this body of research became apparent which currently limit its applicability to the question of intergenerational transfer of skills. In general, the scientists doing cognitive research had not spent much time doing research on the intergenerational transfer of skills. Those conducting basic cognitive research had focused mainly on the understanding of cognitive processes in an individual. This may be due to the fact that experimental cognitive science is a relatively new field and researchers have first sought to understand individual processes. In the area of applied research, the focus has also been on the individual. While there is a large body of work on ways to enhance the cognitive skills of individuals through direct interventions, there is a paucity of research on how to improve a person's cognitive skills indirectly by improving the skills of his or her parents or other social contacts. Again, this is not stated as criticism of the work done in this field but rather as a comment on the usefulness of available research results for the implementation of policies aimed at improving the flow of knowledge and skills between generations.

One of the unique and valuable aspects of this conference was that it brought researchers together with persons who have implemented successful intergenerational education programs. As is widely recognized, too often these two groups have their own professional orbits which rarely cross. From a policy perspective, knowledge gained from research is only as important as its value in addressing pressing policy concerns. Certainly the research on cognitive development and the transfer of skills between individuals is critically important to the creation and improvement of programs aimed at helping parents become their children's first teacher.

It appeared from the discussions that took place at the conference sessions that there has not been enough of this communication in the past. It was obvious that this did not come from any lack of interest on the part of either the researchers or practitioners, but rather as a result of the different training, terminology, and simple lack of professional contact. From a policy perspective this hurts both parties. Researchers are frequently asked to justify their work by explaining how they are contributing to the solution of "real" problems. Practitioners are left on their own to design interventions and services, using mostly prior experience and common sense for guidance. In the current climate of accountability, any information that would help make these programs more effective increases the chances of sustaining funding support.

FEDERAL POLICY EFFORTS

School dropouts, youth unemployment, illiteracy, the underclass—all are seen at the national level as symptoms of a failed effort to develop our human resources. Over the past 4 years a broad consensus has developed among Republicans and Democrats, business and industry, educators and policy makers, that more must be done at the federal, state, and local levels to improve educational opportunities. Both political parties made this issue a major focus of the last presidential campaign, with each candidate competing to be perceived as the better friend of education. The importance of this issue to the business community can be seen in *Children In Need: Investment Strategies for the Educationally Disadvantaged,* a report by the Committee for Economic Development, which is made up primarily of CEOs from Fortune 500 corporations.

While there is general agreement about the severity and urgency of the problem, there is continued debate regarding the best strategy for solving it. There are, however, some basic premises which appear to be influencing the way most policy makers view both the cause of the problem and possible solutions. One of these agreed-upon points is that many intellectual and social difficulties that show up in school-age children and adults have their roots in the early childhood period. Reports such as *Changed Lives,* by the High/Scope Educational Research Foundation, have led policy makers to believe that intensive early educational intervention can have dramatic, positive effects throughout the life of an individual. These results are all the more persuasive to policy makers when accompanied by cost–benefit analyses which indicate that they save money in the long run.

Associated with this belief in the potency of early intervention strategies is the idea that children are embedded in a larger community and culture, and that any successful effort to assist them in their development must involve the other members of that community. The issue becomes, how can adults, especially parents, become more active in assisting children's development? It is thought that, without building this component into day-to-day family and community interaction, any gains achieved in a special program will fade once the intervention ends.

Recent policy initiatives have reflected both the importance of early intervention and the need to involve parents and other adults in facilitating children's development. Adult education programs can become part of an effort to break the "intergenerational transfer" of illiteracy, and early childhood education can explicitly involve parents by helping them become their children's first teachers.

During the 100th Congress, Congressman Bill Goodling (R-PA) introduced legislation that would directly address this intergenerational problem. The *Even Start Act* (Part B of Chapter 1 of P.L. 100–297, The Elementary and Secondary School Improvement Amendments of 1988) has the goal of "providing family-centered education programs which involve parents and children in a cooperative effort to help parents become full partners in the education of their children and to assist their children in reaching their full potential as learners." Even Start really has three goals. The first two involve providing assistance to adults who lack basic educational/cognitive skills and children who are at risk for developmental delay and later school failure. There are, however, existing programs such as Head Start and Adult Education programs which have these purposes. It is the third goal and feature of Even Start which makes it unique. Programs funded under the Even Start Act would enroll both parents and children from the same family and, in addition to addressing their individual needs, work towards the goal of making the parents competent facilitators of their children's development.

The Even Start legislation has received a great deal of support from educators and policymakers. The National Education Association (NEA), International Reading Association, and Parents and Teachers Association (PTA) are some of the major supporters of the program. Several states, such as Kentucky and Pennsylvania, have already begun educational efforts similar to Even Start and were able to provide Congress with successful examples of the intergenerational approach.

The final version of Even Start authorized $50 million a year to fund demonstration grants that would be awarded on a competitive basis through the Department of Education. The Congress recently finished its deliberations on the fiscal year 1991 appropriations bill, which funds most of the Federal education programs. Contained in the legislation is an appropriation of $49 million for Even Start. A notice requesting proposals for grants will appear in the Federal Register early in 1991 with awards made in the spring of that year. These grants provide an excellent opportunity for researchers and practitioners to work together in designing and operating an intergenerational education program.

Chapter 20

Understanding ITCS: A Commentary on the Relationship Between Cognition and Social Change

Daniel A. Wagner
University of Pennsylvania

Embedded within the title of this volume, *The Intergenerational Transfer of Cognitive Skills* (ITCS), are issues which have been of continual interest to social scientists and policy makers concerned with American education. Understanding ITCS would require answers to questions which have been elusive for a long, long time. One might rightly ask: what kind of cognitive skills are we talking about? Between which people or across which tasks are we supposed to study transfer? And what, if anything, do we know about intergenerational change in any psychological processes? Fortunately, there seems to have been an understanding in the conference about what ITCS was supposed to mean.

The implicit meaning of ITCS itself is inherent (or perhaps hidden) in one of the core idealogical metaphors which guides the American conscience—that is, the notion of social mobility. Non-ITCS, then, is not being able to achieve mobility across generations, or even within one's own generation, so that groups of people (by social class, race, ethnic origin) remain relatively immobile at their level in the American social fabric, not achieving the American mobility dream. As one dimension of the problem of social mobility in contemporary America, the notion that cognitive skills can play a role has been around for a considerable period of time—at least since the turn of the century, when the concept of intelligence first began to attract attention in America. Since the early 1900s, and especially during the last several decades, it was widely thought that the biological (and genetic) constraints of nature were such that individuals, or even large groups of individuals (i.e., races), would stay in a given social position due to their own inherent limitations in intellectual ability. The 1970s and 1980s have seen a shift away from such biological tendencies, but there remains in contemporary America a fear that social and economic stagnation are rapidly approaching. Indeed, as Sticht pointed out in his introductory remarks, it is this fear of economic decline which has provided some of the impetus for taking another look at how theories of cognitive science can intervene in a society which, to many observers, appears to be more and more rigid.

One of the central propositions of ITCS is that certain "basic cognitive skills"—such as literacy and numeracy—are "basic" precisely because they are fundamentally part of what it takes to be a productive economic citizen in America. Since these skills are not evenly distributed and in fact tend to correlate highly with one's socioeconomic status, an intervention which could produce an increase in basic cognitive skills, could—so the argument goes—break the cycle of stagnation. At the outset, however, we must be cognizant of the predominant psychological focus of the chapters presented in this volume. This disciplinary perspective tends to necessitate consideration of the building of cognitive skills at the individual level, and the transfer of skills between, say, parents and their children. This is one valid level of analysis, but we might easily work at other levels of analysis that are sociocultural. A sociocultural perspective would lead us to consider issues of class and ethnic relations, world view, distribution of economic resources, and the work of non-psychologists such as anthropologist John Ogbu (1978) and sociologist Pierre Bourdieu (1977). While there are many who would say that a sociocultural level of analysis is essential for trying to adequately consider problems of social mobility, it is also the case that few sociologists or anthropologists have the tools of intervention as much at their disposal as do psychologists, who have had experience in practical intervention programs such as Head Start. Thus, it is not unreasonable for ITCS to be given serious consideration in terms of its intervention potential.

SOME UNIFYING THEMES

When confronted with a set of problems which seem to require an intervention into the established social structure, it often appears that terms such as *incentive* and *motivation* are central for any type of change to take place. The case for ITCS is no different, in that both the system which surrounds potential participants in an intervention program, and people who make up the social structure in which the participants live, may or may not have sufficient incentive and motivation to participate in any kind of program for change. For example, if there are no jobs available for those who become literate through some kind of adult education program, what is the incentive to become literate? If workplaces have little incentive to hire the marginally or recently literate individuals, how can they be expected to be supportive of job training programs?

In the case of literacy programs, it is often said that "empowerment" may be a result of participation in literacy learning; but it is not obvious that all sectors of society, or even many sectors of society, wish poor or less-educated people to become more empowered. Naturally, incentive and motivation are a function of the belief structures which individuals hold. If an individual believes that employment is a function of his or her level of literacy, then motivation for literacy ought to be greater than if the person does not hold such a belief. As Bempachat (Sticht, McDonald, & Beeler, Vol. II, 1991) and others have pointed out, self-attributions can also play a role. If individuals believe that they will fail, then they may not even try. And we know very little about attitudinal and motivational change, particularly within the types of ethnic groups where are normally "targeted" in ITCS-type programs. We know that in other countries, for example, Japan (see Ginsburg, in Sticht et al., Vol. II, 1991), belief structures may provide for classroom and out-of-classroom contexts that contrast dramatically with that found in the United States. However, such cross-cultural comparisons, while interesting, do not easily apply to the American situation. In the Japanese case, for example, it is not clear whether Japanese success in school mathematics achievement is a function of greater classroom control, help provided from interested and literate parents, or simply a more math-intensive curriculum. Separating these variables would be helpful, but they are not sufficient to be directly applicable to the American educational context.

What is meant by the term *cognitive skills* included in ITCS? Does this term mean cognitive skills, literacy, math, practical intelligence, higher order thinking skills, or some other as yet to be defined skills?

And just how many and at what level of expertise do these skills need to be taught? The whole debate over level of literacy skills required is an example of how difficult this issue can be. Long ago, Unesco suggested the idea of *functional literacy,* as if that term could be more easily and simply understood than *literacy* (see Spratt, Seckinger, & Wagner, in press). While literacy seems to have strong support from people with many different social and political agendas, what about numeracy? If arithmetic is seen as useful, how important would calculus be? Again, we see the importance of motivation and incentive; calculus may have great benefit to the adolescent who is planning to go to college, but provides little incentive for the child who is sure that he or she is not going to go to college. Such different belief systems are part and parcel of what is meant by cultural world views, which are resistant to many if not most forms of social intervention.

Mason's program (in Sticht, et al., Vol. II, 1991) for enhancing mother–child reading activities involves the provision of appropriate literacy materials to low-income mothers. However, these materials are at a first-grade reading level; do these mothers need to have a fifth-grade or even high school literacy ability in order to use first grade materials? How much would be gained by giving these mothers additional literacy training, given that they seem to be successful with low-level materials at the present? Of course, this also brings up the issue of how to best spend one's resources. To change an old cliché just a bit: if literacy learning can be accomplished at a low level now, why "fix it" with an upskilling program for mothers?

Within the domain of skill learning, it is also important to consider the *generality* versus the *specificity* of the skills and instructional techniques in question. Should literacy instruction be focused on workplace requirements, or to enable someone to get out of an industrial center and into a white collar job? To what extent does some kind of specific training generalize to contexts and skills which go beyond the actual instruction. Considerable effort has been spent on task analysis in cognitive science (cf. Chipman, in Sticht et al., Vol. II, 1991; also Duffy, this volume); such analyses help to provide a better understanding of the specific skills in question, but provide little in the way of guidance as to which skills ought to be taught, and how they might be useful and generalizable to practical everyday and work-related situations.

Finally, there are a number of serious methodological problems in trying to understand ITCS. The first may be termed *the unit of analysis.* Where should one be focusing the research effort: on the skill, the individual, the family, the school, the community, the ethnic group, the United States, or the world? All of these units are relevant to the problem space of ITCS, but how would one choose the best place to intervene in the system? This is not a trivial question. A related question is that of appropriate dependent variables. If one is to be held accountable for some kind of ITCS intervention program, then what would constitute an appropriate change of behavior that justifies the initial intervention investment? Should this be cognitive/academic test scores, categorical variables such as staying in school versus dropping out, maintenance of skill after a program is finished, or simply the acceptance of the intervention program by the community involved (cf. Datta, this volume)? The choice of dependent variable can be just as important as the intervention itself, since it determines whether the particular intervention is considered a success or failure. The baseline reference point will determine how the intervention program is judged.

RESEARCH QUESTIONS WHICH NEED
TO BE ADDRESSED

It is sometimes said in policy circles that we know enough (or *more* than enough) about such research questions, and we should simply get on with the task of investing in appropriate intervention programs. It should be clear from this volume and its companion (Sticht et al., 1991) that there are major lacunae in what we presume to already know about ITCS in its many forms. Such questions might include the following: Who is to be the clientele? Is the focus to be on children, adolescents, parents, or a combination of these groups? Are target groups to be specified by ethnic or linguistic background? Since cultural and linguistic variables are among the most difficult to resolve in any kind of intervention program, it is unclear how a successful program could be created without substantial attention devoted to these dimensions of any social problem. This also brings up the question, in literacy work, of which language of instruction should be provided if the goal is basic literacy. In the United States the debate over this issue has been intense, particularly within the large non-English-speaking Hispanic population. Should literacy programs be in Spanish or in English for such individuals? Language and culture are also related to the issue of transfer, since what is transferred has to be done in one kind of communication system or another. In addition, how one motivates for change is also bound up in how each ethnic/cultural/linguistic group perceives its own status vis-á-vis the dominant community. Promotion of improved linkages between reseachers, practitioners, and communities is an essential part of the process of change as well.

A whole range of tactical issues on ITCS must also be considered. Should adult learning take place with individual tutors or within classes? Is it appropriate to use computer-assisted instruction (CAI); with which clientele, in which contexts? What about the maintenance or retention of cognitive skills? If several grades of reading achievement can be taught in a matter of months, what do we know about retention of those skills in the months following the intervention? Some evidence (e.g., Wagner, Spratt, Klein, & Ezzaki, 1989) suggests that, at relatively low levels, a fair amount of retention can be achieved, but this certainly depends on the contexts for learning and for retaining. Another important issue in this volume is that of the notion of "small wins" (cf. Datta, this volume) in intervention programs, as contrasted with a "major gain" approach which was often part of intervention rhetoric. This notion of small wins is one that merits serious consideration, since it is more likely to succeed more often, and to succeed in maintaining societal support and program funding over the long haul.

CONCLUSION

The idea that specialists can intervene in ITCS for the purpose of the common social good is one that is very appealing. As we have seen in the chapters in this volume, and in the above discussion, success in an intervention program along the lines of ITCS is certainly subject to a variety of potential pitfalls. Nonetheless, ITCS offers opportunities for direct action which are not commonly part of the critical views offered by specialists with more political or ideological motives in mind. ITCS, indeed, is not designed for the large win, but rather for the small one. Much remains to be done, and much remains to be understood, before serious consequences will result from this relatively new approach to social change. The chapters in this volume are a modest beginning toward trying to understand the uses and limitations of programs for the intergenerational transfer of cognitive skills.

REFERENCES

Bourdieu, P. (1977) *Outline of a theory of practice.* Cambridge, UK: Cambridge University Press.

Ogbu, J. U. (1978). *Minority education and caste: The American system cross-cultural perspective.* New York: Academic Press.

Spratt, J. E., Seckinger, B., & Wagner, D. A. (in press). Functional literacy in Moroccan school children. *Reading Research Quarterly.*

Sticht, T. G., McDonald, B. A., & Beeler, M. J. (Eds.) (1991). *The intergenerational transfer of cognitive skills: Volume II: Theory and research in cognitive science.* Norwood, NJ: Ablex Publishing Corp.

Wagner, D. A., Spratt, Klein, G., & Ezzaki, A. (1989). *The myth of literacy relapse: Literacy retention among fifth grade Moroccan school leavers, 9,* 307-315.

AUTHOR INDEX

Subject Index